Introduction to Political Economy

Introduction to Political Economy
Third Edition

Charles Sackrey and Geoffrey Schneider
with Janet Knoedler

The Economic Affairs Bureau publishes *Dollars & Sense*, a bimonthly magazine. *D&S* explains the workings of the U.S. and international economies and provides progressive perspectives on current economic affairs. It is edited and produced by a collective of economists, journalists, and activists who are committed to social justice and economic democracy.

The Economic Affairs Bureau also publishes the following classroom books: *Real World Macro, Real World Micro, Current Economic Issues, Real World Globalization, Real World Banking, The Environment in Crisis,* and *Unlevel Playing Fields: Understanding Wage Inequality and Discrimination.*

For more information, contact:

Dollars & Sense
740 Cambridge Street
Cambridge, MA 02141
Phone: (617) 876-2434
Fax: (617) 876-0008
Email: <dollars@dollarsandsense.org>
Website: <www.dollarsandsense.org>

Cover illustration by James Schneider
Cover design by Nick Thorkelson
Interior graphics by Matthew R. Daniels
Design and production by Terry J. Allen

Manufactured by Transcontinental Printing
Printed in Canada

Table of Contents

Preface to the Third Edition

We have written this book in order to introduce our readers, we presume mostly students, to what we are calling "political economy." We want to distinguish this kind of economics from the "mainstream" of economics that dominates instruction in contemporary capitalist societies. If you are taking an economics course at almost any U.S. university or college, your teacher has almost certainly assigned you a textbook from what we call the economic mainstream. In the most general terms, how are these two traditions, political economy and mainstream economics, different from each other? We can begin an answer with a passage from one of the very few contemporary textbooks that gives attention to them both.

> Political economy...is more concerned [than mainstream economics] with the relationships of the economic system and its institutions to the rest of society and social development. It is sensitive to the influence of non-economic factors such as political and social institutions, morality, and ideology in determining economic events. It thus has a *much broader focus* than [mainstream] economics. (Riddell, Shackelford, and Stamos 1998, emphasis added)

A bit of historical background will help to make sense of this quotation. What we are calling political economy was first fully developed in the work of Adam Smith, whose 1776 book *The Wealth of Nations* contained a fabulously rich combination of theoretical analysis, historical setting, and copious detail. Smith took into account anything and everything that caught his attention, and to read *The Wealth of Nations* is to discover the broad outlines, and countless details, of British life in the late 18th century. For most of the next century, people studying the economy, among the most prominent of whom were Karl Marx and Thorstein Veblen, followed Smith's lead. They produced broadly cast arguments in which there were no predictable boundaries limiting the kinds of knowledge brought to bear. While Marx and Veblen, and other such political economists, clearly focused attention on economic activity—how people produced their livelihood and how they divided it up—they roamed far and wide in looking for ideas and information that would help them to explain what they saw.

However, after the middle of the 19th century, more and more social scientists adopted a version of the "scientific method," borrowed from physical scientists such as physicists, chemists, and biologists. Successes in these scientific fields starting in the 16th century had recruited many thinkers into taking a scientific approach to their studies, and this was certainly true of economists. By the 20th century, and especially after 1950, economics increasingly came to be expressed in the terms of mathematics and statistics. Presently, the economics profession is dominated, as are the graduate schools that produce professional economists, by economists who exclude from their analyses those things that are not readily measurable or appropriate for quantitative model building.

As the discipline has been narrowed, it has pushed to the margin alternative schools of economics, especially political economy. Political economists who, as Riddell, Shackelford, and Stamos put it, are "sensitive to the influence of non-economic factors such as political and social institutions, morality, and ideology in determining economic events," have gradually found their work shunned by the major economics journals, often because it is considered to be "non-economic." From our view, the most unfortunate consequence of this trend is that the ideas of writers like Marx and Veblen, and others who extended their work, are rarely studied by economists as graduate students, thus less frequently taught by such graduate students when they become professors.

To try to bridge this gap, we have written this book. In our initial chapter, we provide our readers a more detailed look at political economy by comparing its essential ideas and concepts to those of the economic mainstream. We follow this first chapter with two on the central writers in the political economy tradition, Marx and Veblen, whose ideas, as we shall see, provide the structural frame for the rest of the book. In Chapter IV, we take up the ideas of John Maynard Keynes, whose work in the 1930s on the booms and busts of modern capitalist societies revolutionized the way economists understand capitalism and the measures necessary to keep it from collapsing in on itself. Keynes, who actually straddled the fence between political economy and mainstream camps, shared with political economists the practice of casting an exceedingly broad net for useful facts and ideas in his work. Though he had little use for Marx's writings, he often indirectly legitimated political economy by using his grand and eloquent voice to criticize mainstream economists for the narrowness of their studies.

We follow the first four chapters, ones that focus mostly on ideas and systems of thought, with four that analyze the impact of these ideas on our own world. In Chapter V we describe and analyze social classes in U.S. capitalism, in part because they are a central aspect of all political economy analyses of capitalism. We also discuss social classes because they are crucial to how capitalism shapes our lives, and, as we shall see, because they are totally ignored by mainstream economics. We then turn in Chapter VI to the theory of "social balance," developed by John K. Galbraith. In this theory, Galbraith has taken key ideas from Veblen to describe how corporations cajole, trick, and bamboozle us into buying stacks of stuff that we don't need, despite the fact that doing so is destroying the air, water, and public services we need to live. Chapter VII shows how Marx's ideas were extended to current times in the theory of "monopoly capital" advanced in the 1960s by Paul Baran and Paul Sweezy. These two economists used Marx's key idea of "surplus value" to try to understand what they ultimately called "the irrational system" of U.S. capitalism.

In our final chapter, we describe the modern welfare state in Sweden, which has been shaped by political economists in that country for over a century. To study the Swedish economy is to catch a glimpse of life in a society where the public understanding of capitalism, how it works and how it should work, has been influenced more by ideas from political economy than by those from the economic mainstream.

The sequence of chapters we have chosen here has proven helpful to us in teaching the book to undergraduates, yet we suggest that others use the sequence that makes the most sense for their own courses. In order to encourage readers to go through the book in various kinds of ways, we have written each chapter to work mostly independently of the others. A consequence of our making the chapters independent in this way is that our readers will find some repetition as they go along. However, when we repeat ourselves we believe that we only do so in the cases of information or concepts that can bear a second going over. We believe that if this book is read alongside the typical mainstream economics textbook, students will end up with a fairly good introduction to both approaches, and a far richer understanding of capitalist societies. After our readers go through this book and their textbook, they can judge for themselves which approach, or which combination of approaches, works best to help them understand the economic world in which most will spend a lifetime making a living.

Acknowledgements

We have a number of thanks to pass on. First are those colleagues who read earlier drafts of these essays, all of whom gave us good reasons to rewrite parts of each. These helpful critics are: Teresa Amott, Dennis Baumwoll, John Boylan, Lou Casimir, Steve Cohn, Tom Kinnaman, John Kirkland, Catherine O'Connor, Cadwell Ray, Eric Ruckh, Paul Susman, and Amy Wolaver. Also, thanks to Ellen Campbell who helped to write and to edit the essay on the modern Swedish economy. Laurie Dougherty provided us with a fine editing of the first edition.

We want to extend a special thanks to Alejandro Reuss, until recently the book editor at *Dollars & Sense*, and his successor in that job, Amy Offner. For this edition, we have added one essay, that on Baran and Sweezy, and we have thoroughly revised all the other chapters. Alejandro and Amy provided us with pages of detailed suggestions for this new chapter and these revisions. All of their suggestions helped us to sharpen our own interpretations of the ideas we were trying to present and, we believe, ultimately allowed us to make it easier for our readers to use the book.

Finally, our thanks to Janet Knoedler, our colleague at Bucknell, who wrote the chapter on Veblen and part of the chapter that critiques mainstream economics. Further, Jan early on helped us to imagine this project and continues to provide us her counsel as we go from one edition to the next one.

1
Political Economy Critique of Mainstream Economics

Discussions of contemporary capitalism have long been dominated by one line of thinking, which we will define below as the "mainstream" of economics. This mainstream has either ignored, or labored to discount, alternative ways of thinking about the economy, such as those that we described in our preface and that fill up this book. A major consequence of the mainstream refusal to take up alternative ways of seeing the economy is that most students taking economics courses in the United States today will not hear about them. We hope that this chapter will provide a good argument for our readers to push ahead to see what their economics professors have been hiding from them.

WHAT IS THE MAINSTREAM OF ECONOMICS WE ARE TALKING ABOUT?

Like all areas of social theory, the mainstream school constitutes a broad spectrum of often conflicting ideas. Thus, when we refer to "mainstream economists" we are necessarily lumping them into a single category that is an obvious distortion, much like that of any such categorization. Our critique in this essay refers mostly—but not exclusively—to economic models that (1) are narrowly conceived, (2) are quantitative and expressed in complicated mathematical terms, and (3) depend upon certain restrictive assumptions about how people behave, always have behaved, and always will behave. Without question, there are mainstream economists who engage in lively debates on virtually all of the topics we take up in this essay. Many of them move beyond the strict confines of models and assumptions to examine institutional aspects of the economy. And many empirically investigate people's actual behavior, instead of assuming that they all behave in the same, predictable way.

Why, then, do we focus on those mainstream economists who most narrowly conceive the subject? There are two parts to our answer. The first is that this subset of economists dominates contemporary economics and exercises its dominance through its almost exclusive control over graduate training in economics and the most prestigious economics journals. It is also the subset that has produced all but a few of the Nobel Prize winners in economics. The second reason for our focus is that, of all schools of economic thought we know about, this one is least likely to produce results useful to the public. Therefore, a genuinely interesting irony underlies what we write about in this essay: the very "best" economists, in the view of this dominating subset, produce the least useful kind of economics. We recognize that this is a substantial conclusion, and we hope that reading this and the following chapters will lead our readers to consider it at least as reasonable.

A central part of our argument is that there is a critical distinction between *all* versions of mainstream economics and what we call political economy. This distinction is a matter of methodology, or "method of analysis." Mainstream economists are trained to limit the scope of their analyses—that is to limit the breadth of knowledge they bring to bear on an issue—compared to political economists. In choosing a relatively narrow focus, almost all mainstream economists have gradually and systematically excluded from their studies the political economy point of view. The political economy critique presented here is both a general critique of the mainstream methodology, and a more specific critique of the subset of mainstream economics that is most narrow in its approach.

THE DIFFERENCE BETWEEN THE MAINSTREAM AND ITS ALTERNATIVES

Let's consider the following example that demonstrates the wide chasm between mainstream economics and Marxist economics, a principal kind of political economy. How does each view the production of business profits in capitalism? A mainstream economist might put it like this:

> Profits are the payoff to private individuals for "entrepreneurship," for having saved, or borrowed, funds to invest in productive inputs, for having the foresight to know what goods or services to produce with these inputs and the talent to manage how the inputs are used and the goods marketed. Profit-making is the central vehicle by which capitalism is energized because: (1) by investing the funds, producing the goods, and making the profits, the enterprising capitalist

gives jobs to people who are not capitalists themselves and who need those jobs in order to live; (2) the capitalist will make the highest profits only by producing goods and services most demanded by consumers; and (3) it is the competitive quest for profits that gives capitalism its extraordinary dynamism and proven ability to drive from the field all competing economic systems.

On the other hand, in the Marxist view, profit is looked upon in this different sort of way:

Over the past 400 years, through its drive to accumulate profits, the capitalist class — by pillage (such as the enclosure movements), murder (wars against and systematic impoverishment of Third World nations), and domination (of workers, consumers, and the political process) — has come to own the resources, factories, and other capital equipment needed to produce goods and services needed by all. Prior to the emergence of capitalism, most people were peasants who owned enough agricultural tools to produce a livelihood. However, gradually they were stripped of these goods, and in order to live they necessarily became wage workers for capitalists. At their jobs, workers must produce a value greater than their wage, and this excess is called surplus value. This value, created by labor, is seized by the owner and becomes the owner's profits. The profit motive does not always necessarily serve the social good, as the mainstream contends. Competitive pressures, along with generating the dynamic energy of the system, (1) force capitalists to treat their workers as *things*, commodities to be bought and sold like steel ingots or sheets of plywood, and (2) shape many capitalists into predators working against the best interests of the larger society.

It is almost as if two different species of beings were talking about two different worlds. How can such great divisions of opinion exist between economists when they take a look at something as central to capitalism as the profits that fuel it?

POLITICAL ECONOMY: A GENERAL DEFINITION

For our definition of political economy—and we say "our definition" because there are others that refer to schools of thought within the mainstream framework—we will repeat the definition we used in our Preface:

Political economy...is more concerned [than mainstream economics] with the relationships of the economic system and its institutions to the rest of society and social development. It is sensitive to the influence of non-economic factors such as political and social institutions, morality, and ideology in determining economic events. It thus has a *much broader focus* than [mainstream] economics. (Riddell, Shackelford, and Stamos 1998, emphasis added)

Among those who now work in this political economy tradition, as we have defined it, there is a variety of differing, often competing, notions about how capitalism works and which way it is heading. Even though there are important distinctions among them, we are able to talk in the same breath about differing schools of thought in political economy because they agree on the following critical points:

1. Although most mainstream economists claim that they are doing "economic science," their work fails to explain and predict actual events in the real world – an essential test of any scientific work.

2. A principal reason for this inability to explain real events is the restrictive assumption of "economic man" in mainstream economics, along with a parallel assumption that human beings by nature have unlimited wants for consumer goods.

3. Mainstream models are typically not presented in the historical context that shapes all human events. Furthermore, virtually all mainstream economists are ignorant of the history of economic ideas, and thus unaware that the principal assumptions of their analyses have been challenged by political economists for over two centuries.

4. Mainstream economists typically presume a separation between economic activity and political power.

5. Graduate economic programs are largely confined to mainstream instruction, and a particularly narrow version of that school of thought.

ECONOMICS: THE SCIENCE THAT IS NOT SCIENTIFIC

The debate about methodology between the mainstream and political economists has been going on for a long time. The history of this dispute starts at least as early as the fifteenth and sixteenth century in Europe, when essentially religious explanations of the universe gradually gave way to scientific ones, and with stupendous effects on the world. Columbus's voyage to the New World, Galileo's telescope, Harvey's findings about blood circulation, and

Newton's discovery of certain laws of gravity—along with many similarly astounding discoveries in the seventeenth and eighteenth centuries—made inevitable the declining influence of non-scientific explanations of the world. This scientific assault on alternative explanations of human beings and their universe continued, and of course, continues now.

The horrific conditions for many workers crowding into European cities since the early eighteenth century led to the development of a new practical science, public health. The public health movement led governments to promote the habits of healthier living and, especially, to construct systems to protect water systems from sewage. This movement was complemented greatly by the discoveries in the nineteenth century of Louis Pasteur and others unveiling the role of invisible bacteria in the spread of disease. Together, public health and biological science led to a dramatic increase in the life span in industrializing nations after the late nineteenth century. The average life expectancy in the U.S. in 1776 was about 35 years, about 50 years in 1900, and is now about 75 years. Research done by the Museum of Natural History suggests that, "From 1900 to 1990 we have gained about 25 years of life expectancy; nearly equal to what had been obtained in the preceding 5000 years of human history!" (See *www.amnh.org*).

The success of physical scientists in describing the world and improving the quality and length of life in industrialized countries led others to imitate their work. Economists in particular tried to design regular, law-like models for social phenomena. It is true that in the case of the two most influential economists of the eighteenth and nineteenth centuries, Adam Smith and Karl Marx, the former wrote without mathematics, and Marx confined his quantitative analysis to a few simple algebraic notations. However, by the late nineteenth century most economists had adopted some version of the "scientific method" as their approach and, in doing so, marshaled the economics profession toward mathematics and statistics.

Also during the nineteenth century, economists borrowed the idea of "equilibrium" from physics. In doing so, economists made an extraordinary leap of faith about their ability to study and predict human activity. When social theorists use the idea of equilibrium in model building, they are implying that patterns of human life in a fundamental way are analogous to, say, the equilibrating balance of forces in our solar system that keeps Mars from ramming us head on. That is, this idea presumes that the economy is typically *stable*, and when buffeted away from stability, will always return on its own. A critical implication here is that, if the economy is assumed to be stable and self-correcting, it is better to allow it to function on its own, without extensive government interference. Equilibrating systems, whether among the planets or in people's activity, suggested to Adam Smith and to many economists after him, that they were "natural," and this meant they were "God's work." Smith also believed that individuals possessed a natural self-interest that would lead to "the best of all possible worlds," an idea whose modern embodiment we will take up in detail later on.

Alfred Marshall, an influential British economist writing in the late nineteenth century, was particularly important to the shift from imprecise economic language to the precision of quantitative models that incorporated the idea of equilibrium. Though Marshall warned that "economics cannot be compared with the exact physical sciences," he still believed that economics was specially "advantaged" over the other social sciences. He argued:

> [A] person's motives . . . can be approximately measured by the sum of money, which he will just give up in order to secure a desired satisfaction; or again by the sum which is just required to induce him to undergo a certain fatigue.
> (Quoted in Riddell, Shackelford, and Stamos 1998, 8)

This means that the prices we pay for products, the amount we invest to try to make profits, and the wage that will induce one of us to go to work, are all *numbers*, that is *quantities* that can be manipulated by mathematics and analyzed by economists. Marshall and most of his contemporaries thought that the focus of economists should be the prices that emerge in what he called "the ordinary business of life." This meant, for example, learning how self-interested individuals established prices for products, labor, and money (interest rates) in competitive markets.

Marshall and his contemporaries recognized the aggregate economy as cyclical; however, they also thought it was actually formed by all the individual markets added together, and essentially behaved no differently than would a single one of them. Competitive markets were thought to work with equilibrating precision, and in the hands of Marshall, supply and demand, acting as "two blades of the same pair of scissors," were the prime determinants of market price.

Complementing Marshall's system, and developing along with it, was the work of economists who saw markets as driven by "marginal" decisions made by producers, consumers, and workers, that is decisions about whether to produce an additional unit of production, to purchase an additional item of consumption, or to work an additional unit of labor time. In this theoretical world, capitalists made decisions by projecting the revenue and cost—thus also the profit—of the next marginal unit to be produced; and consumers behaved in terms of the marginal satisfaction anticipated from a product measured against its marginal cost. Some practitioners of this sort of analysis, who were called "marginalists," even imagined a system of mathematical notations incorporating the marginal decisions of all economic actors into one giant quantitative model.

The marginalists, in focusing a microscope on the margin of economic actions, were especially important in prompting economists to think narrowly, an ironic consequence of their desire to explain everything with a single giant model. Their method implied the fateful idea that the institutional structure of capitalism outside individual markets, such as its system of social classes and the distribution of income and power, was not within the scope of economics. Marginal analysis also implied an extremely limited role for government. If the system was the outcome of a limitless number of individual marginal decisions made in self-regulating markets, then the thick fist of the government could not be expected to solve any economic problem.

In 1879, Marshall published the prototype for the modern economics textbook, which he called *Industry and Trade*. By 1890, he was calling his book *Principles of Economics*, and in this version, the geometric models of supply and demand that all principles students must now learn appeared as footnotes. Though Marshall kept the diagrams in his footnotes, economists who followed with their own principles texts gradually moved the diagrams from the footnotes up to the text where they came to dominate. Thus began the joyful birth, or sad decline, depending on your point of view, of twentieth-century economics.

Further leading to quantification of economics was the theorizing of the British economist, John Maynard Keynes. In his revolutionizing book *The General Theory of Employment, Interest, and Money* Keynes used geometry, mathematics, and compelling and elegant prose to revolutionize the way that modern economists think about the business cycle. Keynes' work gradually won over most economists in the capitalist world. He preferred a dense prose to mathematics or geometry as a way to express his economic theories, and he differed crucially from the classical school in arguing that capitalism was not a self-equilibrating system. Nevertheless, Keynes' followers constructed diagrams and formulae to carry his theories forward, and these "macroeconomic" models, like the market analysis of Alfred Marshall and the marginalists, successfully lured more and more economists into the encapsulating and often suffocating web of a geometric world.

In 1948, Paul Samuelson of MIT, using his own two-volume mathematical expression of mainstream economics as a model, wrote the first widely used economics textbook. He combined Marshallian analysis, by then called "microeconomics," and Keynesian macroeconomics and called his book *Economics*. This title was, of course, greatly misleading given all the many kinds of economic analysis, most especially political economy, that he simply ignored. Samuelson has, in updating his book over the years, gradually added considerable non-quantitative materials, but the geometric models and other quantitative materials that make up the theoretical core of mainstream economics remain central. Samuelson's amalgamation of microeconomics and macroeconomics has come to be called "neoclassical" economics, and within the economics profession, this term is the common way to describe mainstream economics.[1]

Is this mainstream amalgamation actually doing *science*? To the critique that they have left too many crucial aspects of social life out of their models, mainstream economists typically respond with something like this: "Our assumptions might be unrealistic, and our models might be narrowly conceived, but they work better to predict economic behavior than the theories of our competitors." That is, the proof of models is how well they work.

Well, then, how well *do* they work? A good way to answer this key question is to compare the predictions made by economists to those made by *real* scientists. Consider the example of physicists. It is beyond dispute that they know some things, such as the laws of gravity, more or less for sure. Similarly, while medical doctors may differ on particular diagnoses, they know countless things with a high degree of certainty, such as specific physiological dimensions of, and limitations of, the human body. On the basis of highly predictable outcomes, physicists, medical doctors, and other real scientists have enabled human beings to live longer and to utterly transform their natural habitat, perhaps, even to the edge of ruining it. All these outcomes stem from a scientific method whereby scientists all over the world test hypotheses over and over again until there is wide-spread agreement about this or that aspect of the physical world, or in the case of medical scientists, this or that aspect of the human body.

Yet, and this is the point, there is nothing similar in the annals of economics, and there probably can never be a set of principles, models, theories, conclusions, or predictions comparable to those in the physical sciences on which economists base their methods of inquiry. We are not questioning whether mainstream economists work diligently and honestly, as real scientists do. Nonetheless, economists don't know with any degree of certainty what is going to happen in the next instance with respect to *anything*. And, that is why they always disagree about *everything*. To make the point, we've constructed below a list of central questions about how the capitalist economy operates. As you study economics, no matter what version of it, you will discover that *there is not now, nor has there ever been,* universal agreement on the answers to these questions among people calling themselves economists:

- How should we measure the unemployment rate and what will it be next month?
- Will the aggregate economy go up next month, go down, or stay the same? What will happen to total output if the government increases or reduces personal income taxes?
- How do you measure inflation, and how does it affect various people?
- What has caused capitalism to dominate its rivals? Is it economic freedom? Is it greed? Is it imperialism? Is it brilliant entrepreneurship? Is it the surplus value taken from the hands of workers and made into machines?
- Why are people rich or poor in capitalism? Luck? Greed? Connections? Hard work and perseverance?
- Does free-market capitalism generate the kind of competition that forces firms to operate in society's long-run interest, or do firms, unregulated, run roughshod over workers, small rivals, consumers, and needy politicians, and promote environmental degradation?
- Is economic power distinct from political power; and if they are not distinct, how are they meshed? How do they affect wages, profits, laws regulating the economy, interest rates, prices, exports, and imports?
- Is a growth in GDP a good thing, or a bad thing?
- Is the Federal Reserve System a "neutral monitor" of monetary policy, or primarily concerned with protecting the interests of wealthy bondholders?
- Is a certain amount of unemployment a good thing for capitalism?
- Does capitalism "provide economic freedom directly [and] also promote political freedom" (Milton Friedman, 1963)? Or is advocating capitalism "like the elephant running through the chicken yard, yelling, 'Everyone for himself!'" (Lester Pearson, past Prime Minister of Canada, 1963.)?

If you were to choose at random any professional economist in the world and ask that person any question on the list above, *there is no way to know in advance what his or her answer will be.* If this were true, for example, of the science of physics, in what shape would the space program be?

All this imprecision would help to explain the story about the alumna who visits her old economics professor a decade after graduating. She notices a final exam on the professor's desk, takes a quick look and blurts out, "Isn't that the same exam I took?" The professor replies smugly, "Yes, but that was ten years ago. Now the answers are different."

THE ECONOMIC MAN IN MAINSTREAM THEORIZING

In the view of political economists, the unrealistic treatment of how people behave in capitalist societies is a critical flaw in mainstream economics. The essential assumption of neoclassical economics is that people are utterly selfish, pleasure-maximizing automatons who respond in predictable ways to all stimuli. This theoretical creature is called "economic man," or sometimes "rational man," and this man is not the kind of human being the rest of us would ever know, want to be, or take home.

On this point of human behavior and mainstream models, we can usefully turn to John K. Galbraith, probably the most famous contemporary American economist, and about whom there is a chapter in this book. Galbraith, a long-time critic of mainstream economics, has written that the idea of economic man forms part of a rigid system of thought. According to him, this system:

> ...requires that the ultimately valid propositions of economics be essentially given, like the structure of neutrons, protons, atoms and molecules. Once fully discovered they are known forever. Unchanging also, it is held, is human motivation in a competitive market economy. Such fixed and permanent truths allow economists to view their subject as a science... From this closed intellectual exercise, which is fascinating to its participants, intruders and critics are excluded often by their own choice, as being technically unqualified. And, a more significant matter, so is the reality of economic life, which, alas, is not, in its varied disorder, suitable for mathematical replication. (Galbraith 1987, 284-5)

Along with Galbraith, we do not contest the idea that most human beings will try to serve their own long term interests as well as they can. It is reasonable to assume that in capitalist societies, most of us will seek rewards from the marketplace, whatever our role in it. Yet this readily-observable fact can not help us to know, simply by looking at another human being, what he or she will do in the market *at the next moment.* It is the central practice of real scientists to experiment with the objects of their study until, in their labs, they come to know with some confidence what consistently will happen to Y if they change X? This is not what mainstream economists do because their subject is human behavior, something we can never predict with the kind of confidence that makes real science possible. Therefore, while the scientists are doing science, economists are, as John Maynard Keynes argued, engaging in an exercise in logic based on assumptions that can't be proven.

We want to make our point carefully here, so repetition is in order. We recognize that there are broad patterns of behavior in capitalist markets that are predictable. In fact, almost all of us order our individual worlds in terms of these patterns of behavior. However, to go from *broadly predictable* patterns of behavior to the assumption that all of us, all the time, have the knowledge, time, and inclination to maximize economic gains, carries us from reasonable observation to basing economic models on a badly distorted mirror of real human activity. For example, in order to predict consumer behavior, neoclassical models usually assume that all people have perfect information about all of the goods that they might want to buy, they know all of the prices and qualities involved, they know how much satisfaction they will receive from each product if they buy it, and they are completely rational and self-centered. These assumptions imply that when we shop we are not influenced by store displays or impulses that might interfere with the rational calculation of which good will bring the greatest satisfaction to us per dollar we spend. The assumptions also deny that some of us might actually buy more expensive or slightly lower-quality goods because they are produced under better environmental and labor conditions; that is, they ignore the idea that people might value justice, and not just pleasure. The mainstream view of how human beings shop in modern capitalist cultures is, to put the best light on it, quixotic.

There is a further problem here. In mainstream economics, economic man has also long been the idea of "man with unlimited wants." William Rohlf reveals this central assumption in his mainstream introductory text. As he argues:

> The fundamental problem facing individuals and societies alike is the fact that our wants exceed our capacity for satisfying those wants. (Rohlf 1998, 4)

What could be wrong with this statement? Notably, it is outside history: it is constructed for the sake of analysis rather than inferred from what human beings have actually done. As such, Rohlf bases the economic analysis that follows in his book on a "made-up" human being. Thorstein Veblen, whose ideas we will take up in a later chapter, recognized the failure of this model to explain the complicated ways in which people's desires are actually shaped. Veblen saw economic man as central to what he called "the hedonistic approach" to economics, his description of the central tradition in his own day. By using the term "hedonistic," Veblen meant that humans are looked upon as simple "pleasure machines," looking *only* to maximize their own happiness. In 1919, Veblen wrote that he saw actual human beings as "products of...hereditary traits and past experience cumulatively wrought out under a given body of traditions, eventualities, and material circumstances." (Veblen 1919)

What, then, do we think human beings actually are, for the purposes of studying their economic behavior? For an answer from political economy, we extend these comments from Veblen with some evidence from history.

ECONOMIC MAN AND HUMAN HISTORY

One of the most renowned economists of the twentieth century, Joseph Schumpeter, proclaimed that:

> What distinguishes the "scientific" economist from all other people who think, talk, and write about economic topics is a command of techniques that we class under three heads: history, statistics, and theory...Of these fundamental fields, economic history—which issues into and includes present-day facts— is by far the most important...If starting my work in economics afresh, I were told that I could study only one of these three but could have my choice, it would be economic history that I should choose. (Schumpeter 1954, 12)

History was an essential part of economic analysis, according to Schumpeter, for three reasons. First, a grounding in economic history allowed the analyst to understand economic affairs as processes unfolding in historic time. Second, historical analysis incorporates important institutional "data" that are often excluded from mainstream economic analysis. Finally, Schumpeter argued that those who fail to examine the historical record are likely to commit "fundamental errors" of analysis.

One of the more fundamental errors of mainstream economics has been to insist that the "hedonistic" tendencies of human beings were present from the dawn of time. In fact, the dominant role of these habits has developed in the relatively short era of world history since the rise of capitalism, mostly by those living after 1500 A.D. in Western Europe and North America. Adam Smith argued persuasively that self-interest and the human propensity to barter and trade were natural traits of human beings. Smith reached his conclusions by observing people in his own time making exchanges based on self-interested behavior, and he subsequently decided that the "propensity to truck, barter and exchange"—to offer a good or service to someone else only in exchange for an equally valued good, service, or the equivalent in money— must be a natural instinct. Moreover, Smith argued that the self-interested trader would only trade to become better off, due to the profit motive. Hence, transactions between humans in the capitalist age came to be seen as exchanges between two flinty-eyed, rationally-calculating, self-interested beings who were always looking to profit on any deal. This model left little room for other human inclinations such as altruism, sentimentality, or a concern for justice.

Was self-interested exchange a "natural" tendency of humans? When Smith wrote in 1776, he was ignorant of, or ignored, the writings of those historians of the ancient world who had described a very different system of exchange in the ancient economies of Greece and Rome. In these ancient civilizations, exchange most often took the form of elaborate systems of reciprocity or redistribution. Ancient Babylon and Egypt both operated systems of redistribution whereby most of the produce of the nation was collected, recorded, and then placed in centralized storehouses. In lean times (to which these primarily agricultural civilizations were especially susceptible), the stored produce was not sold to the highest bidder, but redistributed to all of the citizens, be they peasant, weaver, or potter, according to their needs. These economies were organized along the lines of gigantic households, in which all members of the society were expected to make their contribution to the household and in turn to share in the nation's produce. The Biblical story of Joseph describes just such a redistributive system as well as the rationale for the redistribution based on collective capacities and collective needs, rather than individualistic exchange. Recall that the brothers of Joseph, after selling him into slavery years before, came to Egypt in hopes of asking for some of the stored grains so that they could survive the famine in their native land of Canaan. Joseph, in his capacity as manager of the Pharaoh's stores of grains, gave generously to his brothers, despite their mistreatment of him so many years earlier

Other exchange often took place for honorific or social purposes, rather than for economic gain. Another Biblical example describes the honorific exchange between King Solomon of Israel and King Hiram of Tyre. Hiram offered Solomon all the cedar and fir trees that he needed for the temple he planned to build, and in exchange Solomon offered him wheat and oil. This was not economic exchange but an exchange of tributes (1 Kings, 5). Economic historian Karl Polanyi described many such systems of reciprocity—for example, giving gifts of fruit to kin and receiving in return gifts of fish—which existed in pre-capitalist societies. Polanyi argued that this was not barter and trade, but rather a socially-organized system of reciprocity, based on sharing with the rest of the community. To sum up, in *The Great Transformation*, Polanyi argued:

> [A]ll economic systems known to us up to the end of feudalism in Western Europe were organized either on the principles of reciprocity or redistribution, or householding, or some combination of the three....In this framework, the orderly production and distribution of goods was secured through a great variety of individual motives...Among these motives gain was not prominent. (Polanyi 1944, 55)

The obvious implication of Polanyi's point is that the mainstream argument—that self-interest and the instinct to barter and trade is a *natural* trait of human beings—is at odds with historical evidence. The most we can say is that self-interested behavior came to be rewarded in pecuniary terms during the short span of human history elapsed since the rise of capitalism, and that five hundred years of capitalism have probably reinforced self-interested behavior in ways that make it difficult to suppress. But the latter is a very different proposition than to argue that self-interest is inherent in human behavior. And, in some societies dominated by private firms—such as in Sweden—public policy is nevertheless based upon such human motivation as generosity and reciprocity, rather than on the assumption that all people are greedy in all their transactions.

Space does not allow us to tell the stories of how the first markets emerged and then became the ubiquitous markets of economic theory, or how the human yearning to be productive and creative came to be twisted into a labor-leisure tradeoff in modern economics. Suffice it to say that a careful study of history is an essential part of economic analysis and, to borrow an idea from philosopher George Santayana, we might say that economists who ignore history are doomed grievously to misinterpret it. Whether using the lessons of history in formulating present-day policies to make a better future, or testing the theories of modern economics against all of the learning of historians, history is indeed an essential part of the study of economics.

THE MYTHICAL SEPARATION IN THE MAINSTREAM BETWEEN ECONOMICS AND POLITICAL POWER

In addition to concluding that mainstream economics has peopled its models with creatures existing in a historical, psychological, and cultural vacuum, political economists are also highly critical of the mainstream presumption that economics is distinct from politics or power. As a typical example from one economic principles text (an example picked at random from a shelf of them), consider the following statement:

> How did the very wealthy get that way? Of the 400 people on the Forbes magazine list of the richest people in America (with an average wealth of about $500 million each), about one-fourth got rich through inheritance. The other three-fourths, such as Bill Gates of Microsoft, got rich through working, starting their own businesses, inventing new products, and so on. (Stockman 1999, 425.)

In this excerpt and throughout his book, Stockman avoids mention of government, the legal system, or any other institutions related to political power that might have played a role in helping the Fortune 400 amass their wealth. In fact, wealth accumulates in any society, either from inheritance or some other way, because the laws allow it to happen. For instance, as recently as 1959 the highest federal marginal tax rate was 91% for all personal income over $200,000! Since then, the laws have been changed, and now the highest marginal rate—for income over $271,000—is 39.6%. In other words, today's Fortune 400 are accumulating their wealth faster than in 1959 partly because lawmakers changed the laws on their behalf. By comparison, Sweden's welfare state provides all citizens, among other benefits, health care and schooling, and to pay for these benefits Swedes pay over *half* their income in the form of taxes. In the United States, this average tax rate is about 30%, meaning that we have a very different set of rules regarding how much wealth and income individuals keep for themselves and how much will be used for broader, social purposes.

Journalists Donald Bartlett and James Steele (in *America: Who Really Pays the Taxes?*, 1994) demonstrated the extent to which U.S. corporations are subsidized by governments through low or even non-existent, taxes, and by direct subsidy payments. They discovered innumerable examples of this practice, such as government subsidies totaling over $100 million a year to McDonalds, M&M/Mars, and other companies marketing their goods abroad. In 1999, *Time Magazine* updated this research and concluded that in 1997 corporations received almost $200 *billion* in subsidies from state, local, and federal agencies. This huge flow of government payments exemplifies the power of corporations to shape political decisions in their favor, a power that is denied to virtually all citizens except the very wealthy. When did *you* last impose your economic interests on a U.S. Senator or the President, as the owners of large corporations do on a daily basis?

Corporations are able to impose their agendas in this way partly because they give enormous amounts of "soft money" to politicians. One effect of these payments in the past two decades has been lax enforcement of anti-monopoly laws by the anti-trust division of the U.S. Justice Department. Presidents Reagan, George Bush, Bill Clinton, and George W. Bush, who in succession have directed anti-trust policy for more than twenty years, have encouraged the marriage of mammoth corporations, such as the $170 billion merger between Exxon and one of its major rivals, Mobil Oil, and the one between Time/Warner and American Online, which created a $350 billion behemoth. Mergers of this order are sold to the public on the grounds that only giant conglomerates can provide the high-quality, low priced goods for which we are supposed to clamor. Yet, mergers can as often as not mean less competition, higher prices, and a growing challenge to democratic rights in areas where they operate. The devastating social consequences were recently exemplified by the mega-company Enron, whose managers merged dozens of firms in the energy and financial industries and then, blessed by direct contact with George W. Bush, preyed on the whole society.

Our point here is important if we are to distinguish adequately between mainstream economics and political economy. To the former, political power is most often considered part of the background institutional structure which is, as they put it, "taken as a given" and thus is left to political "scientists" or others to worry about. It is this determination to ignore the political consequences of concentrated economic power in capitalism that allows conservative mainstream economists such as Milton Friedman to argue that capitalism always "promotes political freedom." For their part, political economists see capitalism as *intrinsically political:* the capitalist workplace is a rigid hierarchy of control, and the allegedly "neutral" government acts disproportionately –

as even reasonably alert children now know – in the service of the rich and powerful.

Karl Marx suggested that the government in modern capitalist countries is "the executive committee of the capitalist class," that is, of the rich and the powerful. As you will likely discover in an economics principles course, income inequality is now greater in the U.S. than in any other advanced capitalist society, and it has consistently been among the most unequal for over two centuries. This is the case because our laws allow it. The political economist might explain why Bill Gates is worth $90 *billion*, while at the same time about *forty million* people in the U.S. do not have health insurance, in this way: powerful people and corporations have consistently defeated efforts in the U.S. to provide adequate health care to all citizens, while they have spent lavishly to ensure that lawmakers make rules of the capitalist game that allow individuals to accumulate vast fortunes. This political economy view is quite a different explanation from the theory of income distribution that Stockman suggests – the idea that most people get what they earn primarily through hard work and creativity.

Mainstream and Contemporary Graduate Programs in Economics

Since it is probably not by virtue of divine intervention, and certainly not from success in predicting what will happen in the world, why does the mainstream version—and in this context we are talking specifically about the narrow model building we discussed at the beginning of the essay—dominate economic instruction in the capitalist world? As we have said, the answer lies in the kind of graduate programs that now train economists. All but a few of these programs in the U.S. focus on a narrowly-conceived foundation of economic theory, statistics, and mathematics. For example, consider aspects of two such programs always ranked among "the very best," Stanford and M.I.T. Here is Stanford's description of the desirable academic background for prospective graduate students in economics:

> Most of our recent successful applicants have had scores above the 95th percentile on the quantitative GRE, and received excellent grades in economics and math courses. The department requires competence in the calculus of several variables, linear algebra, and probability and statistics as they are used in modern economics. Applicants are not required to have been undergraduate economics majors, but some substantial preparation in economics is desirable (Stanford University web site).

According to the M.I.T. web site, the "core requirements" for its Ph.D. in economics include the following courses:

- Two courses in microeconomic theory
- Two courses in macroeconomic theory
- Two courses in mathematics for economists
- Two courses in econometrics (statistical economics)
- One course in economic history

Most striking about these two programs is not what they include by what they leave out. Here's a list of subjects that one does *not* have to study as a graduate student to get a "doctor of philosophy" in economics at Stanford or MIT:

- Philosophy, religion, ethics
- History beyod a single course, literature, classics, foreign languages
- Art, art history, and music
- Natural or pysical sciences, psychology
- Political Sciece, sociology, anthropology, international relations

Without question, when Ph.D. students go beyond the core requirements, and especially when many of them write their theses, they will do research in other disciplines, particularly the other social sciences and history. However, the core of the typical program makes it quite clear that whatever information is taken from outside economics, it will be filtered through the tiny meshed screen of a narrow definition of economics. Thus, to get a Ph.D., students increasingly need not know anything about the economy, but must understand incredibly complex mathematical manipulations. If it becomes the case that only mathematical economists get Ph.D.s and only Ph.D.s teach economics, the profession will have become self-perpetuating, no matter its failures at being scientific and its exclusivity.

David Collander provides the following look at how survival in the economics profession has narrowed the interests of those studying economics:

In a [1987] study Arjo Klamer and I did of graduate economics education, we asked students what would put them on the fast track. Approximately ninety percent said that knowledge of mathematics and knowledge of modeling was important. Only about three percent said that these were unimportant. *Only ten percent said that knowledge of economic literature was very important and only three per-*

cent said that knowledge of the economy was very important. Sixty-eight percent said
knowledge of the economy was unimportant. In my view, these answers suggest that
something is terribly wrong in the economics profession and in the incentives
that economists perceive. (Collander and Coates 1998, emphasis added)

Of course, as we discussed at the beginning of this essay, the mainstream
school is broad enough to include a variety of approaches, including some
that are skeptical about narrow model building. For example, in 1991, the
American Economic Review—the most prestigious mainstream journal—
invited twelve eminent economists to become the Commission on Graduate
Education in Economics. They were asked to study the nature of graduate
economics training and to report their findings. In describing the contents of
their report, John Cassidy, economics editor of *The New Yorker*, wrote that:

> [The Commission] feared the universities were churning out a generation of
> "idiots savants, skilled in technique but innocent of real economic issues." The
> commission described the state of academic economics in damning detail, but
> five years later little, if anything has changed. "That report took a lot of time
> and energy on the part of everybody involved," Stanford professor Anne
> Krueger, who headed the commission, told me. "Yet, basically, if only the
> report and a pin had dropped at the same time, the pin would have sounded
> noisy." (Cassidy 1996)

It is not just political economists and a few mainstream economists who
are unhappy with the fact that narrowly-trained model builders dominate the
profession. John Cassidy quotes two other people who should know what
they're talking about. One of them is Joseph Stiglitz, an academic economist
who became head of the Council of Economic Advisors to Bill Clinton, and
who won a Nobel Prize in economics. Professor Stiglitz told Cassidy,
"Anybody looking at those [mathematical] models would say they can't provide a good description of the modern world" (Cassidy 1996). The other is
Laurence Meyer, an economist and currently a member of the Federal Reserve
Board. Meyer made the interesting point that the quantitative model builders,
who had come to dominate macroeconomics in the 1970s, actually helped
him indirectly to build an economic forecasting business that depended on
the older, Keynesian models. His firm profited from the fact that more and
more graduating macroeconomists—who could have been his competitors in
the forecasting field—were not trained to build models about the real world

and thus had a declining value to businesses and to governments. Meyer described to John Cassidy the problems of the mathematical school this way:

> When you close your blinds, you don't look out of your window and you don't care what's happening out there. You don't try to build models which are consistent with the real world. With the blinds closed, it's hard to see anything. (Cassidy 1996)

There might be a light at the end of this dark tunnel. Michael Weinstein, writing in the *New York Times*, has reported on foundation money being spent to help de-program graduate economists from their training. Weinstein describes a recent conference in Virginia at which first- and second-year economics graduate students were introduced to "applied topics ranging from the plight of low-income mothers under the 1996 welfare law to the long-term determinants of innovation." The instructors at the conference included faculty from the country's leading economics departments, and Weinstein concludes that their participation may reflect "an unwittingly workable life-cycle" among academic economists. Today, he believes, graduate students are forced to spend their early years submerged in theory because that is the only time in their careers when they are free of other professional demands. As the students become professors, many of them "find their way" into applied subjects. As evidence, Weinstein notes that "[c]ompared with 20 or even 10 years ago, there has been an explosion in the number of academics who are consultants to think tanks for policy analysis, corporations and Government agencies" (Weinstein 1999).

There are, then, alternatives voices shouting down the tunnel, and we can only hope that those in the dark, like the many in economics programs that ignore the real world, will listen.

So What Should Economists Do?

Our position is that the public would do best to listen to economists from all branches of economics, including those outside the dominating mainstream. This, as we now know, surely does not happen, but what would happen if it did? We would like to answer that question by comparing two ways to look at a currently important social issue, environmental pollution. In his popular textbook, Roger Leroy Miller discusses the economist's idea of the "optimal amount of pollution" society should tolerate, and makes the following point:

Recognizing that the optimal quantity of pollution is not zero becomes easier when we realize that it takes scarce resources to reduce pollution. It follows that a trade-off exists between producing a cleaner environment and producing other goods and services. In that sense, nature's ability to cleanse itself is a resource that can be analyzed like any other resources, and a clean environment must take its place with other societal wants. (Miller 1997, 700)

This fairly straightforward argument contains an important point, and it makes sense in trying to decide what to do about pollution that we weigh the benefits of ending a source of pollution against the costs of doing so. What is unstated here, and it is a telling omission, is the assumption that we can actually know all these costs and benefits and be able to measure them. Concerning the costs of controlling pollution, let's take, for example, the case of managing toxic wastes by incinerating them. It is possible to estimate within a useful range the costs of building an incinerator, and we can estimate, but only within a much wider range, its long term operating costs. However, and this is the rub, there are many costs of incinerating toxic wastes that are simply not measurable. As a prime example, the scientific community is divided over the health effects of incineration because a by-product of the process is that certain heavy metals, and often the highly toxic dioxin (the chemical in Agent Orange), are spewed from the stacks during incineration. These enter the atmosphere in very small amounts, but no one knows for sure their effects. What is the cost borne by individuals living next to a possible death machine; and alternatively, if it turns out not to be such a machine, what is the cost to them, perhaps over decades, of worrying about its effect on themselves and their children? Furthermore, incinerators are almost always located in low income neighborhoods against the wishes of the people living there, and we would need to have some measure of the costs to these poor people of having their neighborhood ruined by a big, ugly, smoking incineration plant. Quite simply, it is not possible to measure the full costs of toxic waste incineration.

Though we will not go into the details, difficulties in measuring the social benefits of toxic waste incineration are equally daunting. And once "calculated," we would need to compare the benefits of incinerating toxic wastes to those of leaving them on the ground, throwing them in a landfill, or disposing of them in some other way. Thinking about this matter for just a moment will make it clear that any of these methods of "dealing" with toxic wastes will produce outcomes we cannot know in advance, and which perhaps cannot be measured.

In other words, economists can give us a model that says, in order to decide rationally about pollution, we should measure the costs and benefits of cleaning up any particular polluting source. But that's about it. We are given a conceptual framework in which to think about pollution control but no way to deal with the insurmountable problems of putting dollar amounts on *all* the material and intangible costs and benefits.

Miller's book not only lacks any reasonable procedure for weighing costs and benefits: it also ignores some essential social facts about toxic waste management. There is no mention of our point that poor people—and people of color, especially—are most likely to live close to toxic incinerators; and there is no mention of the fact that the pollution control business is a huge industry with substantial political clout at every level of government. Moreover, Miller seems to have no curiosity at all about the relationship between the roughly three to four *thousand* advertisements the typical adult now sees every day, the rampant consumerism this creates, and the fact that toxic wastes flow naturally from the products of such consumerism. He can ignore those aspects of the issue because, like any good mainstream economist, his job is to take the world as given and make correct scientific statements about it, despite the fact the consumer wants he is taking as given might be leading us toward the destruction of our planet. Miller's analysis of pollution, therefore, is quite typically mainstream in his trust in highly abstract and simple models which promise a good deal more than we think they can deliver.

The political economy world is a far less certain one, in which the political economist works to push away the fog, hoping for a fleeting glimpse of real economic forces. From such a view, with uncertainty the ever-present companion and belief that everything remotely relevant *must be given attention*, the political scientist might look at environmental pollution, in general terms, in something like the following way:

> We believe that human activities that threaten the environment and human health need to be curtailed. And, let's assume—from a large body of persuasive, though not necessarily conclusive, data accumulated from many branches of science and from reputable literary and journalistic sources—that modern patterns of consumption in wealthy countries currently pose a dire threat to the environment and to human health. Then, let's assume it is possible through education to persuade people that it is in their long-term self interest to learn to live with less instead of giving in to the cajoling voices of advertisers. Then, let's establish a principal goal of trying to imagine ways to recon-

struct society so that human beings become gradually less insatiable in the face of the endless swirl of commodities. And, let's plan to do our work with a kind of analysis that will be accessible—and hopefully useful—to others who share our interest in preserving the planet for coming generations.

In this example, we distinguish the political economy approach from the mainstream in four critically different ways:

1. We believe that human nature is pliable and conditional, rather than fixed.
2. We have made explicit value judgments about the way we think the world ought to be.
3. A central basis of our analysis is empirical and historical (and thus inconclusive), rather than theoretical and conclusive.
4. The questions we ask, our method of answering them, and all the other aspects of our investigation, are couched in a language designed for all people who want to build a more reasonable world, rather than symbolic language accessible only to the few.

CONCLUSION

There are, to be sure, a number of other differences that exist between mainstream economics and political economy, as well as disagreements within these groups. We have been describing polar clusters on the great spectrum of economic ideas. After you read the remaining chapters in this book, you can compare them to the mainstream explanations that will almost certainly be the focus of your economics courses. Then, perhaps, you can decide for yourselves what version of modern economic analysis, or what mixture of analyses, makes the most sense.

SUGGESTIONS FOR FURTHER READING

Collander, David and Alfred W. Coates, eds. *The Spread of Economic Ideas*. New York: Cambridge University Press, 1998.

Galbraith, John Kenneth. *The Age of Uncertainty*. Boston: Houghton-Mifflin, 1977.

Keynes, John M. *Essays in Biography*. New York: Harcourt-Brace, 1933.

Myrdal, Gunnar. *The Political Element in the Development of Economic Theory*. Cambridge, Mass.: Harvard University Press, 1965.

Polanyi, Karl. *The Great Transformation*. New York: Farrar and Rinehart, 1944

Routh, Guy. *The Origin of Economic Ideas*. New York: Vintage Books, 1977.

Veblen, Thorstein. "Why is Economics Not an Evolutionary Science?" in *The Place of Science in Modern Civilization*. New York: B. W. Huebsch, 1919.

2
Marxist Thought:
An Introduction

Our goal in this essay is to present a coherent summary of Marx's analysis of economic forces in society and how they shaped human lives. We will do that in two parts. The first briefly outlines a theory of historical change that Marx developed with his long-time collaborator, Frederick Engels. In 1845-6, the two wrote a manuscript, *The German Ideology,* that was largely an attack on prominent German philosophers of their time. It was not published during their lives and, as Marx wrote later, he "abandoned it to the gnawing criticism of the mice in the attic." However, when it was published in the Soviet Union in 1932 readers discovered that its first part, probably written by Marx, contained an explanation of historical change that Marx called "the materialist conception of history." We will provide a structural outline of this conception of history with a few examples to help the reader learn the basic terminology of the system.

We will then examine how Marx applied his theory of historical change to capitalism. This application is spread over thousands of pages of material that Marx and Engels wrote. However, the single most compact presentation is in *Capital*, volume 1, and the second part of our essay will concentrate attention on the arguments about capitalism in that book. *Capital* is by far Marx's most thorough application of his materialist conception of history: one is actually an example of the other, and by presenting them in sequence we hope to clarify the "Marxian" view of capitalism. Marx's analysis of capitalism is an intricate theoretical structure, buttressed by a huge compendium of historical description, and when studied closely it can be genuinely breathtaking in its breadth and depth.

We also want readers to see the great divide between Marx's analysis of capitalism and that of most current mainstream economists, who tend to look upon capitalism as a "given system," and exhibit little or no professional interest in the historical process that gave rise to it. They have ripped economic analysis from its historical context, ignoring the evolution of the capitalist system. As we tramp our way through the Marxist world we will see how substantial this difference is between his work and that of mainstream economists.

MARXIST THOUGHT PART I:
THE MATERIALIST CONCEPTION OF HISTORY BRIEFLY DEFINED

Marx asks a fundamental question confronting all human societies. What must we do to survive? To live, we must mix our intelligence and our energy—our work—with the basic "materials" of the world we find ourselves in; its soil, water, and air. We must work with what's at hand in order to make this today into tomorrow. In 1878, Frederick Engels summarized his and Marx's theory of historical change in the following way:

> The materialist conception of history starts from the principle that production, and with production the exchange of its products, is the basis of every social order; that in every society that has appeared in history the distribution of the products, and with it the division of society into classes or estates, is determined by what is produced and how it is produced, and how the product is exchanged. (Engels 1975, 74)

The economic organization of human society, or the "mode of production" as Marx called it, is therefore the most powerful force in determining social structure. Notably, the way society is organized to produce necessities—for example, into serfs and lords in feudalism, or into owners and workers in capitalist societies—constitutes the "class structure" of society. Since virtually all production involves many different people, Marx concentrated on production as a *social* activity and analyzed the class structure created by the organization of production.

Marx's method of analysis is very different from that of Adam Smith, who focused on how *individuals* behaved within a beneficent, competitive capitalist society. In contrast, Marx sought to understand the forces that cause the economy to change over time. He believed that change resulted from the struggle between opposing, or "dialectical"—what we might think of as "contradictory" or competing—forces inherent in all societies. As an example, one Marx made much of, all economic systems produce hierarchies of social classes, with a top and a bottom, and endless competition and resentment at every level in between. These class struggles emerge in the form of wars, revolutions, democratic reform, and in other ways, and one can find them grinding away in any history book. That is, social classes are inherently contradictory, inherently opposing forces, in every society.

Marx found that the social activity of production took many different forms throughout history, with stages of social organization corresponding to techniques of production. He noted that European society passed through a number of different modes of production, including primitive communalism, slavery, and feudalism, on its way to capitalism. He concluded that capitalism is simply the latest in a series of modes of production and that it, too, will yield to some other mode of production in the future.[2]

The pattern of ownership of tools and materials generally shapes the system of social classes in a society. The two dominant classes in capitalism are the bourgeoisie and the proletariat. Below, we will discuss their relationship and what generates conflict between them, but for now we can emphasize their different stations with a brief look at how wealth in the U.S. is divided between them. According to Doug Henwood, the richest 10% of the U.S. population owns over 80% of all stocks and almost 90% of all bonds (Henwood 1997). Since owning the stocks and bonds of companies means owning their "means of production," the wealth-producing capital of the United States is almost all owned by one tenth of the population. In order to make a living, most of the other 90% who work do so either for these richest 10%, their managers, or in the non-profit sector of the economy.

Additionally, for the past two decades, the U.S. working class has experienced a dramatic decline in income, relative to that of the owners and top managers for whom they work. For example, in 1965, the average CEO's salary was 44 times the average factory worker's wages, but today that ratio is *over 500 to 1*. The changing fortunes of owners and workers in U.S. capitalism are fine examples of what Marx meant by the inherent struggle between workers and capitalists. They also exemplify the inherent contradictions, or "dialectical" pressures, within U.S. capitalism because sustained, relative declines in income for the majority of a society's population tend to produce political upheaval. The interests of Wall Street rarely coincide with those of Main Street, and the conflicts between them can be powerful.

Through his study of history, Marx came to believe that conflict between the classes was the source of most major changes in human society. He summarized this idea in the following passage from *The Communist Manifesto*, written in 1848:

> The history of all hitherto existing society is the history of class struggles. Freeman and slave, patrician and plebeian, lord and serf, guild-master and journeyman, in a word, oppressor and oppressed, stood in constant opposition to one another, carried on an uninterrupted, now hidden, now open fight, a fight that each time ended, either in a revolutionary re-constitution of society at large, or in the common ruin of the contending classes. (Marx and Engels 1998, 34-5)

Marx's focus on social classes in conflict is central to his analysis of capitalism, and we will take it up again in Part II.

Another principal argument in Marx's materialist conception of history is that every mode of production fundamentally shaped other aspects of society. In describing this view, C. Wright Mills, a sociologist influential in the 1950s and 1960s, wrote in *The Marxists*:

> Political, religious and legal institutions as well as the ideas, the images, the ideologies by means of which men understand the world in which they live, their place within it, and themselves—all these are reflections of the economic basis of society. (Mills 1962, 82)

The extent to which political institutions in capitalist countries reflect the needs of the capitalist class can hardly be lost on any person living in the U.S. today, where it seems that government at every level is for sale to the highest capitalist bidder. Less obvious, but as important, consider the symbiosis between religion and the emergence of capitalism in Europe. Religious beliefs in hunter-gatherer societies usually emphasize the importance of nature and the role of people within it, and this reflects the importance of the natural environment to survival in that mode of production. Marx was struck by how convenient to the emergence of capitalism had been the teachings of the early

Protestant religions. These new religions, which developed after Martin Luther's 16th century revolt against Catholicism, stressed that one should accept one's lot in life and that all would be better in the hereafter. Such a belief, of course, made people more willing to accept the dislocations and deprivations so many experienced in early capitalism. In one of his more memorable phrases, Marx described religion as the "opiate of the masses" because he believed that workers in capitalist societies adopted religious beliefs as the only hope in an inexorably grim world.

Marx also argued that capitalism would eventually demean and devalue all that it pulled under its spreading wings. In 1846, in *On the Jewish Question*, he noted that money could transform all things, until money itself was all that was important in life:

> Money abases all the gods of mankind and changes them into commodities. Money is the universal and self-sufficient value of all things. It has, therefore, deprived the whose world, both the human world and nature, of their own proper value. Money is the alienated essence of man's work and existence; this essence dominates him and he worships it. (Marx and Engels 1978, 50)

In Marxist language, alienation derives primarily from a process called "commodification." All things—flesh and blood, inanimate objects, music, poetry, *everything*—ultimately are "for sale" in the capitalist marketplace. We all know countless examples of commodification. Each Christmas, to suggest an obvious one, most of us in Christian countries celebrate the birth of Jesus with an avaricious, competitive, often depressing orgy of consumption of mostly unnecessary products. What was once a simple affair of gift giving to exemplify Christian charity has become in advanced capitalism a gruesome distortion of the original idea. Capitalism, as we all know, incessantly works on all of us to buy things we don't need. However, capitalists pull out all the stops for Christmas. By the time it is over a substantial minority of us need anti-depressants as an antidote to the lack of Christmas joy that millions of advertisements told us the gifts, the cards, and the family gatherings would bring.

Creative output of all kinds is also systematically commodified in capitalist societies, co-opted and transformed by pop culture or the advertising industry. About a decade ago, Paul McCartney of the Beatles tried to buy from a record company the rights to many of the popular songs that he wrote with John Lennon. However, McCartney was outbid by another pop icon, Michael

Jackson, who then proceeded to sell the rights to some of these songs to advertising firms. The Beatles song "Revolution," written in response to the political turmoil of the 1960s, was put in the service of selling sneakers. Some Beatles fans might call this sacrilege, but to a Marxist this kind of commodification is the predictable end road for cultural products in capitalism. "Public" radio stations that increasingly depend upon corporate funds to stay alive, the "Tostitos" Fiesta Bowl, and the Nike swoosh on the uniforms of athletes all over the world exemplify the way by which things that were not once part of the cash nexus have become commodities.

To Marx, the most costly form of commodification occurs when capitalists buy labor power in labor markets. This commodity, labor power, is — as we shall describe in detail later — the irreplaceable aspect of capitalist production, because without hired laborers to produce the output capitalism cannot exist. Even in this age of high technology, labor costs still make up two-thirds of the costs of production for firms, indicating how essential labor remains in the production process. When a capitalist buys labor time, however, he or she must treat that labor power like any other input; it must be bought as cheaply as possible and drained of its last ounce of usefulness for profit-making. The fact that labor power is brought to the market by a human being is, of course, a problem. Human beings, unlike sheets of plywood and computer chips, have imagination, wishes, plans, and dreams, perhaps even to challenge the boss! While imagination and dreams and independence of mind can make for productive workers, such traits can also be problematic for the capitalist who is trying to maximize profits. Who wants an imaginative dreamer—someone who thinks for himself or herself—on the assembly line, or as a secretary, or in the mind-numbing jobs in retail sales and custodial work that are the fastest growing niches in the economy?

Because workers are interested in many things other than their jobs and, in fact, many workers hate their jobs, capitalists face the complicated problem of focusing their employees' attention on the work at hand. The modern capitalist workplace, particularly in the United States, is usually a dictatorship, where all the rules are made by the bosses and followed by all workers who want to keep their jobs. Capitalists want ordered work from conforming, non-complaining bearers of crucial labor power. They want a "thing," rather than a human being. This is the commodification of labor – a linchpin of Marxist analysis.

Globalization, a major social transformation now engulfing everybody, everywhere, provides a good example of the materialist conception of history, particularly its dialectical and contradictory nature. Globalization is the ultimate expression of the free market system, as capitalism expands inexorably around the world in search of new markets and cheap, desperate labor. Marx described this search for desperate labor power in his often-flamboyant style by suggesting that "The worshipful capitalists will never want for fresh exploitable flesh and blood, and will let the dead bury their dead" (Marx and Engels 1978, 215). For capitalists, globalization can be immensely profitable as they search the globe for the cheapest labor and resources to minimize their costs of production. Capitalists can also increase the scale of both production and profits by adding customers from the furthest reaches of the world.

However, capitalists are not the only actors. As often as not, their behavior produces countervailing responses and unintended consequences. Consider the unintended consequences of capitalist globalization. In recent decades, an immediate, *intended* consequence has been the decline of the real wages of the working class in the United States. U.S. laborers cannot easily maintain their own wage levels when they are in competition with low wage workers in developing countries all over the globe making as little as a quarter an hour. Yet Marx saw clearly that low wages in capitalism would mean that the system could produce more than could be sold, with the result an international crisis of "underconsumption." Furthermore, the increasing inequality generated by globalization tends to destabilize the political institutions of developing societies. As evidenced in the political turmoil in Argentina, a developed country, and in other developing countries, workers in such societies will not accept low wages and limited human rights forever. In the Marxian view, out of this new set of conflicts generated by globalization, this new dialectal situation, will arise new societies, which we now can only imagine vaguely, but which will be driven into being by the very historical processes produced by the spread of capitalism.

To sum up Marx's theory of history: he believed that in order to survive, people must construct economic systems — modes of production — and that in all societies these modes principally determine the way people behave. Capitalism, now the dominant mode of production in the world, is no exception to this rule, and we have looked at a few of the ways this system shapes our lives. Marx argued that capitalism is a system of social classes that are in conflict and that the "cash nexus," as Marx once referred to capitalism, will in the end make commodities of all things and people.

How, then, does capitalism actually work? How does it make us into what we are, and especially into commodities? We have only hinted at the answer to this question, and now we turn our attention to the broader and deeper answer developed in *Capital*.

MARXIST THOUGHT PART II:
MARX'S CRITIQUE OF THE CAPITALIST MODE OF PRODUCTION

After Marx and Engels developed their materialist conception of history, sporadically between 1845 and 1857, Marx began work on a longer project to describe and explain the "laws of motion" of capitalism. The overall structure of that explanation had been presented compactly in the first part of The Communist Manifesto, but its dozen or so pages gave only a fleeting glance at the complete story. The expanded version was published in 1867 in the first volume of what was to be a multi-volume project, and Marx gave it the title Capital: A Critical Analysis of Capitalist Production. The book was first published first in German, and later editions in French (1872) and English (1886) made his critique available to most parts of the industrialized world. Marx was emphatic that the purpose of this book, and of all his analysis, was not just "to understand the world, but to change it."

The first volume of *Capital* was the only one published during Marx's life. Volumes II and III were prepared by Engels from Marx's notes, and Volume IV, more a massive compendium of economic ideas than an extension of his critique, was edited by a German Marxist, Karl Kautsky, between 1905 and 1910. We will focus almost entirely on Volume I because in it Marx presents his most fundamental arguments about capitalism, especially the relationship between the owners/managers of capital and wage earners who work for them. By focusing on *Capital*, we do not want to leave the impression that it is a compact statement of all that Marx wrote, for his other voluminous writings have influenced virtually every aspect of modern thought in the social sciences and the humanities. Nonetheless, as an argument about how the production system of capitalism came to be, how it functions, and the crucial implications of those functions, *Capital* works well on its own.

Despite the wide influence of *Capital* for over a century, few people outside of universities have the time or inclination to read the book. Inside U.S. universities, new interest in Marx emerged in the 1960s and 1970s, and then waned until quite recently. Despite this lack of access to an ordered and protracted discussion of *Capital*, its central ideas are quite easy to understand when placed in a modern context, using the experiences common to people who live in capitalist culture. It is our purpose here to take up the major themes in Marx's critique of capitalism in precisely that kind of context. We will begin our analysis by elaborating on the principal players we alluded to above, as Marx dramatically did in his own writings.

Players on the Capitalist Field, I:
Owners/Managers and their Competition

Marx argued that most people engaged in economic activity in the capitalist mode of production would fall into one of two major groups. First, there are the capitalists and their managers, or what Marx called the "bourgeoisie." Their identifying trait is that they own or manage the capital equipment of society, the buildings, furniture, materials, and everything else needed to produce commodities (goods and services) for sale. Like the classical economists before him, such as Adam Smith and David Ricardo, and mainstream economists in our time, Marx believed capitalists have the single goal of accumulating and maximizing profits from their investments in machines, materials, and labor power. And, like those before him, he had a high regard for the power of this capitalist accumulation process to accomplish gigantic tasks. As early as 1848, in the *Communist Manifesto*, Marx wrote this:

> [The capitalist class] during its rule of barely one hundred years, has created more massive and more colossal productive forces than have all preceding generations together. Subjection of nature's forces to man, machinery, application of chemistry to industry and agriculture, steam navigation, railways, electric telegraphs, clearing of whole continents for cultivating, canalization of rivers, whole populations conjured out of the ground – what earlier century had even a presentiment that such productive forces slumbered in the lab of social labour? (Marx and Engels 1998, 40-1)

Few in our own capitalist age would disagree with this claim, though others might use less florid language to make it. Marx says elsewhere in the *Manifesto* that capitalists can be depended upon constantly "to revolutionize the means of production," by which he meant that the owning-managing class will never stop imagining ways to make their production more efficient and therefore less costly. A new technique, a new revolution in the means of production, will give the individual capitalist the power to make extra profits until the inevitable occurs and competitors adopt the same technique, or perhaps even better ones. Less industrial societies will have their "walls battered down by cheap commodities," as Marx put it in the

Manifesto, for no mode of production can compete with capitalism in its capacity to drive down costs and shape the world after its own image. The globalization of capitalism that is now restructuring the world economy is a process Marx saw with uncanny accuracy in 1848, as reading the *Manifesto* will demonstrate.

For Marx, when the capitalist brings together land, labor, and capital, he or she produces a volatile mix that inevitably produces conflict. This view that struggle preeminently characterizes the capitalist workplace puts him at odds with Adam Smith and most others in the classical school, and with mainstream economists. It is, of course, not lost on mainstream economists that owners often have conflicts with their workers. Yet, anything beyond a perfunctory mention of the relationship between labor and capital, or what Marx called the social relations of production, is left outside the province of mainstream economics. From his different perch, Marx saw market competition compelling owners to see their workers as two-sided creatures. On the one hand, workers are crucial for production. On the other, they are unpredictable and resistant to change and authority. They are given to slowdowns if not monitored carefully, and, if united, they possess the collective power to demand higher wages and different working conditions. They can even halt production altogether. This threat means that workers must be continually controlled, their rebellions squelched at their inceptions.

Marx concluded that this world of hostile workers and hungry competitors would ultimately corrupt even the most saintly capitalist. It doesn't matter whether he or she is a Christian, Muslim, or Jew; is friendly or mean-spirited; is Asian, Latin American, or what you will. Ultimately, the forces of competition would entice the most well-intentioned capitalist to close the factory, reduce wages when possible, break the law, buy the politicians, adulterate the product, or do whatever else was necessary to maximize profit. Whereas mainstream economists see competition as the "invisible hand" that gives capitalism great moral authority over other economic systems, Marx saw competition as an unrelenting pressure that threatens to drag all capitalists down to the moral level of the most unscrupulous ones. As an example, Marx emphasized in *Capital* that without laws against child labor, *some* capitalists will hire children if doing so will lower costs, and the advantage thereby gained will force competitors downward into a squalid moral abyss. This imperative to follow the least scrupulous leader produces the assaults of the capitalist class on their customers, on their workers, and on the environment that one can find described daily in any newspaper.

Assessing the great power of competition to shape the actions of capitalists, Marx wrote this in chapter 10:

> To the out-cry as to the physical and mental degradation, the premature death, the torture of over-work, [capital] answers: Ought these to trouble us since they increase our profits? But looking at things as a whole, all this does not, indeed, depend on the good or ill will of the individual capitalist. Free competition brings out the inherent laws of capitalist production, in the shape of external coercive laws having power over every individual capitalist. (Marx 1967, 257)

Later in *Capital*, Marx vividly exemplified these effects of competition on capitalist morality by quoting a contemporary, T. J. Dunning, who had written:

> With adequate profit, capital is very bold. A certain 10% [profit] will ensure its employment anywhere; 20% certain will produce eagerness; 50%, positive audacity; 100% will make it ready to trample on all human laws; 300%, and there is not a crime at which it will scruple, nor a risk it will not run, even to the chance of its owner being hanged. (Marx 1967, 760)

Marx's description of owners differs dramatically from the mainstream version, in which the capitalist stands triumphantly on a pedestal, a heroic risk-taker who has brought together land, labor, and capital. To paraphrase Marx's view of that version, "Mr. Capital and Mr. Labor combine with Madam Land to produce the best of all possible worlds for them all."

Players on the Capitalist Field, II: The Workers

Estranged Labor Beginning in his early writings, Marx assigned great importance to the oppression of workers under capitalism. In 1844, Marx wrote a long manuscript, clearly intended to be a book, that provided a structural overview of his thinking about "economics" at the time. The notes lay undiscovered for almost a century, yet when they were published in English in the 1950s as the Economic and Philosophic Manuscripts, they generated great interest among Marxist scholars, who found a modern-sounding and compelling view about how capitalist wage labor limits human freedom.

In particular, the *Manuscripts* contained a section called "Estranged Labor," in which Marx described what, for him, were the fundamental conditions of labor under capitalism and the reasons that he found them so appalling. Marx argued that workers in capitalism are alienated from their work, their fellow employees, and themselves, and this argument became a preeminent theme for him and for all those who followed in his footsteps. According to Marx, workers' alienation stemmed from historical processes starting in 14th century England that gradually separated (alienated) workers from the land and tools with which they had forged a living as peasants. Eventually their survival depended on being hired as wage laborers. Marx described the terrible consequences of alienation for workers in what has become the most famous passage from "Estranged Labor":

> [Labor] is external to the worker, i.e., it does not belong to his essential being;…[I]n his work, therefore, he does not affirm himself but denies himself, does not feel content but unhappy, does not develop freely his physical and mental energy but mortifies his body and ruins his mind. The worker therefore only feels himself outside his work, and in his work feels outside himself. He is at home when he is not working, and when he is working he is not at home. His labor is therefore not voluntary, but coerced; it is forced labor. It is therefore not the satisfaction of a need; it is merely a means to satisfy needs external to it. Its alien character emerges clearly in the fact that as soon as no physical or other compulsion exists, labor is shunned like the plague. External labor, labor in which man alienates himself, is a labor of self-sacrifice, of mortification. Lastly, the external character of labor for the worker appears in the fact that it is not his own, but someone else's, that it does not belong to him, that in it he belongs, not to himself, but to another….it is the loss of the self. (Marx and Engels 1978, 74)

This conclusion that "lost labor" is a "lost self" perhaps says it all, yet does so in a far too general way. Fortunately, soon after writing the *Manuscripts*, Marx entered into his long collaboration with Frederick Engels, and they turned out thousands of pages in the form of essays, books, newspaper articles, and letters about capitalism. An ongoing burden of these pages was to explain to workers the nature of the system that oppressed them and to urge them to rise up against it. What follows are the key ingredients of this explanation.

Divided Labor In *Capital*, Marx had a good deal to say about the causes of estranged labor, and his analysis was more in the language of classical economics and less in the philosophical language of his earlier writing. In three key chapters of the book (13-15), Marx outlined the evolution of what 19th century economists called the "division of labor" (what we now call "special-ization"). Marx saw that a central reason for the estrangement of factory labor was the fact that it was profitable for owners to break tasks down into small-er individual units of work. As production was reduced to repetitive, mindless tasks, workers suffered physical injuries and mental frustration. Marx quoted from a French economist of the time to describe the grim consequences:

> To subdivide a man is to execute him, if he deserves the sentence, to assassi-nate him if he does not.... The subdivision of labor is the assassination of a people. (Marx 1967, 363)

The words are a bit different here than in the *Manuscripts* of 1844, but the argument is the same: *the capitalist mode of production, by necessarily and sys-tematically dividing labor to the greatest extent possible, denies most working people the opportunity to do the kind of creative work that Marx thought was essential to their humanity.*[3]

Controlled Labor How do capitalists force workers to do jobs that are so physically and spiritually deadening? With the development of manufactur-ing (used in this context to mean, "production by hand") in 17th and 18th century England, and with the industrialization that followed, production moved from homes to factories. Small farmers and cottage industry produc-ers had never had much control over the prices paid them by large mer-chants, but industrial workers had even less control over all parts of their work. Because factory workers toiled for owners rather than for their own immediate benefit, the owners monitored their efforts carefully. Indeed, industrial production created the need for a new kind of worker — man-agers and supervisors — to keep other workers doing increasingly alienating work. The division of labor, Marx put it, gradually separated "the hand from the brain" in capitalist workshops by generating ever more tasks demanding simple, repetitive motions but not much knowledge or control of the whole production process. This knowledge, originally held by workers, was trans-ferred to managers. Marx often compared the factory system to the way mil-itary officers keep the ranks in order. As he put it in *Capital*, when produc-tion begins, the capitalist:

> ...hands over the work of direct and constant supervision of the individual workmen, and groups of workmen, to a special kind of wage-laborer. An

industrial army of workmen, under the command of a capitalist, requires, like a real army, officers (managers), and sergeants (foremen, overlookers), who, while the work is being done, command in the name of the capitalist. (Marx 1967, 332)

To Marx, the increasing complexity of production in capitalist systems demanded ever more complex and sophisticated ways to keep workers performing jobs they typically do only in order to pay their bills.

What people involved in capitalist firms want from the experience varies with their relationship to the firm: do they own, manage, or supervise the work, or do they do it themselves for wages? The owners want brisk, timely, committed work, done as quickly as quality standards will allow. They want workers to be there promptly in the morning, to stay as long as they are supposed to, and longer if possible, and to perform flawlessly, efficiently, and without complaint. Workers, though, compelled to make a living, would prefer a friendly, flexible environment, over which they have some measure of control. Thus, workers keep their noses to the grindstone only when forced to do so by managers, supervisors, electronic monitors, spies, or whatever else the owners can use to compel them to greater productivity.

In brief, then, the major players on the capitalist field are capitalists hustling profits and workers hustling a wage or salary. We have described the two classes in the way that Marx chose to describe them, "in relation to each other." By this he meant that the term "capitalist" refers to someone who hires "wage laborers," that neither can exist without the other. Their relationship to each other produces the central dramatic action of the capitalist mode of production. Like all good dramatic action, this one is a waxing and waning struggle, and, in this case, what is being fought over is what Marx called "surplus value."

Surplus Value

For Marx, the origin of profit in capitalism was surplus value. This if a very different explanation of profit than that offered by mainstream economists. To appreciate the difference, consider the following (quite typical) version from a popular mainstream principles textbook:

> Profit can be looked at as the reward you get for taking a chance for society, and winning. If you hire some factors of production and make something the people want, and if you do it efficiently, you will be rewarded. Your profit is your reward. But if you guess wrong you get no reward. You lose. Your loss is

your "punishment" for using society's resources in ways the society didn't want its resources to be used. (Bowden and Bowden 1995, 63)

Let's look at Marx's alternative tale about how profits emerge in capitalism. Marx defined surplus value simply as the difference between the value of what a worker produces and what he or she is paid. Capitalists take this as profit, although it comes from the labor of the workers. In his analysis, Marx adopted what he calls "socially necessary labor time" as his standard of value for products exchanged in the market. The exchange value of a good or service is determined by the average number of hours of labor time that went into its production. In other words, Marx advanced one version of the general argument that the value of goods is determined by the labor that goes into them. The issue of what gave products their value had been debated by social theorists before Marx, and Adam Smith and David Ricardo were only the most prominent among the many who had put forward this kind of "labor theory of value."

Marx's own version of this theory was much more closely argued, and he used the first several chapters of *Capital* to work out its internal consistencies and logical implications. In these chapters, Marx assumed that value, as he defined it, would in the long run determine (more or less) market prices. In Volume III of *Capital*, at least in the version Engels fashioned from Marx's notes, Marx attempted to prove that the labor theory of value could be used as a basis for determining market prices. However, many critics have not been persuaded, and the debate continues. Fortunately for us, the framework Marx established about value is useful in analyzing capitalism, and this is true whether value determines prices, as Marx argued, or not. In the example below, we will work with the market prices of labor, materials, capital equipment, and products, rather than their embodied "socially necessary labor time." And, as we shall see, doing so does no harm to the analysis.

The idea of surplus value is easy to understand for anyone who has worked for wages or for a salary. Take for example, a young woman, a recent graduate from college who is offered $26,000 dollars a year to work for a capitalist company. What can we surmise about this transaction? The former student will likely be taking such a job because she is making an important transition in life and will soon pay the bills heretofore paid by her parents. She will probably have surveyed the possibilities and taken the best job available, given all her needs. What we know for certain is that the owner will be looking for one thing from the work of the student, and that thing is profit. In a nutshell, then, our new worker will be expected to produce something over $26,000 of new value, net of the cost of any materials used while doing it. Pure and simple. Our ex-student knows the rules, too, we can be sure. She knows that if she does not produce an amount of value greater than what she is paid, she will unceremoniously be ushered out the door.

None of this would be news to anyone raised in a capitalist society, though mainstream economists choose to look at it differently. Of course, they know that workers are hired to make profits for a firm, yet they typically avoid analyzing the historical processes that created that distribution of income and power. However, Marx was centrally concerned with the way this distribution came to be and how it shaped profit making, once established. To answer these questions, Marx developed a detailed historical description of how the land and tools necessary for production were stripped from peasants and artisans, forcing them to work for wages in order to survive. Under capitalism, when the entrepreneur and the worker arrive at the workplace to seek their fortunes, the principal rule that emerged from this historical (rather than natural or divine) process is that the worker must labor to produce surplus value for the entrepreneur.

Marx explained the ways in which capitalists extracted surplus value from workers in his analysis of the working day. In this discussion, to which we now turn, he probed a number of interesting questions that mainstream economists long ago stopped asking.

The Working Day

At the beginning of his great historical essay called "The Working Day" (chapter 10 of *Capital*), Marx broke down the day into two parts, creating a very simple model but one with complex implications. He asked the reader to look at the day of the typical employee as comprised of two parts, as follows:

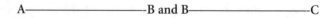

A————————————-B and B————————————-C

The first of these parts, A—B is the part of the day it takes for the worker to produce enough output (again, net of any material costs) to pay for his or her wage. We can more clearly exemplify this if we extend the example we began earlier with our recent graduate making $26,000 a year. We have chosen that apparently random number on purpose because it allows us to draw a simple example to make the point. Such an annual salary would come to $500 a week, or $100 a day. This means that, on average, *each day* this worker

must add extra value to the firm's output of more than $100 in order to jus-
tify continued employment.

To extend the example, let's assume that this employee adds value to the
firm's output of $160 a day or, assuming the typical eight-hour day, $20 an
hour. Already, we can see that the employee is making surplus value (profit)
for the owner, because the $160 of added value is more than the $100 daily
salary. As we take one step further into this analysis, we move away from the
de-politicized firm of the mainstream and into the world seen in Marxist
terms. That step is simply to say this: if the employee is adding $20 per hour
of extra value, she will have produced enough extra value to pay for her wage
during the first five hours of the day. Given the eight-hour workday in our
example, that means for the last three hours our ex-student will be producing
surplus value for the capitalist, the only reason why she was given the job in
the first place. Marx called the first five hours of this day "necessary labor" and
the remaining three hours "surplus labor" to differentiate the part of the day
the worker was working for the wage, and the part of the day spent toiling to
produce the owner's profits.

Marx focused the whole center section of *Capital*, several hundred pages,
on these last three hours, or the B—C part of the day. He did so because this is
the part that provides the capitalist surplus value, the quest for which is the dis-
tinguishing trait of capitalism. Marx did not, in his theorizing anyway, pass
judgment on the process of creating and maximizing surplus value in capitalism. As we have already learned, the capitalist is only doing what is necessary
to survive, and the worker is doing the same thing. The nature of the working
day, in Marx's view, is a way to look at the experience of most people who live
in capitalist culture, because most of them do work to produce surplus value
for someone else. What did Marx make of this particular configuration of the
day? The answer is "just about everything," and here we will take up the most
important things.

Extending the Working Day To begin with, we can ask ourselves a simple
question: what are the ways the owner of a firm can increase the B—C part of
the day? One immediate way would be simply to extend the length of the
working day. Marx called surplus value generated this way "absolute surplus
value," to distinguish it from "relative surplus value," which we will take up
soon. If our recent graduate worked 10 hours a day, rather than 8, this would
generate roughly another $40 of surplus value for the firm. The rub, of course,
is that it is illegal for the owner to do that in most modern capitalist countries

without paying a premium for "overtime" hours. Marx describes the political realities of the length of the working day this way:

> But when the transaction was concluded, [the worker] discovered that he was no "free agent," that the period of time for which he is *free* to sell his labor-power is the period of time for which he is *forced* to sell it, that in fact the vampire will not let go "while there remains a single muscle, sinew or drop of blood to be exploited." For "protection" against the serpent of their agonies, the workers have to put their heads together and, as a class, compel the passing of a law, an all-powerful social barrier by which they can be prevented from selling themselves and their families into slavery and death by voluntary contract with capital. In the place of the pompous catalogue of the 'inalienable rights of man' there steps the modest Magna Carta of the legally limited working day, which at last makes clear "when the time which the worker sells is ended, and when his own begins." (Marx 1967, 416, emphasis added)

Some of the more compelling periods of U.S. and British history, and of that of all capitalist societies, describe the battle waged over the length of the working day. When Marx was writing *Capital* in the 1860s, both British and U.S. laborers were engaged in protracted and often bloody battles with owners over the conditions of work in virtually every industry. To Marx, this struggle over the length of the working day was an inevitable outcome of the capitalist mode of production, and focusing on the B—C part of the day made it obvious why this was the case. Both parties, owner and worker, have diametrically opposed needs: the former has strong incentives to work the worker as long as possible, while the latter will typically do anything to make the workday shorter.

Laws concerning the workday, along with a tangled forest of others that have sprung from the same soil, exist in all advanced capitalist countries. In the early part of this century in the U.S., company violence against workers, including the use of the militia against them, combined with sorry working conditions to produce a reform movement led by working people that continues today. The unending political battles in the U.S. for the past sixty years over workplace safety, social security, unemployment compensation, minimum wages, welfare, trade, monetary and fiscal policy – to name only a suggestive list of issues – attest to this fact.

Once the length of the working day is fixed, the essential nature of the "contested terrain," as economist Richard Edwards described the workplace, does not change. Surplus value remains the goal of owners and high wages and good (if not easy) work conditions the goal of workers. What's a poor owner to do? Consider again the working day, A———-B———-C. If "A———C" is limited by law to represent eight hours in total, and the owner wants the part of the day in which the workers produce surplus value, B———C, to be as long as possible, what are ways to expand that part of the day? The answer must be to restructure work so that the laborer pays for the wage earlier in the day; or, in terms of the diagram, to restructure work so that "B moves to the left." Marx called profits made by such changes *relative* surplus value, and distinguished them from greater profits made simply by lengthening the working day.

Technological Displacement of Workers Marx was quite explicit in one example concerning relative surplus value. Market competition and the hunger for surplus value always force owners to replace their workers with machines when it is profitable do to so. Making workers more productive with better, faster machines means that they pay for their wage earlier in the day. Marx took up the issue of machinery at great length in chapter 15 of Capital. Although his argument concerns British industrial capitalism in the 19th century, his point remains relevant. He says at one point:

> [A] machine immediately becomes a competitor of the workman himself. The self-expansion of capital by means of machinery is thenceforward directly proportional to the number of the workpeople, whose means of livelihood have been destroyed by that machinery. The whole system of capitalist pro-duction is based on the fact that the workman sells his labor-power as a com-modity. Division of labor specializes this labor power, by reducing it to skill in handling a particular tool. So soon as the handling of this tool becomes the work of a machine, then….the workman becomes unsaleable…. That portion of the working-class thus by machinery rendered superfluous, either goes to the wall in the unequal contest of the [other outmoded industries] or else floods all the more easily accessible branches of industry, swamps the labor-market, and sinks the price of labor power. . . . (Marx 1967, 405-6)

Of course, this is the natural process by which technological unemploy-ment occurs in capitalism. As an example from our own capitalist world, assume a capitalist firm that can make 1,000 units of a commodity at an aver-age price of $1.00, with a process that uses one machine and 100 workers.

Then, a supplier drops by with news about a new machine which will allow the owner to produce the same 1,000 units but with only 50 workers and at a cost of $.80 per unit. Will the capitalist fire fifty of his workers? Probably, though he or she might first of all use the threat of the machine as a way to speed up the work and increase productivity that way. Over the long run, though, as that machine is replaced by the next and "better" one, some workers will need to look for work elsewhere.

In the two preceding chapters, 13 and 14, Marx had demonstrated, as he had in *The Communist Manifesto*, a genuine appreciation for the ability of the bourgeoisie to develop technology rapidly enough to transform the world with a theretofore unprecedented breadth and speed. He remained committed to the idea that machines could, in a mode of production designed for "free men," deliver people from the drudgery that has been the lot of most of them throughout human history. Yet, with the emergence of a system whose central dynamic is the production of surplus value, the machine becomes the agent of the worker's displacement, it promotes the exploitation of women and children, and, most horribly, it crushes workers between its moving wheels. Selected quotations from the chapter will make his point. On the moral imperatives of capitalism and the machines, Marx wrote:

> In so far as machinery dispenses with muscular power, it becomes a means of employing laborers of slight muscular strength....The labor of women and children was, therefore, the first thing sought for by the capitalist who used machinery. (Marx 1967, 372)

and:

> [M]achinery sweeps away every moral and natural restriction on the length of the working day. Hence, too, the economic paradox, that the most powerful instrument for shortening labor-time, becomes the most unfailing means for placing every moment of the laborer's time and that of his family, at the disposal of the capitalist for the purpose of expanding the value of his capital. (Marx 1967, 385)

Concerning dangers of the factory, Marx had this to say:

> [In the factory] every organ of sense is injured in an equal degree by artificial elevation of the temperature, by the dust laden atmosphere, by the deafening

noise, not to mention danger to life and limb among the thickly crowded machinery, which, with the regularity of the seasons, issues its list of the killed and wounded in the industrial battle. (Marx 1967, 401)

On this last point, Marx was, as we have said, writing about industrial capital rather than U.S. capitalism today (with its 70 percent of the workforce in the services industries), but we should not presume his comments about safety are outdated. In 1995 for example, 5,300 people were killed on the job in the United States and another 3.9 *million* received disabling injuries, meaning that the mechanized capitalist workplace remains a threat to life and limb. For those workers who remain on the job, and ambulatory, what else can the owner do to get them to pay for their wage earlier in the day?

Cutting Wages Let's assume that the student from our earlier example is toiling away for $26,000 a year in a capitalist firm with one hundred workers. Assume further that the owner decides to cut wages for all of them. Doing so would increase surplus value by moving the "B" part of the work day to the left, if we assume productivity doesn't change, because at a lower wage workers will provide enough extra value to pay for their wage earlier in the day. Will the workers accept these wage cuts like good soldiers? It depends, of course, and Marx made it clear he believed this battle over wages, like that over all the other conditions of work, would wax and wane.

As an excellent example of this ongoing struggle between capital and labor over wages, for about twenty-five years after World War II, real wages (that is, wages after accounting for inflation) rose regularly. This was because of steadily rising productivity and because, with roughly one-third of the workforce unionized, including virtually all wage earners in the big industries, labor unions had genuine collective power at the workplace and on the national political scene. However, for several reasons, including a declining manufacturing sector, globalization, and the intentional strategies of major capitalists to reduce the rate of unionization, labor's power relative to bosses began to decline in the early 1970s. Since then, the rate of unionization has fallen dramatically: in 2000 only 13.5% – and just 9% of the labor force in private firms – were union members. Now real wages for an hour's work are lower for most workers than they were in 1970. The current generation of "bottom line" employers is no more cold-blooded than their counterparts from, say, 20 years, or 120 years ago. The difference is that the weakened political power of workers allows the cold-bloodedness, ever lurking in capitalism, to prevail where it could not before. To put it another way, if we ask when employers try to lower the wages of their employees, the answer comes quickly to any of us: whenever they can get away with it.

Speeding up the Workplace Consider again our student and her ninety-nine fellow workers in the hypothetical capitalist firm. Let's say that this company provides consulting services to other firms.[4] Maybe fifty of its workers use computers to keep information flowing through the office, or to keep tabs on costs, or what have you; maybe the other fifty are outside the office consulting, drumming up customers, or hanging out when they can get away with it. How could the owner speed up the work of these hundred employees? Or, formulaically, how can he or she make them more productive and, by doing so, enlarge the B—C part of the workday? The owner could monitor the work of those fifty on the computers, rank them according to their speed, and publicize the rankings. Or, the owner might devise ways to speed up the efforts of the outside workers by increasing the number of contacts they must make, or by transferring to them some of the computer work usually done in the office. When, we ask again, will the owners/managers speed up the work of employees? The answer, again, is: whenever they can get away with it. Further, given the nature of work in most capitalist firms, we can also predict when workers will not do the work their bosses want them to: whenever they can get away with it.

Moving the Production Somewhere Else Another method by which owners try to enlarge the B—C part of the day is to seek out lower wages somewhere else. Most of the shoes worn by Americans used to be made in mills in New England, produced by family-owned firms which dominated local economies but nonetheless provided relatively high wages and a good measure of security. Now, only a few such shoe mills continue to exist in New England. First, the plants were moved to the southern U.S. because wages were lower there and, stemming from the same conditions that generate low wages, there was a relative hostility to organized labor. But before long, producers were moving their mills further south to places like the Dominican Republic, where wages were even lower; then, the move was to Taiwan and South Korea. This quest for the lowest wages reached its nadir when the Nike Corporation moved its production to Indonesia, where in the early 1990s, its subcontractors hired young women to make Nike shoes for 14 cents an hour.

To sum up Marx's arguments about "relative surplus value," he showed that confining the length of the working day to a maximum number of hours did not change the essential dynamic of the capitalist mode of production. It simply mandated that capitalists "intensify labor," to use Marx's term, in order to maximize surplus value. Concretely, this meant cutting wages, speeding up work, replacing workers with machines, and marching around the globe in search of low-wage workers.

The Industrial Reserve Army

In chapter 25 of Capital, Marx theorized about the debauched conditions endured by so much of the working class in Britain. His guides into this territory included dozens of reports of Parliamentary investigations, as well as Frederick Engels, whose book *The Condition of the Working Class in England* had early on helped draw Marx's attention away from philosophy and toward political economy. In chapter 25, Marx paid particular attention to the nature of what we call "unemployment" and the reasons that it regularly occurs in capitalism. What distinguishes Marx's treatment from current ones is in part the tone of his writing. Marx called those without jobs in capitalism "the industrial reserve army." His words conjure complex images that present a far richer notion about workers without jobs than the abstract mainstream term "unemployment." Consider the implications of Marx's term. First, he uses a military metaphor, "army," reminding us that those without jobs are foot soldiers in some capitalist's army and, like their counterparts in the real army, utterly at the mercy of the "generals" directing the struggle. More important, however, is the word "reserve," which in Marx's definition carries crucial political and economic implications.

The unemployed in Marx's system are "in reserve" in the sense that capitalists always need a pool of them in order to make surplus value. Consider an economic recession, where production and employment spiral down together, the decline in each bringing about further declines in the other. The first workers to get the axe will be the last ones hired back, and they will be those considered the least skilled, least educated, least desirable for whatever reasons. If the contraction is great enough and long enough, an increasing number of those losing jobs will be more educated and experienced.

We all know this, but Marx adds the emphasis that for capitalism to function, these people must take their lumps, if not in silence, at least without posing a political threat. In other words, capitalism *absolutely depends upon* a class of people at the bottom who can be fired without explanation and who also are not able to organize resistance to the system that has tossed them out. Instead of resisting, capitalism demands that these workers graciously blame their lot on themselves, rather than blame a production system that makes their unemployment necessary and predictable. Further, capitalist systems need the reserve army to hold down wages: a pool of unemployed, financially desperate workers reminds those who remain they can easily be replaced if they make demands on their employers. And finally, the reserve army serves the needs of capitalism in times of economic growth. When the economy starts expanding, it won't grow for long unless there are people "in reserve" who can be absorbed back into the system. Naturally, he capitalists' hope is that those in reserve will not have made themselves into a real "army" in the meantime.

Throughout *Capital*, Marx fulminates and rages, in between the lines of his dense theoretical arguments, about the lot of workers in capitalism. It deeply provoked his moral outrage. Yet in mainstream economics, unemployment is hardly considered a moral issue, but a short-term failure of the system or a long-term failure of hopeless individuals. The relationship between joblessness and the political system is also generally ignored because, as is usual in mainstream economics, politics and questions of power are cavalierly ignored.

Social Classes

The idea of the army of unemployed points to the fact of social classes in capitalism, about which Marx had much to say. One of the more intriguing aspects of life in U.S. society is that those who shape opinions, including many professors, deny the existence of social classes. Instead of concepts such as "working class" or "ruling classes," they have substituted entirely different ideas and metaphors, such as "social status" or the "melting pot." The "American Dream" anchors a mythical understanding of ourselves, and in it any lad or lassie can, by trying hard enough, make it to the top. Those who actually have done so are paraded through our media and our history books as proof of typical experiences, though they are not that at all. Research debunks the myth with a crashing finality by showing that the best way to get to the top is to be born to parents already there.

Marx wrote often about social class, both theoretically and through his accounts of key events of his times. However, his theory is quite undeveloped, and he never abandoned what he argued early on in the *Manifesto* that society is ultimately divided into the two great camps of the bourgeoisie and the proletariat. In his system other classes were fated to extinction. "Petit bour-geoisie" is Marx's term for owners of small firms, intellectuals, and all others who did not hire wage laborers. He also referred to those truly outside the production system as the "lumpenproletariat," a term very close to the current idea of the "underclass." Marx believed that smaller firms would ultimately fail to compete with big firms and the petit bourgeoisie would be "hurled into the proletariat" along with all those intellectuals who did not end up as apol-ogists for capitalism.

Some later thinkers have criticized Marx's division of society into two classes as overly simplistic. A crucial question arises: Who is truly a worker, and who is not? Are supervisors workers? Are medical doctors? How about teachers in public schools, or in private schools? These are important ques-tions, not always answered clearly by Marx's choice to put everyone into two warring groups. Yet, a two-part class system is not as superficial as it might seem. Consider U.S. society, where most of us work for wages or salaries in positions where the following conditions prevail: we do not control what we produce, how it is produced, or how it is priced; we have nothing to say about whether our workplace will be open tomorrow; we must take the wage offered us, even if it is not enough to live on (unless we can easily get another job or are part of a union that will collectively fight for higher pay). And, our labor is "divided" as a matter of course, and it will be sub-divided into ever-smaller tasks as long as it is profitable for owners to do so. If these are the conditions of your job, you are a worker in the Marxian version of the capitalist world. On the other hand, if you do have some control over these matters, you are a capitalist, or a high ranking official in a capitalist firm; that is, you are in the capitalist class.

Without question, this classification is oversimplified. Owners of small firms typically have much less control over their affairs than do the owners of large, powerful ones. And, there is an obvious difference in the significant control over work held by a carpenter working for a construction company and the gofer who spends all day bringing nails and wood the carpenter needs to the do the job. Marx was aware of these differences, and this com-plexity of the modern world has led latter-day Marxists to construct varia-tions on Marx's themes, mostly by adding classes that don't fit very neatly into any of his categories. For instance, Pat Walker's *Between Capital and Labor* (1978) describes a "professional managerial class" made up of profes-sionals such as doctors, lawyers, academics, and others who have some con-trol over their working environment but who do not typically hire wage laborers and earn surplus value. Other scholars have, in this same vein, tried to account for these "in between" classes. In their accounting for professionals, these theorists are not abandoning the Marxist framework but are trying to modernize it so that it remains a viable paradigm in which to think about capitalism.

Implicit in Marx's discussion about social class is the quite limited number of roles that can be played out in modes of production. As an example, presume that a youngster reads captivating books that make him or her want to be a shining knight, or a provincial duchess, or a hardy English yeoman, or a plains Indian warrior, or a pioneering woman ready to prove herself when pushed up against the rough elements of the weather (not to mention patriarchy), or the fair-minded leader of a workers' council in a democratic socialist country. It is not possible to play these, or any number of other roles, if one resides in modern capitalism, because you can only be an owner, a worker, a government servant, or someone else inhabiting a role shaped by capitalism. And inside your role, you must play it to the hilt to survive: as an owner you must worship the bottom line, and as a worker you must obey the owner. This does not mean, of course, you have no agency—no free will—but as Marx put it so very well:

> Men make their own history, but they do not make it just as they please: they do not make it under circumstances chosen by themselves, but under circumstances directly encountered, given and transmitted from the past. The tradition of all the dead generations weighs like a nightmare on the brain of the living. (Marx and Engels 1978, 595)

By placing people in social classes according to "their relationship to the means of production," Marx introduced new language and a larger, powerful theoretical framework. Discussions of social class continue to ignore Marx at a cost. As one economist, Teresa Amott, put it recently:

> ...No matter how far from *Capital* the debate [about social class in capitalism] has strayed, Marx's original conceptions continue to define the shape and logic of the argument. In fact, one could argue that the burden of twentieth century thought on class has been the task of rehabilitation, elaboration, deconstruction, and contestation of Marx's original construction of class, that to criticize Marxist concepts of class, one must stand in the space that Marx cleared. (Amott 1996)

As Amott argues, though Marx did not himself give the same kind of full the-oretical treatment to social class as did many other writers, he established the framework for a discussion about social classes in capitalism that continues today. How could there not be social classes in our society when even small children know that the people who own or control the businesses also own houses, cars, food, clothes, and all the rest, that are better than those of the people who work for them?

Other Economic Arguments about Capitalism

Capital is a book of about seven hundred pages, and in it Marx wrote about many aspects of capitalism. We have taken up those arguments that dominate the book and which remain mostly germane, even eye opening, to readers in our own day. We have ignored some of his arguments because they do not have a great deal to say about our own world. Still other claims Marx made do not merit much explanation in this kind of review, because they are now so commonly accepted. However, we will mention two of the latter kind of argu-ment because they have a particular importance to *Capital*. We will also say a few words about Marx's theory of revolution.

Booms and Busts In mainstream economics, John Maynard Keynes is gen-erally considered to have founded the modern study of the business cycle in the mid-1930s. However, the history of economic thought is now rarely taught in graduate schools, and thus economists usually do not know that others, including Marx, had developed complex and persuasive theories of the business cycle. One problem is that Marx scattered arguments about the instability of capitalism throughout all four volumes of *Capital*, and few read-ers have taken the time to compile and assess his claims. Marx's arguments are also largely unknown to mainstream economics for ideological reasons, and, as we have pointed out, economists have gradually come to ignore all that he wrote. Despite their ignorance, Marx made a series of strikingly modern argu-ments about the business cycle. One argument from Volume II is this:

> The ultimate reason for all real crises [recessions/depressions] always remains
> the poverty and restricted consumption of the masses as opposed to the drive
> of capitalist production to [produce as much as possible]. (Marx 1981, 484)

This idea is now central to all modern mainstream theories, and interest-ingly, it has gathered considerable attention recently. Many economists, including prominent ones in the United States, are beginning to fear that the increasingly unequal distribution of world income is creating a "restricted consumption of the masses," just as Marx described. These economists suspect that consequent underconsumption could bring the world economy into a serious depression.

In the second and third volumes of *Capital*, Marx developed other intriguing theories of the business cycle. One of them was a clear precursor to Keynes, and in it, Marx argued that there is interdependency between the investment and consumption sectors of a capitalist economy. In Volume II, he showed with fine logical consistency that over- or under-production in one of these can produce a "realization" crisis, or what we call a recession or depression. It is only because British economists, who with Keynes developed modern macroeconomics, were not reading Marx that they did not see that much of their own work only extended what he had already written about.

The Centralization of Capital Marx was the first major social theorist to predict that capitalism would lead to a growing centralization of power in the hands of a few capitalists. Marx meant what we call horizontal, vertical, and conglomerate mergers (firms merging, respectively, with one of their competitors, suppliers, or firms from a completely different industry. In Chapter 25 of *Capital*, Marx explained how capitalists' need to mechanize production would produce ever more costly machinery and buildings. These expensive new technologies would drive down costs, and smaller firms not able to buy the newest machinery would be driven out of business or gobbled up by the bigger ones. The financial industry, too, would verge toward centralization. Ultimately, both it and these large financial and industrial firms would shape business regulations in capitalist states to allow for more centralization in the future. Marx's arguments on these matters are more interesting for their prescience than as new information. Yet interestingly, Marx tied the centralization of capital to the eventual collapse of capitalism, because he thought that as monopolies grew in power, they would hurl more and more workers, and the owners of small firms, into an increasingly immiserated proletariat. The result, he predicted, would be unrest and then revolution.

The centralization and immiseration that Marx described have clearly been underway in most capitalist societies. Consider the effect of the immense Wal-Mart chain. Its monopolization of retail sales has made it ever more difficult for main street merchants to compete with it. Wal-Mart has two princi-pal advantages over its smaller competitors: its huge stores spread the over-head for each sale over hundreds of thousands of products in the typical store. And, Wal-Mart now directly purchases almost one quarter of the total output of another giant, Proctor & Gamble. This gives it the market leverage to buy at volume prices considerably lower than those charged to smaller outlets. Direct purchases such as these immediately wipe out whole strata of small wholesalers and threaten all retailers that compete with the giants. Millions of small business owners, particularly those who are not highly educated or do not have professional skills, hurled into jobs with low pay and no control over their work.

The Theory of Revolution In one rhetorical outburst in the next-to-last chapter of *Capital*, Marx predicted that capitalism was doomed and that it was but a matter of time before the capitalist "expropriators" – another of his terms for capitalists who steal surplus value – were themselves "expropriated" (p. 715). Marx argued that booms and busts would grow increasingly tumul-tuous, each one leaving more small firms driven from the field and more workers in ever-greater misery. That tumult eventually lead to an overthrow of the capitalist class. That this has not happened is a testament to the resilience of capitalism, and its great capacity to adapt to technological and political changes. Marx was aware of this adaptability, and in particular he thought that in democratic capitalist societies workers might restructure the system and make it more "civilized" without overthrowing it. In his view, however, capitalism could never be a *just* system, and efforts to reform it would simply prolong the oppression of the working class. To some degree, this is what happened in the capitalist welfare states in Northern Europe, as we shall see in the essay on Sweden.

Whether the workers of the world will ultimately "unite" and overthrow their oppressors remains to be seen. Recent estimates place the current level of worldwide unemployment as high as 150 *million* people. We can only expect these numbers to grow as industrialization in developing countries drives more rural people to cities looking for wage labor. Further, the number of unemployed could increase if the current depression in Japan continues and if the stock market slide in the U.S. ushers forth a recession that slows economic activity the world over. At what level of world unemployment would Marx's prediction about revolutionary upheaval come true? It remains to be seen.

The Moral Standing of Capitalism

In the last six chapters of *Capital*, Marx took up a fundamental question: where does accumulated capital originate? He answered that it had begun with slavery and imperialism. The substance of his answer is generalized in chapter 31, in which he wrote

> The discovery of gold and silver in America, the extirpation, enslavement and entombment in mines of the aboriginal population, the beginning of the conquest and looting of the East Indies, the turn of Africa into a warren for the commercial hunting of [black people], signalized the rosy dawn of the era of capitalist production. (Marx 1967, 703)

These examples follow two chapters on the enclosure movements, particularly in Britain starting in the sixteenth century and continuing up to Marx's time. Enclosure was the process in which the crown joined with land barons and the church to drive most of the agricultural work force, comprised of the peasants and the yeomanry of Britain, off the land and into the cities as vagabonds or wage laborers.[5] For British peasants whose livelihood was stolen, enclosure was brutality, and it led Marx to argue that capital originated in plunder and violence. It had been seized from the whole population, he wrote, first by the nobility and the Church, then by the emerging capitalist class. Because wealth and power are passed down from generation to generation, this early pillaging remained the foundation of the distribution of wealth and power in Marx's time. Later on in the chapter, Marx hurled forward this verbal thunder:

> If money, according to Augier [a Frenchman writing in 1842] "comes into the world with a congenital blood-stain on one cheek," capital comes dripping from head to foot, from every pore, with blood and dirt. (Marx 1967, 760)

In these last six chapters, Marx made two interconnected claims. The first was that capitalism was born in pillage and murder, and the second was that it is a system of unremitting oppression and violence against working people. Do these claims have any merit as descriptions of modern capitalism? Was U.S. capitalism built on violence and plunder? Does it remain oppressive to the majority of the people who live in it? The answer, of course, depends on whom you ask. The history of the United States has received countless tellings, offering dramatically different answers to these questions. Were John

D. Rockefeller and J.P. Morgan "robber-baron" criminals, as some historians have concluded? Or, was their inexorable drive to accumulate profits, and their need constantly to revolutionize the means of production, the forces that brought modern industrial capitalism into being? Or were capitalists both plunderers *and* revolutionaries, as seems to be Marx's position? For those who adopt the benign meritocratic view of capitalism, its inequalities of opportunity and outcome can be justified with the claim that it has always been an open system in which all who genuinely make the effort can rise to the top. This view is, without question, the dominating one in our times.

Others, though, see things quite differently. They argue that central to modern capitalism are owners and managers who *by definition* live off surplus value produced by someone else; who *must* create mindless tasks for most of their workers; who *must* withhold loyalty to their workers; and who *must* fire, or replace, or even harm their workers' health if doing so will increase their surplus value; and who *must* monitor their workers' efforts to keep them on jobs which many hate.

This is a language of force and oppression, and to a Marxist it is also the language of plunder and pillage. Surplus value, stolen from the workers only because the capitalists control the productive system, is the means by which these owners build their fortunes, amass their political power, and dominate the capitalist world. And capitalists' quest for surplus value requires them to do damage to everything in their path. Consider tobacco executives who kill their customers for surplus value, or Nike's Phil Knight, who has become a billionaire off workers toiling under wretched conditions, or the countless chemical companies that have dumped toxic materials onto fields where children now play. Consider marauding executives from Enron, WorldCom, and Arthur Andersen who stole from everyone in their path: workers, customers, suppliers, and owners of their stock. Finally, consider the refusal of all these actors to take responsibility for their human and environmental destruction. Are such characters on the modern capitalist stage any different from the "blood sucking werewolves" of Marx's world? Like everything else, it depends on your point of view.

CONCLUSION

Marx was prodigious writer, and this introduction is meant to urge readers to look into his work for themselves. Whereas we have tried to explain Marx's conception of history, and the basic ideas about capitalism advanced in the first volume of Capital, the other works of Marx and Engels contain thoughtful elaborations of their ideas, often in powerful and elegant language.

If one wants to take on *Capital*, or some of Marx's other more demanding texts, the best way to do so is in a college course or a reading group. On the other hand, much of what Marx and Engels wrote is quite accessible, and interested readers can certainly browse and read independently. Our readers should give Marx another chance and not listen to those who claim from the rooftops that "Marx is dead!" Quite frankly, that is a claim that could only be made by someone who has never read his works.

SUGGESTIONS FOR FURTHER READING

In the case of the works of Marx and Engels cited below, there are many publishers of each item. We have thus confined reference information to the initial publishing date of each of them.

Engels. *The Condition of the Working Class in England,* 1845.

Engels. *Socialism: Utopian and Scientific,* 1880.

Marx and Engels. *The Communist Manifesto,* 1848. (The 1998 Verso edition of the *Manifesto*, subtitled "A Modern Edition," contains a useful introduction by British historian Eric Hobsbawm.)

Marx. *Wage-Labor and Capital,* 1849.

Marx. *Capital,* Vol. 1., 1867.

Marx. *The Civil War in France,* 1871.

Marx. *The Critique of the Gotha Program,* 1875.

About Marx-Engels and their thought:

Brewer, Anthony. *A Guide to Marx's Capital.* London: Cambridge University Press, 1984.

Cohen, G.A. *Karl Marx's Theory of History: A Defence.* Princeton, N.J.: Gerald Allen, 1941.

McClellan, David. *Karl Marx: His Life and Thought.* New York: Harper-Row, 1974.

Applications of Marxist economic theory:

Baran, Paul, and Paul Sweezy. *Monopoly Capital: An Essay on the American Economic and Social Order.* New York: Monthly Review, 1966.

Bowles, Samuel and Herbert Gintis. *Schooling in Capitalist America.* New York: Basic Books, 1976.

Braverman, Harry. *Labor and Monopoly Capital: The Degradation of Work in the Twentieth Century.* New York: Monthly Review, 1974.

Carver, Terrell, ed. *The Cambridge Companion to Marx.* Cambridge: Cambridge University Press, 1991.

3
Thorstein Veblen and the Predatory Nature of Contemporary Capitalism*

INTRODUCTION

Thorstein Veblen is another of the radical econo-mists whose theories of the economy diverge sig-nificantly from the standard neoclassical (i.e., mainstream) analysis that is offered in the standard economics textbooks. Veblen's system of analysis has some similarities to that of Marx. Veblen treats the modern American economy as dominated by business interests and inherently prone to cyclical crises, rather than resembling the mythical perfect-ly competitive world created by Adam Smith. Veblen makes conscious use of learning from the other social sciences in order to analyze the factor that he thought to be most important for understanding the economy—economic and social change.

Before we proceed, let's dismiss one of the common complaints about Veblen: his unique writing style. Critics, and even many admirers, of Veblen characterize much of his writing as irony, and many dismiss his work as humorous satire. As one example, a famous quote from Veblen examines the role of habit in human thought processes:

> The patriotic spirit, or tie of nationalism, is evidently of the nature of habit . . . .
> More particularly is it a matter of habit what particular national establishment a

* This chapter was written by Janet Knoedler

given human subject will become attached to on reaching what is called "years of discretion" and so becoming a patriotic citizen. The analogy of the clam may not be convincing, but it may at least serve to suggest what may be the share played by habituation in the matter of national attachment. The young clam, after having passed the free-swimming phase of his life, as well as the period of attachment to the person of a carp or similar fish, drops to the bottom and attaches himself loosely in the place and station in life to which he has been led; and he loyally sticks to his particular patch of oose (sic) and sand through good fortune and evil. It is, under Providence, something of a fortuitous matter where the given clam shall find a resting place for the sole of his feet, but it is also, after all, "his own, his native land" etc. It lies in the nature of a clam to attach himself after this fashion, loosely, to the bottom where he finds a living, and he would not be a "good clam and true" if he failed to do so; but the particular spot for which he forms this attachment is not of the essence of the case. At least, so they say. "It may be, as good men appear to believe or know, that all men of sound, or at least those of average, mind will necessarily be of a patriotic temper." (Veblen 1998, 134-135)

Veblen's writing was often characterized by such subtle sarcasm, but the sarcasm masked cogent and important analysis. To quote his most famous student, Wesley Clair Mitchell, "there [was] always an aura of playfulness about his attitude toward his own work in marked contrast to the deadly seriousness of most economists" (Quoted in Galbraith 1972, v). The humor sometimes employed by Veblen may have softened his message somewhat. As John Kenneth Galbraith put it in his introduction to a 1972 reissue of *The Theory of the Leisure Class*, "That Marx was an enemy whose venom was to be returned in kind, capitalists did not doubt. But not Veblen. The American rich never quite understood what he was about—or what he was doing to them."

As we will see, Veblen coined a number of phrases well-known to us today: phrases such as "conspicuous consumption," "leisure class," "sabotage," and "captains of industry." These were not mere clever turns of phrase, but rather theoretical concepts as central to his system of analysis as concepts such as self-interest and profit maximization are to neoclassical analysis. To understand the importance of conspicuous consumption or to see the role played by the captains of industry, we will situate those terms within his system of analysis.

THE ROOTS OF VEBLEN'S UNDERSTANDING OF THE ECONOMY

Veblen was a careful observer of the changes taking place in the United States economy at the beginning of the twentieth century and an innovating economist who specialized in studying economic change. Many of Veblen's views of the economy were conditioned by his father's experience as a late nineteenth century farmer in Minnesota contending with the changing economy of the post-Civil War United States. In the early 1870s, Midwestern farmers had taken advantage of new agricultural technologies to improve wheat processing and, in turn, to expand their production. As you will learn when you study the operations of competitive markets, a bumper crop causes a rightward shift in the supply curve that tends to lower prices, a good thing for consumers, but not necessarily for farmers. Lower prices led to falling incomes and economic misfortune for many farmers. Farmers attributed their financial woes to the groups who seemed to be prospering. To quote Joseph Dorfman, biographer of Veblen, farmers reacted with a "wave of bitterness against the business interests . . . from the country-store trader and banker to the railroad company" (Dorfman 1961, 14). Fellow Minnesotan and chief lecturer for the Grange, Ignatius Donnelly, lamented in 1873: "Could the ordinary man retain his economic independence, or must he become the wage slave of the possessor of great wealth?" (Dorfman 1961, 16).

Midwestern farmers believed themselves to be victimized by several groups of villains: the railroad tycoons who raised their rates and made it costlier for them to ship their produce to the East, the bankers who advanced them loans and then demanded payment even when falling prices destroyed the farmers' profits, the jobbers or wholesalers who bought the farmers' produce at low prices and resold these products at higher prices. To the typical farmer, it appeared that he was doing all the productive work and losing money while the railroads, middlemen and financiers were profiting at his expense. Yet the decisions of the railroads, middlemen and financiers, at a remove from the farmers and workers, dictated the economic fortunes of the actual production workers. Below we will explore this distinction between what Veblen called industrial and pecuniary activities in more depth. (This same clash of monetary and real values is found in Marx.)

Veblen also examined other conflicts which he thought were central to the pace and direction of economic change. For Veblen, the conflict between scientific or "matter-of-fact" thinking and superstitious or animistic thinking explained the often slow pace of change in our increasingly technological society. According to Veblen, past-binding thinking locked society into habitual ways of thinking and being. Even today we can find examples, ranging from persistent superstitions about Friday the thirteenths, to the persistent gender and racial stereotypes that hinder women and minorities from rising to the top of corporate hierarchies or earning the same average salaries as their white male counterparts. In the same way, the conflict between what Veblen once referred to as "imbecile institutions" (his term for past-binding behavior) and the logic of the machine process, his metaphor for modern production techniques. This conflict could impede technology's path and even alter its beneficent consequences. In one obvious example, the modern school year in the United States still includes a three month summer break, even though that summer break no longer serves its original purpose—to free children to work on family farms during the busy summer months. As a result, U.S. children attend school on average two fewer months during the year than Japanese children.

VEBLEN'S EVOLUTIONARY ANALYSIS

Veblen, like many early economists, was first trained in philosophy, so he took great pains to examine the philosophical foundations of the received economics of his day. He found that those foundations were outmoded for understanding the kind of economics emerging in the twentieth century. Mainstream economics then and now relied on the philosophical underpinnings of natural law that swept social science thinking in the late eighteenth century. This was the period during which Adam Smith wrote *The Wealth of Nations*. Smith and other early classical economists were influenced by the work of Isaac Newton, and they described the social world in the same terms that physical scientists used to describe the physical world. The physical universe was seen as an immense clock set into motion by a divine Clockmaker, and the social universe was seen to be similarly well organized and mechanically ordered. Just as the Newtonian laws of physics kept the physical world operating in orderly fashion, the "natural" economic laws of the marketplace would channel the self-interested actions of human beings toward mutually beneficial outcomes for all. The natural order of the social universe was believed to be a system of free markets, with humans free to consume and to work as they pleased, but controlled, if not by the Divine Clockmaker, then by his close counterpart, the "invisible hand." Adam Smith developed this metaphor to describe the impersonal market forces which he and his followers believed regulated the economy, and the idea precluded intervention by earthly (government) regulators.

The Newtonian world-view led economists to see a world that was for the most part fixed and immutable. To quote David Hamilton, these early economists assumed that "the social order of their day was the natural product of sufficient reason and therefore fixed" (Hamilton 1991, 22). Most economic historians agree that Adam Smith's England did in fact resemble the microeconomic model of perfect competition, even though great joint stock companies dominated much of England's international trade (Heilbroner 1999).[6] Hence Smith could justifiably construct a model of a perfectly competitive economy, where many small producers competed and self-interest alone sufficed to maintain social order and to produce the greatest economic welfare. Influenced by natural law philosophical thinking, Smith also assumed that the economic world had reached its ideal form with the flourishing of competition in late eighteenth century England. Analysis of change was deemed irrelevant, because the "classical" economists believed they were describing the archetypal economic system that would henceforth prevail always and everywhere. In such a world, analysis of economic change could be restricted to the temporary—and, in theory, unnatural—movements away from competitive market equilibrium. The main question to be answered, then, was: When demand rises for one product or falls for another product, how will the market reach a new equilibrium price and quantity?

Veblen argued that an evolutionary model was more useful for understanding the economy. Writing one hundred years after Smith, and observing the economic changes that had so concerned Marx, Veblen, like Marx, declared that the social universe was not fixed and immutable. Smith had described a transitory epoch, according to Veblen. Writing in an age where a Darwinian model of evolution was being adopted in the biological sciences and imitated in the social sciences, Veblen adopted an evolutionary model to explain the cumulative causation and constant change that he observed.[7] Indeed, during the period that Veblen wrote most of his major works, 1898 to about 1923, evidence abounded that economic and social change was a permanent feature of the economy. New technologies allowed for mass production of goods and services, transforming industries that may have once conformed to Smith's model of atomistic competition, into industries now dominated by a few large multinational firms. Moreover, a huge wave of mergers and acquisitions at the turn of the century created huge national and multinational business firms that dominated their industries and transformed the nature of competition. The economists who clung to Smith's theories and applied them to the greatly changed economy of the late nineteenth century assumed that the natural order of the world (in the form of placid price competition) would quickly restore Adam Smith's ideal economy.

Veblen's use of the Darwinian approach did not mean that Veblen believed in survival of the fittest, despite the fact that Veblen actually studied under

William Graham Sumner, one of the architects of social Darwinism. Veblen took from Darwin and Sumner a different scientific method, "which studies humanity in its process of continuous adaptation to both its social and natural environment and which sees the conditions of human existence as subject to ceaseless change" (Tilman 1993, xxvi). It is not survival of the fittest that is relevant to understanding economic and social change, but rather the simple fact of evolution itself. As a simple example, the modern practice of men wearing ties—a non-utilitarian adornment that fits tightly around the neck of most men who move in professional circles—for important social or professional occasions, dates to an era where men used their ties or cravats to wipe their faces while eating. Over time, ties evolved into the quintessential symbol of the gentleman of business, even though the modern businessman would no sooner wipe his face on an expensive silk tie than he would appear in public with a cheerful checked napkin wrapped around his neck. Less obviously, perhaps, but more importantly, Veblen observed that the nature of the work performed by entrepreneurs, or to use his word, "undertakers," also evolved considerably as large multinational firms came to dominate the U.S. economy. Businesspersons in the mid-nineteenth century conducted the financial and managerial affairs of their businesses, but also spent time on the shop floor working alongside their own workers. Thus they had constant exposure to the working conditions of the average production worker. By the end of the nineteenth century, the undertakers had become "captains" of industry and finance who managed their operations for their own pecuniary gain rather than to meet the needs of the community.

THE LEISURE CLASS

To understand why Veblen, and other heterodox economists after him, saw analysis of economic change from an evolutionary approach as crucial to understanding the dynamics of any economic system, we will look at his most important economic ideas in their appropriate context. Veblen wrote at a time when many social scientists (but few economists) were beginning to use evolutionary narratives to examine social phenomena. Veblen began his analysis of the economy with the concept of the "leisure class." which he singled out as "an economic factor in modern life." He presented this in his most famous book, *The Theory of the Leisure Class*, which set forth many of the basic concepts of his analytical system, and made explicit use of his evolutionary understanding of the modern economy. The book was written as the excesses of the Gilded Age of the late nineteenth century began to reveal themselves in the lavish entertainments and opulent mansions enjoyed by the wealthy capitalists of the era. However, Veblen began his analysis not with these wealthy robber barons, but with the feudal cultures of Japan and medieval Europe, because he believed that modern economic behavior had evolved slowly from those beginnings. In Veblen's view, any careful analysis had to unearth the long historical roots of our modern institutions (Lerner 1976, 22).

A common theme ran through economic history, according to Veblen: "Wherever the institution of private property is found, even in slightly developed form, the economic process bears the character of a struggle between men for the possession of goods" (Veblen 1973, 34). The word "struggle" conveys Veblen's view of competition—not merely placid price competition of the sort described by Smith, but the "slash and burn" competition more common in our modern business landscape. Veblen also recognized that property had held a dual role throughout history: one economic, one symbolic.

In that struggle for subsistence, according to Veblen, there has always been a "warrior" or "leisure class" and a "menial" or "productive class." This taxonomy is similar to the class distinctions made by Marx. The leisure class first emerged in early hunter-gatherer societies. Veblen defined this group as the class of persons exempt from menial labor and for whom the "honorable employments" of hunting were reserved (Veblen 1973, 21). In these early cultures, the gender division of labor between men and women was strictly observed: the men hunting for food, the women gathering and farming and preparing the food. Both sets of activities were, of course, equally indispensable to economic survival, but not equally honored.[8] The hunters constituted the first leisure class: "in [the hunter's] own eyes, he is not a laborer, and he is not to be classed with the women in this respect; nor is his work to be classed with the women's drudgery, as labor or industry" (Veblen 1973, 23).

Over time, the leisure class came to include the entire class of persons who were exempt from the more routine and menial tasks necessary for economic survival; the leisure class was not exempt from work of any kind, but was exempt from menial labor. These invidious distinctions between different lines of work have persisted over time, Veblen insisted, meaning that our modern ranking of methods of making a living is rooted in our deep anthropological past. While a modern industrial economy no longer depends on a class of hunters to provide a large portion of society's means of subsistence, the higher honor accorded those engaged in "predatory" pursuits has endured, and the low repute accorded those engaged in actual productive work has also persisted. The modern day robber barons were, in Veblen's analysis, the economic descendants of the warring nobles of medieval Europe and the warrior class of Japan, struggling not against nature or against other clans for control over land and property, but against other robber barons for control of their industries. We can see similar struggles today. The U.S. government's antitrust trial against Microsoft exposed Bill Gates' ruthless tactics to increase use of Microsoft's Internet Explorer, such as forcing computer manufacturers to install IE on their computers or withholding Windows from manufacturers, such as IBM, building operating systems that might compete with Windows.

In the Veblenian system, then, the modern leisure class would consist of those whose ownership of wealth and whose control of the means of production permits them to engage in the same kind of relentless competition and predatory activity carried out by their barbarian forefathers, and more importantly, to be exempt from the menial jobs performed by ordinary workers. Modern leisure class activities would include high finance, corporate law, management, and other activities undertaken by those concerned mainly with "conversion of goods and persons to [their] own ends, and a callous disregard of the feelings and wishes of others, and of the remoter effects of his actions" (Dorfman 1961, 184). The modern menial class would thus consist of those who are not owners of property and thus must work for wages or salaries for someone else.

For Veblen, the leisure class was also the wealthy class, and that too has historical precedents. In ancient cultures, Veblen believed that wealth came to be equated with social status: as he argued, "possession of wealth confers honor" (Veblen 1973, 35). Initially, wealth consisted of the booty dragged back from wars with neighboring clans or nations; the items seized, be they treasures or slaves, were the spoils of battle and therefore served as a very public sign of physical prowess. Possession of wealth came over time to represent "a trophy of successes scored in the game of ownership carried on between the members of the group" (Veblen 1973, 36-7). Over time, mere possession of wealth came to confer reputability on the possessor, as if the wealth itself signified the superior strength of the leader of the household. By the late nineteenth century, robber barons such as Rockefeller, Vanderbilt, and Morgan were considered both successful and honorable largely because they were wealthy, despite their destructive and often dishonorable business practices. Moreover, ownership of property came over time to be seen as an indication of the prowess of the owner, and thus "it becomes indispensable to accumulate, to acquire property, in order to retain one's good name" (Veblen 1973, 37). With wealth thus equated to esteem, humans strove to emulate and surpass the wealth of their neighbors: as Veblen concluded, "[I]t becomes indispensable to accumulate, to acquire property, in order to retain one's good name. ...A certain standard of wealth in one case, and of prowess in the other, is a necessary condition of reputability, and anything in excess of this normal amount is meritorious" (Veblen 1973, 37-8).

CONSPICUOUS CONSUMPTION

Of course, mere possession of wealth does not confer upon the possessor an honorific position in society unless the rest of society perceives that the wealthy are indeed wealthy. Therefore, the wealthy must engage in "conspicuous consumption." Conspicuous consumption was an important element of Veblen's understanding of human behavior. To quote Veblen at length on this point:

> The quasi-peaceable gentleman of leisure [by which Veblen means the modern robber baron 'descended' from the early warrior], then, not only consumes of the staff of life beyond the minimum required for subsistence and physical efficiency, but his consumption also undergoes a specialization as regards the quality of the goods consumed. He consumes freely and of the best, in food, drink, narcotics, shelter, services, ornaments, apparel, weapons and accoutrements, amusements, amulets, and idols or divinities. . . . Since the consumption of these more excellent goods is an evidence to wealth, it becomes honorific; and conversely, the failure to consume in due quantity and quality becomes a mark of inferiority and demerit. (Veblen 1973, 64)

Conspicuous consumption is the way the wealthy demonstrate their wealth, and thus their success in war or in business. By purchasing the finest houses, autos, suits and shoes—all visible and public signs of financial success—they gain the respect and admiration of their peers and subordinates. Today, the BMW parked outside the office, the Armani suit for everyday wear, and the Kate Spade bag slung casually across a shoulder, tell the casual onlooker that the owner is a successful (i.e., wealthy) person.

Veblen referred to this as "conspicuous waste" because, "in order to effectually mend the consumer's good fame, [a conspicuous expenditure] must be an expenditure of superfluities" (Veblen 1973, 77). Those expenditures are "traceable to the habit of making an invidious pecuniary comparison"—to demonstrate the level of income and wealth held by the conspicuous consumer (Veblen 1973, 79). In other words, the Lexus owner would be as ably transported around town by a Chrysler Neon, or the Range Rover owner would have his or her needs just as efficiently and dependably met by a Chevy truck. The point of making an expensive purchase is precisely to demonstrate to those who can not afford the Lexus or the Range Rover the superior social status of the conspicuous consumer.

Juliet Schor confirms that this motive still dominates in our modern era in her recent book, *The Overspent American*. The ubiquitous "visible logo"—be it the Nike swoosh, the Hilfiger label, or even the Starbucks name on a disposable paper cup—tells observers that the purchaser has bought the real deal (Schor 1998, 46). One nationwide poll of women revealed that half of the respondents participated in status buying, with 80% of the respondents—a percentage that would not have surprised Veblen at all— admitting that purchases were more often based on the designer label than on the intrinsic quality of the goods. Robert Frank recounts how some "nouveau" millionaires in both Silicon Valley and suburban Chicago have demolished large modern homes, valued in the hundreds of thousands of dollars, so they could build even larger homes on the same sites to suit their elevated social status. As one new executive for America Online declared, the "scraper" that he razed "was definitely livable. I just wanted something bigger" (Frank 1999, 28-39).

While luxury SUVs or demolition of perfectly good homes carried on by the wealthy may be obvious examples of waste, Veblen even disparaged those forms of conspicuous waste that were practiced on a daily basis. Conspicuous waste in his view was anything that did not contribute to a "fuller unfolding of human life" (Veblen 1973, 94). For instance, Veblen argued that our tendency to prefer hand-wrought items to machine-made goods was based on the honorific status imparted by the costlier, hand-made item. In other words, our preference for a hand-crafted spoon over an ordinary spoon found in a diner was not based on the beauty of the hand-crafted item, but rather "a gratification of our sense of costliness masquerading under the name of beauty" (Veblen 1973, 79). Veblen himself once received as a gift an expensive brooch from a woman student who had become alarmed at his habitual use of a safety pin to hold together his jacket. When presented with the gift, Veblen simply chided, "You haven't listened to a word I have heard all semester" (Dorfman 1973).

Related to Money — copying Someone

PECUNIARY EMULATION

Mainstream economic theory has long taught that consumers make purchases based on rational assessment of the intrinsic utility of the item in question.

Veblen rejected that analysis as overly simplistic in one of his most famous paragraphs:

> The hedonistic conception of man is that of a lightning calculator of pleasures and pains, who oscillates like a homogeneous globule of desire of happiness under the impulse of stimuli that shift him about the area, but leave him intact. He has neither antecedent or consequent... Self-imposed in elemental space, he spins symmetrically about his own spiritual axis, until the parallelogram of forces bears down upon him, whereupon he follows the line of the resultant. When the force of the impact is spent, he comes to rest, a self-contained globule of desire as before. (Veblen 1919, 75)

The mainstream theory of consumer choice reduces all of the complex processes and influences involved in human consumption to a simple and overtly rational choice. The mainstream preconception is that products generate utility, i.e., that the smoker derives utility from consumption of his or her cigarette. Consumer tastes and preferences are then taken as given, with the relative price being the main factor that causes consumers to buy more or less of some commodity, such as shoes or cigarettes. Veblen recognized that this approach ignored the social influences on consumption: advertising, peer pressure, the symbolic nature of commodities in a capitalist culture, and many other external influences.

In particular, Veblen argued that mainstream economics ignored a powerful motive for consumption, the motive of pecuniary emulation: the imitation of the spending habits of our peers and those above us on the social ladder. As Veblen argued, "Goods are produced and consumed as a means to the fuller unfolding of human life . . . . But the human proclivity to emulation has seized upon consumption of goods as a means to our invidious comparison" (Veblen 1973, 94). Consumption decisions are driven by the need to fit in with our peers or, in popular parlance, to keep up with the Joneses. Again, to quote Veblen:

> [T]he standard of expenditure which commonly guides our efforts is not the average, ordinary expenditure already achieved; it is an ideal of consumption that lies just beyond our reach... The motive is emulation—the stimulus of an invidious comparison which prompts us to outdo those with whom we are in the habit of classing ourselves...each class envies and emulates the class next above it in the social scale, while it rarely compares itself with those below or with those who are considerably in advance. (Veblen 1973, 81)

Veblen thought that this "propensity for emulation" was among the strongest economic motives. In fact, a more recent proponent of this theory, economist Robert Frank, has called people's concern about social position " a deep-rooted and ineradicable element of human nature" (Quoted in Cassidy 1999).

Veblen's argument that conspicuous consumption and pecuniary emulation are the driving forces behind much of the consumption we observe in capitalism is persuasive but not necessarily pejorative. This is true for two reasons. First, human beings are social beings and we cannot help but to emulate much of the behavior of those around us, in fact, to try to outdo others (Lerner 1976, 24). Second, and perhaps more importantly, pecuniary emulation, or our emulation of the spending habits of our peers and those above us on the social ladder, takes place in a context of capitalism. In capitalism, social status is heavily tied to income and wealth, and is demonstrated visibly by the accoutrements of wealth—fancy clothes, luxury cars, and stately houses. To maintain our status in our desired communities, we endlessly strive to "keep up with the Joneses." Imagine for a minute the businessperson who arrived at an important meeting in a polyester suit, wearing coke-bottle glasses and carrying papers in a shopping bag rather than an expensive leather briefcase. Would he or she be given the same attention at that meeting, or receive promotions? Similarly, the student who wanted to join the most popular sorority on campus, but showed up for rush events in sweats and sneakers would most likely be hastened out the door. While both individuals might have much of substance to contribute, their outward appearance would signal their desired peers that they just wouldn't fit in.

MARGINAL PRODUCTIVITY AND INDUSTRIAL EMPLOYMENTS

Another tenet of neoclassical economics that Veblen disputed was the theory of marginal productivity. This theory, that the wage earned by any given worker would naturally tend to be equivalent to the marginal productivity of that worker, was articulated by Veblen's own former professor, John Bates Clark. At the time Veblen began to write his *Theory of Business Enterprise*, many economists considered the high incomes received by the robber barons to be simply their fair returns, the hard-earned fruits of their intense and stressful labors. As entrepreneurs, they organized the production process, and their earnings were the equivalent of their contributions to the firm, just as the factory worker or the shop clerk earned his or her wage in proportion to the productivity that they contributed to the firm.

Marginal productivity theory is still a central element of mainstream labor economics; it is used, for example, to explain the high salaries of professional athletes: as the argument goes, they receive high salaries because they sell tickets and advertisements. Marginal productivity is also used to argue that it would be inefficient to raise the minimum wage. In recent years, marginal productivity theory has been used to justify the enormous and growing pay gap between CEOs and workers—a gap that now exceeds 500 to 1—and to justify the growing inequality of income. According to this argument, top management has increasingly had to make tough decisions, thus earning the millions of dollars that they are paid. Alternatively, some argue that good managers are a scarce commodity and it is simply the working of supply-and-demand that elevates executive salaries.

Veblen argued for a different taxonomy to compare the work of the robber barons to that of ordinary workers. Within the modern firm emerging at the turn of the century, Veblen saw two basic groups of workers: those who made goods (those engaged in industrial activities, as he called them) and those who made money (those engaged in pecuniary activities). This is not quite the same as the breakdown between the owners of property and the property-less described by Marx, for Veblen includes among those engaged in pecuniary employments many who hold no property at all—for example, people working in advertising, middle managers, corporate lawyers. In other words, Veblen thought that the modern-day businessman or businesswoman had the same class identity as a capitalist. Veblen argued that the work of the typical business person was directed at making the product of their firm vendible—i.e., marketing and selling the product. Thus they were engaged in buying and selling, negotiating and contriving, merging and financing, but not actually involved in producing anything.

For Veblen, this distinction between different kinds of work and workers —some involved in production, others acting as "undertakers" in managerial, administrative, and financial positions – reflected facts about people's social functions and interests. He argued that businesspeople—the captains of industry, financiers, lawyers, CEOs and others at the top ranks of Wall Street or corporations today—were chiefly concerned with the distribution of wealth and the fattening of their own wallets. They were not concerned with providing needed goods and services to consumers. To quote Veblen, their concern was with the "exchange values of goods and . . . the vendibility of the items with which they are concerned, and on the necessities, solvency, cupidity, or gullibility of the persons whose actions may affect the transaction contemplated" (Quoted in Dorfman 1961, 193).

By contrast, actual production was carried out by those engaged in "industrial pursuits"—engineers, craftsmen, assembly line workers. These workers were, in Veblen's view, actively furthering the "material interests of the community," or more precisely, "adapting the material means of life, and the processes of valuation constantly involved in the work run on the availability of goods and on the material serviceability of the contrivances, materials, persons, or mechanical expedients employed" (Dorfman 1961, 192-3). Taken to its logical conclusion, this dichotomy suggests that profit-seeking businesspersons can be at least as interested in marketing products in clever and creative ways as they are in improving the actual product. As an example, consider the following: in recent years, Nike has spent more to hire Michael Jordan to hawk its shoes than it has paid to its entire Indonesian work force to produce the Air Jordans. Nike contracts out most of the production work for its shoe lines, relying on labor-intensive production technologies and low-cost labor, leaving Nike as little more than a large marketing company.

Veblen analyzed the changes in business firms since the halcyon days of Adam Smith in the same evolutionary terms he used to explore the evolution of consumption. In the early stages of manufacturing, dating back to the British Industrial Revolution and even before, the typical owner-entrepreneur was also a producer, who often manufactured or at least handled the goods that he sold. The master who crafted horseshoes, for example, might spend a portion of his day checking bank statements and logging orders, but would also work side by side with his journeymen and apprentices making the actual product. To quote Veblen here, this early "captain of industry" "was business manager of the venture as well as foreman of the works, and not infrequently he was the designer and master-builder of the equipment, of which he was also the responsible owner" (Veblen 1997, 103). As firms became larger and the management of those firms required more and more of the owner-manager's time, "industry and business gradually split apart" (Veblen 1997, 106). The captain of industry—originally "a cross between a business man and an industrial expert"—became removed from the shop floor and did not deal with matters of production, spending more and more of his time engaged in financial management of the firm (Veblen 1990, 59). He became a "captain of finance," rather than a captain of industry, far removed from the production lines. As his daily activities changed, so did his interest, as he became less interested in production and more interested in profit. To quote Joseph Dorfman, Veblen's biographer:

> The modern captain is not interested in the permanent efficiency of the industrial system or of any plant, but in the control of a segment of the system for

the strategic purpose of influencing the security market for the flotation of securities, the maneuvering of a coalition or any other well known method of manipulation . . . . The modern captain does not create opportunities for increasing industrial efficiency, but only watches for opportunities to put his competitors in an uncomfortable position; cut-throat competition, rate wars, duplication, misdirection, wasted efforts and delay of improvements long after they are advisable are the price the community pays. (Dorfman 1961, 125-6)

In a later, famous quote, Veblen described this watchful waiting carried out by modern businessmen as being similar to the activities of toads sitting on a country road:

Doubtless this form of words, 'watchful waiting,' will have been employed in the first instance to describe the frame of mind of a toad who has reached years of discretion and has found his appointed place along some frequented run where many flies and spiders pass and repass on their way to complete that destiny to which it has pleased an all-seeing and merciful Providence to call them; but by an easy turn of speech it has also been found suitable to describe the safe and sane strategy of that mature order of captains of industry who are governed by sound business principles. There is a certain bland sufficiency spread across the face of such a toad so circumstanced, while his comely personal bulk gives assurance of a pyramidal stability of principles. (Veblen 1997, 109-10)

With captains of industry making no direct contribution to production, Veblen argued that their salaries could not be attributed to marginal productivity.

INDUSTRIAL SABOTAGE

According to Veblen, it is not placid Smithian price competition that characterizes the modern industrial economy. Instead, it is savage and predatory competition. The efforts of John D. Rockefeller to smash his competition exemplify Veblen's ideas of competition and business sabotage of the industrial processes.

By 1869, at the age of 30, Rockefeller was already a major oil refiner in Cleveland, the early center of the oil refining industry in the United States. He came up with the idea of negotiating lower shipping rates from several key railroads to gain a competitive advantage over rival oil refiners. At the time, most of the markets for refined oil were on the eastern seaboard of the United States; thus transportation represented a major cost for oil refiners. Using his clout as Cleveland's largest refiner and therefore an important bulk shipper of oil, Rockefeller secured preferential rates for shipping his oil. (Recall that the railroads during this same period were raising the rates charged to farmers.) This gave him an enormous cost advantage over smaller competitors who could not guarantee bulk shipments to the railroads. Rockefeller believed that he was simply exploiting his "economies of scale," but critics at the time argued that he was instead using his "special power to compel railroad-freight concessions" (Chernow 1999, 114).

In 1872, Rockefeller devised an even more ambitious scheme, innocuously named the "South Improvement Company," or SIC. Under SIC, all refiners who joined their operations with his would receive up to a 50% rebate from the railroads on their shipping costs, not only for their own oil but for all oil shipped by rail, including oil shipped by their competitors.[9] The SIC included most of the major refiners and all the major eastern railroads, in effect forming a double cartel. The SIC in turn guaranteed the major railroads a steady flow of oil shipments. To quote Ron Chernow, "the railroads acquired a vested interest in the creation of a giant oil monopoly that would lower their costs, boost their profits, and generally simplify their lives" (Chernow 1999, 113). The provision that the SIC refiners would receive rebates for oil shipped by their competitors has been described by one Rockefeller biographer as "an instrument of competitive cruelty unparalleled in industry" (Chernow 1999, 136). In fact, the SIC oil refiners would now have a huge advantage over their smaller independent rivals: "the harder their competitors worked, the more money Rockefeller and associates would make" (Dillard 1967, 410). Moreover, this same provision in the SIC agreement would give SIC members precise pricing and shipping information about their competitors, permitting the SIC oil cartel to undercut their rivals at every turn.

While it is true that this SIC contract violated no actual law (this was two decades before the first federal antitrust laws were passed), rumors leaked out about the "scheme of gigantic combination among certain railroads and refiners to control the purchase and shipment of crude and refined oil from [western Pennsylvania]" (Chernow 1999, 138). A firestorm swept the local newspapers in the affected regions; the railroads abandoned the agreement; and the Pennsylvania legislature canceled the SIC's charter in 1872. So the SIC never actually went into effect. However, during the six weeks in early 1872 that the SIC rumors were spreading, the remaining competition realized that if they didn't sell out, they would be driven out of the industry. 22 of the 26 remaining Cleveland refiners sold their operations to Rockefeller during that six week period, most of them later acknowledging the implicit SIC club held over their heads by Rockefeller (Chernow 1999, 154ff; Dillard 1967, Ch. 23; Porter 1973, Ch. 3).[10] This was not the friendly competition between small local blacksmiths that drove prices down, as Adam Smith had described. Instead, Veblen saw that the nature of competition had changed, and he used words like "sabotage" to describe the brutal tactics of Rockefeller and the other robber barons.

More generally, during the period Veblen wrote, most of the firms that were to become important American corporations, like John D. Rockefeller's Standard Oil, began to employ modern mass production technologies. These relied increasingly on the use of knowledgeable engineers and trained personnel to keep the production lines running (Porter 1973). One feature of mass production—what Veblen referred to as the "machine process"—was the need for standardized production processes and interchangeable parts. For Henry Ford's assembly line to run smoothly and efficiently, every part had to be made precisely to the same specifications, so that an individual worker could simply insert the widget into the gizmo as it rolled across the work station. Interchangeable parts eliminated the need for hand crafting of each automobile from top to bottom and greatly improved both the quantity and quality of output. Parts suppliers—firms supplying the steel chassis, the nuts and bolts, the frames and engines—were required to meet exacting specifications. Production became less and less a matter of individual discretion and craftsmanship and more a matter of technological expertise and mechanization.

The mass production that accompanied the Second Industrial Revolution in late nineteenth century America created both huge productivity gains and great economic growth (Ratner, Soltow, and Sylla 1993, Ch. 12). Specifically, American dominance in the machine tools industry, which promoted mechanization of hand-crafted tasks, and its early use of industrial research to develop new products and manufacturing processes, led to large production and distribution facilities, new technologies, and the big business that we know today.

However, in Veblen's analysis, these vastly superior machine technologies and improved capacity remained under the control of the captains of finance, who managed them with an eye toward greater profits rather than greater productivity. Productive capacities were great indeed, but Veblen believed that the captains of industry prevented industrial capacity from becoming even greater. Observing the great merger movement that occurred at the turn of the century, when nearly 3,000 firms disappeared into mergers with larger rivals, Veblen argued that businesspersons were taking control of large segments of the nation's industrial apparatus in order to carry out "industrial sabotage" on a large scale. For Veblen, industrial sabotage was a "conscientious withdrawal of efficiency." More fully, industrial sabotage could take the form of "any degree of obstruction, diversion, or withholding of any of the available industrial forces, with a view to the special gain of any nation or any investor, unavoidably brings on a dislocation of the system; which involves a disproportionate lowering of its working efficiency and therefore a disproportionate loss to the whole; and therefore a net loss to all its parts" (Veblen 1990, 73).

This was sabotage in Veblen's view because the increasingly interconnected industrial system needed rapid and reliable flow of goods and services from one sector to another—steel to the auto and rail industries, raw materials to the chemicals producers, railways transporting disposable food stuffs—and needed to be free of all obstructions to those necessary intersectoral flows. However, businesspersons could often profit from disrupting those flows or holding up supplies, raising prices and increasing profits.

Industrial sabotage continues today. For instance, Microsoft Corporation was found in its recent antitrust trial to have engaged in a wide variety of predatory and exclusionary activities to promote its own operating and desktop software at the expense of competitors and its own customers. In one example brought out at the trial, Microsoft waited until the last possible moment to make a deal with IBM for its Windows O/S, and then raised the price by nearly 900 percent. This, of course, placed IBM machines at a huge disadvantage with its PC competitors. Enron, in similar fashion, now stands accused of manipulating electricity supply in California – in particular, creating 'phantom congestion' on power grids in 1999. This manipulation exacerbated, or even created, the famous California energy crisis that summer, and produced enormous profits for Enron until its accounting crisis brought the firm to bankruptcy court.

Veblen also believed that businesspersons engaged in sabotage when they chose to rely on obsolete but profitable methods of production rather than to move to more modern and innovative production techniques or to produce products that would better serve the consumer. In a famous example, J.P. Morgan, a captain of finance par excellence in Veblen's time, gathered hundreds of previously competing steel producers into a new behemoth, U.S. Steel, that dominated all segments of the steel industry. Having removed most of the relevant competition by merging with them, U.S. Steel was able to curb its costs by slowing its pace of innovation to a crawl. This set the stage for a pattern of sluggish innovation and noncompetitive behavior that persisted for the rest of the century. By the early 1980s, the American steel industry spent less as a percentage of sales on research and development than any other American industry except textiles (Adams and Mueller 1986). Similarly, one has only to ponder the story of the American automobile industry during the second half of the twentieth century or the dismal performance of corporate giants such as GM and IBM in the 1980s to see what Veblen meant. It was not internal lobbying by GM engineers that prompted GM to develop more fuel efficient cars, but the gradual erosion of GM's market share and the superior cars made by foreign competitors that finally prompted some changes (Adams and Brock 1995, 65-92).

By using the term sabotage, Veblen did not mean that the captains crept by dark of night into the factories that they controlled and meddled with the machines. He took a broader view of sabotage, one grounded in the notion that modern production technologies were so productive that they could allow humankind to produce sufficient goods and services to alleviate all poverty and human want. However, Veblen believed that modern business practices subverted these possibilities by prizing profit over production and thus keeping industrial plants operating inefficiently, i.e., below full capacity.

Veblen argued that industrial sabotage was pervasive and that it had serious macroeconomic effects. In his view, businesspeople valued pecuniary or profit-making activities over industrial or productive activities. Given those priorities, he argued that industrial depressions occurred when "the business men engaged do not see their way clear to derive a satisfactory gain from letting the industrial process go forward on the lines and in the volume for which the material equipment of industry is designed" (Veblen 1978, 213). In other words, Veblen saw business cycles as primarily caused by business sabotage of industry. For that reason, Veblen disparaged the term "overproduction," believing the term instead referred to the business "difficulty . . . that not enough of a product can be disposed of at fair prices to warrant the running of the mills at their full capacity, or running them at a rate near enough to their capacity to yield a fair profit" (Veblen 1978, 217). In other words, business persons would rather reduce production or close plants until supplies dropped and prices were restored to profitable levels.

For Veblen, sabotage was also waste, albeit a different form than conspicuous waste: it was the consequence of deliberate idling of production and labor, and a direct consequence of the businessperson's profit seeking. Idle capacity and waste were systemic and substantial, argued Veblen, and harmed the community welfare. Hence the irony observed by Veblen in many of his writings on the captains of industry and finance: by the turn of the 20th century. As Veblen observed, the tremendous productive capacity of modern industry should have eliminated the problem of unemployment and privation by the turn of the 20th century, but the predatory and pecuniary practices of modern business seemed if anything to have exacerbated them. In short, for Veblen, modern business organization and the quest for profits created an inevitable tendency toward idle industrial capacity and unemployed labor.

Veblen's writing on sabotage recalls Marx, who also acknowledged the enormous productive capacity of modern technology. Veblen and Marx also agreed that modern capitalism placed pecuniary values above all others, so that greed, corruption, and invidious consumption eroded the productive potential of modern industry. Thus, capitalism generated enormous inequality and universal dissatisfaction with the goods already possessed. Both believed that if pecuniary values could somehow be displaced and the common welfare honored, enormous productivity could be harnessed for all peoples. It is a utopian view of an economy, surely, but one that has merit as we contemplate the growing inequality in our modern world and the great need still faced by so many. In fact, a recent UN report argued that we would need to redistribute no more than one percent of global income to eradicate poverty in the world (UNHDR, *Human Development Report*, 1997). In other words, as Veblen argued one hundred years ago, we have the material means to provide a decent living for every person on the planet. The question is, how to permit sufficient output of the needed goods and services, ranging from basic foodstuffs to good schools, and how to distribute these goods and services to meet the basic needs of all people on the planet.

Veblen's analysis of sabotage also resonates with Marx's analysis of the reserve army of the unemployed, and the relentless drive of the bourgeoisie to keep wages low and profits high. Veblen adds to Marx's arsenal of capitalist strategies the use of mergers, buy-outs, and all other business tactics that are used to garner profits rather than benefit consumers or workers. To quote Veblen, "in no such community that is organized on the price system...can the industrial system be allowed to work at full capacity for any appreciable interval of time, on pain of business stagnation and consequent privation for all classes and conditions of men. The requirements of profitable business will not tolerate it" (Veblen 1990, 43). In other words, it is imperative for business interests who serve pecuniary and not industrial ends, to use Veblen's terms, that industrial capacity be kept below its potential. Otherwise, supply would increase too rapidly, prices would fall, and profits would suffer. Was he referring simply to business downturns? Veblen argued that even in periods of high profits, business interests would act to make those high profits even higher: "it is considered doubtful whether an increased production, such as to employ more workmen and supply the goods needed by the community, would result in an increased net aggregate income for the vested interests which control these industries. A reasonable profit always means, in effect, the largest possible profit" (Veblen 1990, 45).

CONCLUSION

Veblen saw that the economy was constantly evolving, and he strove to understand the nature of economic and social change. At the same time, he understood that our anthropological roots influenced our modern economy in important if unrecognized ways. Most importantly, he argued that the predatory nature of competition, the prevalence of pecuniary standards of success, and the failure to use modern technologies to alleviate human want and misery were all symptoms of a capitalist economy that placed pecuniary values above all others. As a consequence the economy no longer functioned primarily to provision all its inhabitants. Veblen is remembered today mostly for his colorful analysis of the leisure class, but his criticism of business interests, his understanding of the importance of economic change in economic analysis, and his belief that the economy could be used to alleviate all the genuine needs of all human beings, remain his important if ignored contributions to the discipline of economics.[11]

Veblen's writings not only contain trenchant critiques of the received economics of his day, but also offer alternative forms of analysis that could lead economists to new conclusions. Veblen was critical of the view that human beings were merely self-interested. In his many other writings not reviewed above, he expanded on his affirmative view of human nature, and argued that what really promoted human welfare was not self-interest, but rather the instinct of workmanship and the parental bent. To state these ideas briefly here (the reader can read Veblen's *Instinct of Workmanship* to learn more), the parental bent extended beyond concern for one's own children, and, according to Veblen, was a culturally instilled proclivity to provide for the next generation and to contribute to the common good. The instinct of workmanship was the human proclivity to improve things, to make things work, to be both creative and efficient. We can only imagine how different mainstream economics might be if it had started from these alternative premises.

4
John Maynard Keynes

INTRODUCTION

Human beings are both weak and strong, and of their several frailties none is more complex than their ability to believe strongly in things that are clearly not true. We all fall prey to this folly. For example, in the fifteenth century there were those who warned Columbus that the earth was flat. And today, mainstream economists pretend that social classes do not exist in U.S. capitalism. It can be quite costly to trudge forward into the cold and piercing winds of life on the basis of wrong ideas, and especially so if we are experts with an audience.

One such costly idea was held for almost two centuries by the classical school of economics and, like so much of modern thinking about the economy, this one started with Adam Smith. The idea was simple enough: capitalist economies cannot experience *long term* "gluts," producing more output than customers could buy, because of natural, internal forces that automatically end overproduction before it becomes a recession or depression. Despite being at odds with the downturns that occurred with awful regularity in all capitalist economies, this classical theory held sway in economic thinking roughly from the late eighteenth century until the middle of the Great Depression in the 1930s. It was John Maynard Keynes who dealt it a crushing blow in a 1936 book, *The General Theory of Employment, Interest, and Money*, sometimes called *The General Theory*. This book swept away much of the debris of classical thinking about business cycles, and `what to do about them.

To the economist in the classical school, the self-regulating character of capitalism meant that the government's role in the economy could be limited. Adam Smith, also a principal source of this idea, wrote his famous treatise *The Wealth of Nations* in 1776 primarily as a tract against the "mercantilist" thinking of his time. The mercantilists believed in government economic policies that would foster favorable trading conditions with other nations. This required a mosaic of government rules and regulations, including favoring monopolies in crucial trading industries. Under mercantilism, the state was an instrument for the benefit of a few industries and individuals, often to the detriment of everyone else. Smith and the biggest fans of his ideas, members of the emerging capitalist class in Britain and France, believed that unregulated capitalism would, in contrast, benefit all groups in society. By allowing all economic classes to seek their self-interest in a competitive system, capitalism would produce the most productive outcome possible, argued Smith; therefore, government intervention in the economy could only be harmful. Smith allowed for a few government functions, such as education, police protection, and national defense. But he thought an economy that was largely unregulated by government would be both superior and self-regulating.

In the central tradition of economics,[12] then, between 1776 and 1936 business cycles were ignored as a legitimate subject of study, and public policy to lessen their damaging effects was out of the question. In the United States during these years, the classical school's domination of economic thinking among both academics and capitalists claimed countless victims. President Herbert Hoover, responding to the ravages of the Great Depression of the 1930s, could only bleat to a disbelieving public the classical article of faith: "Prosperity is just around the corner." Irving Fisher, among the most respected U.S. economists of the time, no doubt helped to confuse Hoover by declaring, just prior to the 1929 stock market crash that began the Depression, that the economy was on a "permanently high plateau." It was into this theoretical morass that Keynes stepped in 1936 with *The General Theory* to change forever the way we all think about the capitalist business cycle.

So, who was this Keynes fellow?

JOHN MAYNARD KEYNES, THE PERSON

Keynes was an Englishman who lived from 1883 to 1946, and after 1913 produced a torrent of books and articles about the economic world. In the course of his 63 years he was: a brilliant student at England's most famous prep school; an equally brilliant student and then professor at Kings College in

Cambridge; a financier who made a fortune for himself, and later for Kings College by overseeing its endowment fund; president of a life-insurance company; patron of the arts; husband of a famous Russian ballerina; member of the influential "Bloomsbury set" of intellectuals; esteemed official of the British Treasury; board member of the Bank of England; and the principal designer of the international financial system after World War II. Most important to his lasting fame, Keynes' writing held the rapt attention of the political and intellectual world during his adult life, and continues to have lasting influence half a century after his death.

The General Theory is only the most famous of his economic writings. One of Keynes' earliest works was an acclaimed book on probability theory. Another early book, *The Economic Consequences of the Peace* (1919), catapulted him into an international spotlight that never dimmed while he was alive. In this book, Keynes argued with impressive foresight that the victorious allies in World War I had exacted such heavy reparation payments from the Germans that the German economy would sink into ruin, producing dangerous political chaos. From the 1920s on, Keynes focused mostly on economics and, as we shall point out later, he often paused to write sharp critiques of the methods and analyses of other mainstream practitioners.

While Keynes was a powerful critic of some aspects of mainstream economics, his work was clearly different from the political economy practiced by Marx and Veblen. Keynes never gave up the idea that capitalism was the best of all possible modes of production. Indeed, given what he saw as human nature, he believed that competitive markets in capitalism were uniquely designed to minimize the often deadly effects of human competition. Thus, Keynes championed government intervention in capitalism because he believed that without it, the system he preferred would collapse into economic and political chaos. In other words, Keynes wanted to save capitalism from itself.

Rather than the reforms Keynes sought in government policy, Marx called for revolutionary overthrow of the capitalist class and the development of a socialist system. And Veblen imagined a grand reconstruction of capitalism, based on the rising power of engineers and scientists compared to that of capitalists. Therefore, if we look only at the political policies Keynes called for, in comparison to those advocated by Marx and Veblen, we can see that he was a very different kind of political economist than they were. Despite their fundamental differences, all three shared two principal conclusions that set them aside from most of those in the central tradition. The first is their view that unregulated capitalism is, for various reasons, a disaster waiting to happen;

and second is their belief that economists in the central tradition had so narrowly defined their discipline that they had come to misunderstand, or completely ignore, crucial dimensions of capitalism. We will discuss these two points later in this chapter, but first we turn to Keynes' critique of the classical explanation of business cycles.

Defining Our Terms

Business cycles have enormous effects on life in capitalist societies, and economists have given much attention to their nature and causes. In the process, they have developed an array of names for the business cycle. In the early nineteenth century, some economists referred to economic declines as "gluts" or "overproduction." Later in the nineteenth century, these gave way to the more ominous "economic crises," popularized by Marx.

During the 1930s, the collapse of U.S. capitalism was so deep and prolonged that it came to be known permanently as the "Great Depression." However, when the economy took another dip in 1937-38, after four years of slow growth, economists came up with "recession" as a way to distinguish that dip from the Depression. A few mainstream economists, their thoughts clearly under the mesmerizing spell of the classical school, tried in the 1950s to popularize a peculiarly hopeful term, "rolling readjustments." Fortunately, this term didn't stick but it's useful to note that profoundly different political ideologies are embedded in the concepts "economic crisis" and "rolling readjustment."

We will use the term "business cycle" in a general sense, and we will use other terms—gluts, recessions, depressions, or crises—as they fit what we are discussing. As with all descriptive language, one's choices among these terms often reveal personal biases. One oft-quoted analysis of these choices roots them completely in subjective circumstances: "If you lose *your* job, we're in a recession; if I lose *mine*, we're in a depression."

No matter what they were called, capitalist business cycles produced a long-standing debate throughout the nineteenth century, and the two sides can be succinctly expressed:

The Classical School: Economic recessions and depressions are natural and localized consequences of capitalism that are automatically self-limiting.

The Alternative Schools: Economic crises are complex, inevitable, and unpredictable consequences of the capitalist order.

THE CLASSICAL SCHOOL AND BUSINESS CYCLES

Until Keynes exploded their theory, economists in the classical school believed that "overproduction" – the production of goods that could not find buyers – was impossible except in the very short run. Economists in this school believed that when some firm, or even an entire industry, produced too many goods, automatic adjustments would occur that would put the economy back on track. We will take some time shortly to describe the analysis, but the ideological importance of this claim is easily explained. Classical economists, like most of their successors in the central tradition, did not question that capitalism was the best of all possible economic systems. This firm stance gave them the inclination to ignore unsightly aspects of capitalism, like social classes and the dominance of the state by the capitalist class. It also encouraged them to try to explain away imperfections in the system that are obvious even to children. An imperfection such as the business cycle, both obvious and potential politically destabilizing, especially needed explanation. How did the classical ideologues explain away the business cycle?

To answer this question, we will construct a hypothetical model of an early nineteenth century capitalist economy with three classes of economic actors: wage earners, capitalists, and landlords. Let's suppose that during a given year, the owners of capitalist firms produced $10 billion of goods and services and were successful in selling it all during the same time. To produce that level of output, the capitalists would have had to buy materials, labor time, and rent space from landlords. Thus they would have paid out most of the receipts from their sales in material costs, wages, and rents. Whatever was left after making all the payments to these "factors" of production could be kept as profits.

The process we are describing here is a key one to understand because it means this: at the aggregate level of the economy, the process by which the capitalists produce goods is the same as the one by which participants in the economy receive income to buy back the output from the capitalists. If we break into this flow of income and spending at the beginning of production and look at just one part of the stream during a particular month, we can see that, in exchange for their labor time, households received wage payments. And during the same month that they receive this income, they will send most of it back to the capitalists in exchange for consumption goods and services. This interdependence between producers, consumers, and workers is now called the "circular flow of income and output," and you were part of it the last time you cashed your paycheck and headed off to buy something. The circular flow is so crucial to an understanding of aggregate economics that there is always a circular flow diagram early on in principles textbooks. Because it is the conceptual center of macroeconomics, it will help the beginner to study such a diagram long enough to understand its basic meaning (perhaps before you go on here).

Now, let's go back to the circular flow of our own model and assume that as the $10 billion in sales revenue flowed into the capitalist coffers during the year, they paid it out as follows:

$7 billion went to laborers as wages
$1 billion went to the landlords as rents
$2 billion was kept by capitalists as profits

We are going to suppose that the laborers spent *all* their $7 billion of wages on goods and services, and the landlords spent *all* their $1 billion on consumer goods, too. This $8 billion, as you now know, will have gone back to the capitalist producers during the same year, and it will be the biggest part of what they have in order to start up the next year's cycle of production.

Now consider the $2 billion going to the capitalists this year. Let's suppose they spent $1 billion on consumer goods for themselves, and "saved" $1 billion. We'll also make the reasonable assumption that the $1 billion they saved was soon put back into the spending stream when they purchased—"invested in"—new capital goods, such as machinery and factories. Machines wear out and new technologies emerge that could lower costs for the capitalist, so that each year capitalists use up part, or all, of that year's savings to buy these new capital goods. This process is sometimes called "capital accumulation." In our model, the upshot is that the capitalists will have put all their profits back into the spending stream by purchasing $1 billion of consumer goods and $1 billion of capital goods.

We can sum up the results of our hypothetical model in this way: during the year, capitalists produced $10 billion because they thought they could sell it. They actually did sell it all because every dollar they paid out in the form of wages and rents, as well as the profits they paid themselves, came right back to them in the form of someone's consumer spending, plus their own spending for capital goods.

This model embodies the theory that all output will find a buyer – a theory that formed the core of classical thinking about the business cycle until Keynes's *General Theory*. The theory became known as "Say's Law," named for the French economist Jean Baptiste Say. What's the basic problem with this theory? *Not all savings are automatically converted into spending during the same year, month, or six months, or whatever time period we might be analyzing.* Going back to our example, let's take a closer look at the $1 billion saved by our capitalists. What might the capitalists in our economy have done with that $1 billion if, during the year, threatening events—such as epidemics, war, catastrophic weather, or a financial crisis—had produced a sweeping wave of pessimism among them? Such events might also have frightened the other potential savers in the economy, the landlords, and what would be the effect of their fears on their own spending? Both of these classes might reasonably have responded to fears about the future by saving for the coming bad times, rather than using all of their income to buy consumer or capital goods. If they had done this, that is, not put back all the $3 billion we gave them in our model, there could only have been one result: the capitalists would have produced goods that were not then sold, causing them to accumulate unwanted, unsold goods—inventories—and very likely to produce less output during the next time period. An economic downturn would have begun because all of the supply would *not* have created its own demand.

Despite the reign of a modified version of Say's Law in the central tradition up to the 1930s,[13] some economists saw through the classical error. Thomas Malthus in the early part of the nineteenth century, Karl Marx in the middle, and John Hobson at the turn of the twentieth century, are only the most well-known who argued that savings not returned to the income stream quickly enough could cause a downturn. Marx probably spoke for many of these ignored and heretical economists by referring to Say's analyses of the aggregate economy as "trivial," "tedious," and "insipid nonsense." Whatever they might have thought about Say and his Law, these critics could not break its transfixing hold on classical economists. That break would have to wait for Keynes in 1936.

We now turn to a second foundation of classical thinking: the idea that sustained involuntary unemployment in capitalism is not possible.

THE CLASSICAL THEORY OF UNEMPLOYMENT

The classical economists believed, with good reason, that work for capitalist wages was essentially irksome. This meant that below a certain level of wages nobody would work and that as wages rose more people would offer their labor power to the highest capitalist bidder. Given the two sides of this labor market, if the supply of labor were to remain constant, for instance, but capitalists decided to increase their output, they would need more workers and this would drive up wages. Alternatively, if the supply of labor remained constant, but the demand for labor time fell, wages would fall.

To connect this theory of a single labor market to the classical theory of unemployment, consider the following example: take a hypothetical large city with an active labor market for skilled carpenters. Let's assume that the going wage is $15 an hour, and as we begin our analysis there are 10,000 carpenters on the job. Suppose that, for whatever reasons, there is a substantial decline in the demand for construction throughout the whole region. This event will likely reduce the selling prices of construction projects and thus the value of the output of the carpenters who work on them. As the value of what carpenters produce declines, their services will also be less in demand, and given that, we would expect their wages to fall. However, suppose that these wage rates don't fall because the carpenters make it clear they will fight wage cuts individually, or collectively through labor unions, or in other ways. This kind of resistance produces what is known as "wage rigidity," and in response to it, if the decline in construction demand is steep enough, some employers will lay off some of the carpenters.

Suppose the capitalists lay off 2,000 carpenters, and the remaining 8,000 of them continue working for the old wage. Now, in terms of the classical theory, here is a crucial question: are these 2,000 laid-off carpenters "unemployed"? According to the classical economists they are unemployed, but *voluntarily* so. That is, they are *choosing* to be unemployed, and if they would lower their wage demands enough, construction firms would once again find it profitable to hire more carpenters. Perhaps, if all the carpenters were willing to take $10 an hour, and if that wage fit the new market conditions, it would again be profitable for the capitalists to hire all 10,000 of them. In other words, as long as carpenters are unwilling to accept lower wages in the face of falling demand for their services, there can be no *in*voluntary unemployment. The implicit and connecting idea here is that hiring the carpenters at a lower wage will allow the builders to sell their output at a lower price. This lower price will produce a greater demand for the projects, and that will lead to an increase in the demand for carpenters. In other words, our unemployed carpenters are out of work because of their resistance to wage cuts.

The classical school generalized this theory—that without wage rigidity all individual markets were always at, or tending towards, full employment—to the entire economy. So strong was the hold of this model on the minds of economists in the central tradition that it was, as Guy Routh reports, "maintained right into the depths of the depression of the 1930s," when unemployment in both Britain and the U.S. was about 25%. As a prominent example, consider the comments made in 1932 by the president of the Royal Economic Society, the principal organization of the British classical school: "General unemployment appears when asking too much is a general phenomenon.... [The world] should learn to submit to declines of money-income without squealing" (Routh 1986, 57).

To sum up this quick review of the classical school's explanation for economic downturns and the consequent unemployment, we have the following: (1) aggregate supply will always equal aggregate demand, except temporarily, because capitalists will automatically use any savings out of the income stream to purchase capital goods; and (2) deviations from full employment in *all* individual labor markets result from worker resistance to falling wages in contracting industries. How, then, did Keynes go about putting these models, more or less, into the dustbin of history?

THE BROAD OUTLINES OF THE "KEYNESIAN REVOLUTION"

We want to be clear about our purposes in this section. The central structure of the Keynesian macroeconomic framework is formed by interrelated theories of consumption, investment, government spending, net exports, and the way in which behavior in these various sectors causes a capitalist economy to expand and contract. Such a framework is central to any introduction to modern macroeconomics, and all economics students will thus be made to learn its structural outlines and most important details. We will leave to economics courses the proper development of macroeconomics and take up only what helps us to explain the broad impact of Keynes' ideas on economics and on public policy, and of course, the relationship of these to political economy.

In 1936 when Keynes published *The General Theory,* many economists eagerly seized its details and implications, especially their relation to the causes of the Great Depression all were living through. Most of these economists were young and from the United States, many from Harvard's economics department. At the same time, the book produced a great debate among economists throughout the capitalist world, and many were not then, nor are they now, convinced of its usefulness. However, enough economists in the United States and Britain were converted to his way of thinking to begin to sink the classical ship. One such young economist, Harvard's Paul Samuelson, legitimized Keynesian economics by putting it on a par with classical microeconomics in a 1948 principles textbook that remains the model for most such books.

Another reason that Keynes' critique took hold was that others outside the central tradition, who understood and accepted his principal conclusions, had already developed much of his critique. As early as the 1700s, thinkers outside the mainstream had already advanced arguments about savings, involuntary unemployment, and the policy measures that might solve the problem of depressions. In the 1860s, Marx had developed a number of ideas about business cycles, including the idea that they resulted in part from an imbalance of spending in the investment and consumption sectors of the economy. Toward the end of the nineteenth century, in 1899, the Englishman John A. Hobson had argued that unemployment was caused by "over-savings." Hobson, however, was soon to realize that he had made a heretical argument and would be punished for it. As he later wrote, there were several negative responses to the book:

> The first shock came in a refusal of the London Extension Board to allow me to offer courses of Political Economy. This was due, I learned, to the intervention of an Economics Professor who had read my book and considered it in rationality as equivalent to an attempt to prove the flatness of the earth...[The second came] when suddenly, without explanation, the invitation [to offer a course to a charitable organization] was withdrawn. Even then I hardly realized that in appearing to question the virtue of unlimited thrift [savings] I had committed the unpardonable sin. (Quoted in Keynes 1936, 365-6)

By the late nineteenth century it had become, at least according to Hobson and Keynes, an unpardonable sin not to agree with the classical explanation of the business cycle! And as we have seen, right up to the point when Keynes was writing *The General Theory*, Britain's most widely respected economists were still telling the world that the only way out of the Great Depression was to lower wages all around.

More substantive than these largely ignored critiques of the classical theory were the actual practices of one European country, Sweden, which had implemented its own "Keynesian" policies before *The General Theory* was published. John K. Galbraith has described how, since the early part of the century, Swedish economists and government planners had instituted policies that made sure that "over-saving" in the Swedish economy was offset by government expenditures (Galbraith 1987). Swedish fiscal policy, in practice before Keynes argued for it, was part of the Swedish "middle way" we discuss in another chapter.

All this theory and practice was well known by Keynes, a fine student of history and of his own discipline, and he drew upon both to build his own system. He also chose as a specific strategy in *The General Theory* to write the theoretical parts in the language of the classical school and, many parts of his analysis begin from one or more of the conceptual foundations of that school. If you were to try to read the book, you would almost certainly be cornered by confusion. Yet, if you plowed on you would find that the book opens up at the end because, quite intentionally, Keynes wrote the closing chapters for the general public. There he took up the implications of his theory for public policy in a discussion that justifies his renowned eloquence as a writer.

THE KEYNESIAN CRITIQUE OF SAY'S LAW

A major contribution of Keynes's *General Theory* was its critique of Say's Law. Keynes argued conclusively, in terse theoretical parts of his book, that this "law" was the wishful thinking of those who dreamed of a self-regulating capitalist system. The assumption that savings would always be spent on capital goods during the same production period was not quite so far-fetched when made by Adam Smith. In his time the merchant and landlord classes did virtually all the saving, and it appears that usually—but certainly not all the time—they quickly converted their savings into capital goods in order to profit from rapidly expanding capitalist markets. However, Keynes noted that by the nineteenth century, and certainly by the early twentieth century, industrial capitalist systems had become vastly more complex.

Even in a world in which the economic role of government was supposed to be minimal, governments had become ever more involved in economic affairs. Thus, the saving "leakage" from the economy was joined by the "tax leakage," because whatever governments took in taxes reduced the circular flow of income. Like savings, these taxes could lead to underconsumption if the tax leakages were not put back into the income stream by government. Still a third leakage occurs when people in the U.S. buy imports which, dollar for dollar, reduce the amount they would have bought from U.S. firms. In fact, from the point of view of Say's Law, we can think of taxes and imports as identical to savings: they are a drain from the system that must be returned or overproduction will occur.

We can express Keynes' idea more clearly if we consider the magnitudes of these leakages from the spending flow in our own economy. In 1997, for example, U.S. business firms employed over 120 million people and these people produced output that was sold for over $8 trillion. As this $8 trillion flowed through the U.S. economy, most of it, about $4.7 trillion, was put back in by household consumption spending. However, much of it was drained out of the expenditure stream as leakages:

- More than 10 million businesses firms saved—"accumulated"—about $1 trillion to help finance their expenditures for capital goods.[14]
- More than 90 million household units saved about $267 billion and put most of that in banks or other financial institutions to be lent out to others.
- All the levels of government took a total of about $1.5 trillion out of the expenditure stream through taxation.
- Households and firms spent about $.5 trillion on imports, another leakage from the domestic expenditure stream.

This means that during 1997, the tax, savings, and import leakages out of the flow of income were almost $3.3 trillion, or about 40% of all the expenditures! Of course, at the same time that these leakages were occurring, "injections" were taking place as well. Governments were putting money back into the expenditure stream by buying such things as military hardware and education; business firms were adding to the stream by buying machinery and equipment; banks were lending the savings out to all kinds of spenders; and there were exports sold to foreigners.

These figures lead us to the relevant theoretical point: while U.S. capitalists were deciding to produce the $8 trillion of output during 1997, they had no idea, of course, how much of the income they generated would be lost to leakages, and how much would be gained back by injections. *The reason is that these leakages and injections result from an impossibly large number of decisions by people who, at the time they save, tax, or spend, do not typically know anything about how others are putting money into, or taking it out of, the income stream.* The capitalists in this process are not operating in total darkness, because they have past sales experiences to draw upon. However, the volume of output that the capitalists produce for sale, say, next month, depends upon hunches, or other best guesses, about something they *cannot know*: the level of leakages and injections that will occur as the income their production generates flows through the economy. If their estimates of sales are not realized—which, in theoretical language, will occur if there are too many leakages that are not offset by injections— they will likely accumulate inventories, and during the subsequent time period they will likely produce less total output. Thus, when the *typical* business firm is not selling all the output it is producing, there will be general overproduction, and this will ultimately lead to a decline in output, employment, and income.

The Multiplier and the Liquidity Trap

Two other parts of Keynes' critique of Say's Law merit a brief description here. Keynes developed the first of these, called the "multiplier," with other Cambridge economists, and it was a powerful addition to his model of the macroeconomy. We will explain the multiplier with a simple example. Imagine a rosy scenario in which the local billionaire decides to pay back the community by giving the first person he or she sees a $100 bill. Suppose you are the lucky recipient, and you spend it on that tattoo of your favorite professor you've been aching to put on your arm. Your purchase alone increases spending in the economy by $100, and it also increases the income of the tattoo parlor by $100. Suppose the owner of the parlor spends $80 of it for a new hairdo. This will add $80 of new spending and income to the $100 spent for the tattoo, both of them additions to spending brought about by that initial $100 the billionaire gave to you. The beautician now has some more money to spend, and on down the line each new level of spending creates multiples of its own.

These successive transactions thus "multiply" the first round of spending — the $100 spent on the tattoo — and make the total change in spending some multiple of that first round. The multiplier adds a certain speed and energy to upward and downward movements of the economy, and it added to the new macro-theory that Keynes used to undermine the classical theory. It is also carries with it depressingly bad news for those committed to laissez-faire, for our $100 bill would have produced a similar multiplier effect had it been new government spending for goods and services, or simply handouts to needy citizens. We'll say more about that later.

The theory of the "liquidity trap," another of Keynes' principal ideas in *The General Theory*, has recently resurfaced in public discussion in relation to the current long-term depression of the Japanese economy. In trying to explain the depth of the Great Depression, Keynes argued that societies could wallow in a slump for long periods of time even if interest rates—which at low levels are supposed to induce capitalists and consumers to spend more and end the downturn—fall to zero. He called this problem a "liquidity trap," and argued that it would occur if there were a collapse in confidence among consumers and capitalists that encouraged them to seek "liquidity," meaning they would choose to hold on to money, rather than buy things, until they perceived that the economy was improving. We will briefly return to this idea in another context below.

KEYNES AND THE CLASSICAL THEORY OF UNEMPLOYMENT

Keynes developed several critiques of the classical claim that there could be no long-lasting *involuntary* unemployment, and we will concern ourselves with the two most prominent ones. Remember that for classical economists, lasting unemployment resulted when workers were not willing to take lower wages in declining product markets. Thus, their suggestion for unemployment policy—even in the middle of the Great Depression, when the unemployment rate was 25% in both the United States and Britain—was for the working class to take lower wages. Keynes saw at least two fatal errors in this thinking. The first had partly to do with the relative power between workers and their bosses, for it was apparent to Keynes, and almost everyone else, that unless there was a sustained and deepening downturn, workers mightily resisted wage cuts. However, because the classical economists ruled out government intervention as a way to lower wages, nothing was left to do except to wait for workers to see the light and accept the necessary wage cuts. When they didn't—which was almost always—this meant that wages never fell quickly in recessions, preventing the economy from self-adjusting as the classical theorists believed it would. To the classical school, this resistance from workers to falling wages also meant that the recessions should be blamed on them, rather than on the system itself. Thus, the first big mistake of the classical school was to substitute wishful thinking for observable facts about how promptly wage rates would fall in declining labor markets. In reality, wages were sticky and did not adjust quickly enough to end recessions.

The second error of the classical school can be explained like this: suppose that an economic contraction becomes deep enough, and sustained enough, to lower the demand for labor in all the principal labor markets. There would be a point in such a contraction at which wages would begin to fall, when and by how much depending on countless conditions. We have already pointed out that according to the classical economists, falling wages would lower costs and prices, thus inviting a greater demand for goods and services. In turn, they believed that this greater demand would *automatically* turn around the economic decline. Keynes pointed out, however, that a *general* fall in wages— the largest single part of national income—would likely cause an eventual *decline* in the demand for goods and services that workers buy, rather than an increase encouraged by lower prices.

Keynes offered several other possible consequences of a fall in wages, some of which might be expected to raise expenditures by business firms, but he did not see them as having the capacity to offset the decline in total spending that would come from falling wages. Falling wages, if they did have the effect of reducing total consumer demand, could also greatly reduce the optimism of the capitalists and lead them to reduce their spending on new equipment. This latter possibility was important to Keynes because he knew that the sustained and deep depression of the 1930s had, by 1936, done exactly that in the leading capitalist countries. In general, such a progression would mean that the decline in consumption spending, along with the decline in capitalist spending on capital goods, would send the economy spiraling downward even further.

To Keynes, then, the levels of employment and unemployment depended on a series of factors: the collective decisions of people to spend as consumers and capitalists and to fund government spending programs, the decisions of foreigners to buy U.S. products, the multiplier, and all the remaining parts of his theoretical framework. That is, in his model the unemployed are victimized by crises in capitalism, *and the classical solution of lower wages would only make the crises worse.* In his argument, Keynes came closer than he probably would have liked to Marx's idea of an "industrial reserve army" of unemployed that we discussed in the essay on Marx. What these two theories share is the conclusion that unemployment is an inevitable feature of capitalism over which workers have no control. Unemployment goes up when aggregate spending declines, and thus if we are looking for culprits to blame, it would have to be the millions and millions of individuals in households and business firms deciding to cut back on their spending. Unemployment in capitalism, therefore, is *systemic and inevitable,* rather than the result of individual decisions to work or not to work at market wages. It is hard to imagine a more resounding rejection of classical economics than this Keynesian conclusion about unemployment.

THE CURRENT STATUS OF KEYNESIAN ECONOMICS

Aside from pushing from the limelight central parts of classical economics, the principal long-term influence of The General Theory has been to broaden the focus of macroeconomics. Today, aggregate sectors of spending, and their dynamic interrelationships, are understood as central to the study of the capitalist business cycle. Keynes had no particular qualms about the microeconomic models that his own mentor, Alfred Marshall, had been so important in bringing to the mainstream; and his principal work in 1936 built on many of the theoretical foundations of the classical school. For this reason, as we have said, Keynes never really left the central tradition of economics. In fact, the macro-theory he produced gradually became part of the mainstream, a process that led Paul Samuelson to write in the 1964 version of his textbook that:

> [Today] the broad fundamentals [of Keynes' theory] are increasingly accepted by economists of all schools of thought, including, it is important to notice, many who do not share Keynes' particular policy views and who differ on technical details of analysis. (Samuelson 1964)

Samuelson's point here does not mean, by any stretch of the imagination, that there have not been challenges, before and after 1964, to Keynesian ideas. These have come particularly from economists unhappy with his conclusions about the need for government intervention in the economy. Two of these challenges, called "monetarism" and "rational expectations," have come from the economics department at the University of Chicago, which has been one of the strongest bastions of anti-Keynesian sentiment in the United States academy since the 1930s. There are also "post"-Keynesian economists, and they compete for the attention of other academic macroeconomists and the policy makers in government.

It is far beyond the scope of this essay to go into the current academic debate about macroeconomic theory.[15] We will merely present fresh evidence of the fact that, even after 60 years of challenges from many mainstream economists, Keynesian ideas continue to play a role in current academic debates about the macroeconomy. As an example, Keynes' theory of the "liquidity trap" has surfaced recently in the attempts of several economists to explain the current sustained depression in Japan. One of these economists, Paul Krugman, traveled to Japan in the late 1990s to see conditions for himself. Economic columnist Louis Uchitelle described Krugman's conclusions:

> He constructed a mathematical model, a standard tool of modern economics, to demonstrate that printing more money and lowering interest rates, even down to zero, would succeed in stimulating demand and expanding an economy. "Instead, I succeeded in proving to myself that this was not necessarily true," he said. He concluded that a liquidity trap was possible after all. It was no longer just a historical curiosity —a fading memory of the Depression and the teachings of Keynes. It had happened in Japan.... Among professional

economists, Mr. Krugman was not the first to conclude that Japan had fallen into a liquidity trap. A small group of Keynesian economists already had this in mind. And as early as 1996, some conservatives, among them John Makin of the American Enterprise Institute, who does not consider himself a Keynesian, wrote that Japan was caught in a liquidity trap.... (Uchitelle 1999)

In our view, a particularly interesting aspect of this article is that it takes us back to the 1930s, when Keynes launched his major attack on the classical school's theory of economic crises, ushering in a debate that won't go away. Today, it is remarkable to see mainstream economists like Professor Krugman scurrying back to Keynes when capitalism begins to slip and slide. Keynes' run has been a long one.

KEYNES, THE POLITICAL ECONOMIST, I: ECONOMIC METHODOLOGY

We now want to expand our argument for having included Keynes in a book on political economy. The Keynes you will encounter in your regular textbook will seem to conform to the "scientific method" used by mainstream economists. But there was another important political economy side to Keynes' thinking—a side that demonstrates the broad sweep of his ideas. We will let Keynes demonstrate this by speaking for himself at some length here and below. Writing in 1931, he said:

The study of economics does not seem to require any specialized gifts of an unusually high order. Is it not, intellectually regarded, a very easy subject compared with the higher branches of philosophy or pure science? An easy subject, at which very few excel! The paradox finds its explanation, perhaps, in that the master economist must possess a rare *combination* of gifts. He must be mathematician, historian, statesman, philosopher—in some degree. He must understand symbols and speak in words. He must contemplate the particular in terms of the general, and touch abstract and concrete in the same flight of thought. He must study the present in the light of the past for the purposes of the future. No part of man's nature or his intuitions must lie entirely outside his regard. He must be purposeful and disinterested in a simultaneous mood; as aloof and incorruptible as an artist, yet sometimes as near the earth as a politician. (Keynes 1963, 140-1)

Referring more precisely to the quantitative techniques of the mainstream economists, Keynes wrote in *The General Theory*:

Too large a proportion of recent "mathematical" economics are mere concoctions, as imprecise as the initial assumptions they rest on, which allow the author to lose sight of the complexities and interdependencies of the real world in a maze of pretentious and unhelpful symbols. (Keynes 1936, 98)

As an example of the kind of ideas that Keynes was willing to entertain, consider his explanation of what motivates economic actors in capitalism. In the following passage from *The General Theory*, where his specific focus is what motivates capitalists to invest in capital goods, note that Keynes implicitly dismisses as badly misleading the constricted creature called economic man.

[A] large proportion of our positive activities depend on spontaneous optimism rather than on a mathematical expectation, whether moral or hedonistic or economic. Most, probably, of our decisions to do something positive, the full consequences of which will be drawn out over many days to come, can only be taken as a result of *animal spirits*—of a spontaneous urge to action rather than inaction, and not as the outcome of a weighted average of quantitative benefits multiplied by quantitative probabilities.... Thus if the animal spirits are dimmed and the spontaneous optimism falters, leaving us to depend on nothing but a mathematical expectation, enterprise will fade and die—though fears of loss may have a basis no more reasonable than hopes of profit had before....In estimating the prospects for investments [in capital goods], we must have regard, therefore, to the nerves and hysteria and even the digestions and reactions to the weather of those upon whose spontaneous activity it largely depends. (Keynes 1936, 162-3, emphasis added)

If we take these three passages together, we can see in Keynes' methodology a far-flung net—or a particularly big vacuum cleaner if we use the metaphor of U.S. economist Robert Solow—in which to catch things that might help his analysis. For Keynes, apparently, the entire universe of ideas and knowledge had potential for helping theorists understand the world outside the swirl of prejudices and confusions inside their heads. His methodology for studying economic activity broke all the self-imposed bonds of the central tradition. Though he insisted often that economic *theory* was a matter of simple logic, it seems hardly to have mattered to him whether economics was a science. In other words, though Keynes's ideas about the economic world were in some ways deeply embedded in classical thinking, they were outside it in critical ways. Perhaps now, after reading about Veblen and Marx, one can see how much closer his research impulses were to theirs than to those of the economic mainstream. His method of work was that of a political economist.

KEYNES, THE POLITICAL ECONOMIST, II: THE POLITICAL KEYNES

By the early 1920s, Keynes had come to believe in the need for government intervention in certain areas of economic life, and thus the policy prescriptions he offered in *The General Theory* merely extended ideas he had held for some time. The specifics of his antirecession policies will not come as a surprise to readers at this point. When an economy is mired in an economic contraction, Keynes argued, it is a consequence of inadequate spending in all the key sectors. Economic downturns were most likely to originate from a decline in capitalists' purchases of capital goods, because volatile and unpredictable "animal spirits" ruled these expenditures. When the spirits led the capitalists to reduce their spending on buildings and equipment, all those who had been supplying such products before would now be out of jobs and income, and the effects of their declining spending would spill over into the consumption sector, causing a decline there as well. Further dragging the economy down would be a negative multiplier effect, and soon enough an economic crisis would be underway.

Given this theory of how the aggregate economy could quickly slide into a recession, the solution seemed obvious to Keynes: as investment and consumption spending fell, the government should take up the slack in demand by borrowing money to increase its own expenditures, or reducing interest rates to encourage spending in other sectors of the economy. And it didn't matter for what those expenditures were made. As this spending worked its way through the economy, it would ultimately produce a better outlook for businesses, which meant more investment on capital goods. With the help of the multiplier, this would start the whole process moving back upward to recovery and economic growth.

Aside from the Swedes, who tried this kind of fiscal policy before Keynes argued for it, other capitalist governments did not readily jump on the Keynesian bandwagon. The New Deal in the United States generated a spate of new government programs such as unemployment compensation, federal welfare, and public works projects that gave jobs to the unemployed, but the government was not ready to risk the huge deficits that Keynesians were urging on it as the way to end the Depression. However, starting in about 1940, Keynesian policies were "tested in the field" by most capitalist governments during World War II. In the United States, government leaders tossed aside the classical school's admonition against government intervention in the economy, including its rule against deficit spending, to fight the war against Japan and Germany. Running massive deficits to finance the construction of bombs, planes, and ships, federal government spending led to a massive recovery. By 1943-44, the unemployment rate fell to its lowest recorded level, about one percent of the work force.

With the war as a gigantic lab experiment that seemed to prove the Keynesian theory, most in the scholarly and political world gradually came to adopt it. After World War II, most capitalist nations passed laws, such as the Employment Act of 1946 in the United States, making the maintenance of stable prices and full employment a job for the federal government. These were laws in part written by, and certainly reflecting the views of, Keynesian economists. A symbolic high point of the influence of Keynes occurred in 1963, when in a speech at Yale University John Kennedy used the idea of the Keynesian multiplier to justify the cut in personal income taxes he was urging on the Congress as a way to cause a sluggish economy to grow faster. The essentially Keynesian basis of domestic U.S. economic policy remained in place for about 25 years, and in 1971 an economic conservative, Richard Nixon, argued that "we are all Keynesians now."

Even as Nixon spoke, the U.S. economy had already begun to develop a number of structural problems, particularly pockets of hard-core unemployment and rising inflation, that could not be readily resolved by Keynesian policies. These problems in the United States and in Britain in the 1970s deepened through the decade and they propelled into power Margaret Thatcher in Britain in 1979 and Ronald Reagan in the United States in 1980. The public elected these two because it succumbed to their espousal of the old laissez-faire slogans of free enterprise, individual initiative, and especially the sentiment that government in principle was a bad thing for the economy. By the middle of the 1980s, the U.S. Republicans and British Conservatives held sway with an increasingly antigovernment rhetoric that is now the stated economic philosophy of the major political parties in both countries. By the end of the 1980s, it was virtually impossible in the United States to be elected to public office at any level if one championed higher taxes. According to many political analysts, George Bush was pushed from the presidency by Bill Clinton in 1992 because he went back on his famous "read my lips" pledge not to support tax increases.

For his part, Bill Clinton jumped on the bandwagon when he came into power as a "new Democrat," claiming that "the era of big government is over.

"His economic policies – including "ending welfare as we know it" — were largely indistinguishable from those of the Republicans. Catering to business and financial interests is now considered "economic policy," justified by the essentially specious argument that their good fortunes will trickle down to the rest of us. Partly, Clinton moved toward the Republicans in order to get elected and re-elected; partly he did so because, more than any Democratic president before him, he aggressively and successfully financed his campaigns with money from rich individuals and powerful corporations.

Not surprisingly, given his family background and his conservative economic policies as Governor of Texas, George W. Bush continues to pour out the laissez-faire rhetoric. Indeed, he campaigned both to be governor and to be president crucially on the grounds that he was a successful "entrepreneur" who knew about capitalism and how it worked because he had made a fortune in the market place. In fact, as all know now, he used insider trading to turn a small investment in a failing company into almost a million dollars and used that to turn himself into a part owner of the Texas Rangers. His insider trading, and failure to report it in a timely fashion, provoked an investigation by the Securities and Exchange Commission. The SEC, then headed by one of his father's appointees, a man who had been a family attorney, found that George W. had not violated any laws. Then Bush and his Texas Rangers partners got local politicians to invoke the laws of eminent domain to allow them to grab privately owned real estate for their own gain, actions that produced lawsuits by some of the private owners whose land was seized (some of which suits remain unresolved.) The partners, along with the politicians, also persuaded locals to pass a ½ cent sales tax to pay for a new stadium. Last of all, when, as Texas governor, Bush sold his small share of the Rangers, his business partners paid him an extra $10 million because he had been one of the "general managers" of the team. Thus, while he has bellowed loudly in the laissez-faire choir, Bush has depended upon the federal government to disregard his shady dealings and upon local government to add greatly to the riches he had already inherited from his family.

In other words, all this anti-government posturing is mainly the rhetoric of politics, and it is utterly at odds with the extensive role government plays in the U.S. economy. Federal spending was 21.7% of Gross Domestic Product in 1980 when Reagan started his rhetorical war against government. By 1992, when George Bush's defeat ended twelve years of Republican control of the White House, this proportion had actually risen to 22.5%. Looked at another way, between 1980 and 1992, federal spending per capita—the average amount the federal government spends on each of us each year—actually increased from $4,232 to $5,610, after taking account of inflation. Thus, while Republicans were claiming to be delivering a laissez-faire utopia, in fact, the governments they largely dominated at every level responded to our demands to spend more on each of us each year. And, for his part and for obvious political reasons, the current president, George W. Bush, has allowed hefty import duties on steel imports and continues to sign legislation providing multi-billions of dollars to agribusiness. For all these politicians, sloganeering about the evils of government works as a political strategy. Their actions, however, reveal that they are no more antagonistic to government action than was Keynes, if not being so fits into their re-election strategies, or can add to their personal gain in other ways.

A principal reason the U.S. economy is currently not in crisis is that most people are confident that the national government will not hesitate to intervene, and massively if necessary, should the economy turn downward. Before Keynes, and certainly in the middle of the Great Depression, no one could reasonably have had that confidence. If people believed the economy were slipping into recession, they would not tolerate their president, or other economic policy makers like the Federal Reserve Board, pronouncing week after week that government would only make things worse if it intervened in the economy, and that prosperity was "just around the corner." This widespread involvement of government in capitalism is the political reality in all modern capitalist countries, no matter what their politicians say in speeches or at press conferences about "keeping government off of peoples' backs." These same people expect their governments to manage the macroeconomy, and presidents who have failed to do so in the public perception—Jimmy Carter and George Bush—are two recent examples—don't get a second term.

KEYNES AND INTERNATIONAL CAPITALISM

There is a counterpart to all of this regarding the international economy. Keynes achieved much of his fame for having been the principal designer of the post-World War II system of international finance. In 1944, representatives from the allied nations met in Bretton Woods, New Hampshire to plan a framework for developing world capitalism once the war was over. The system that Keynes and others designed was in place from 1945 until the early 1970s. It formed a matrix of regulations analogous to Keynesian domestic policy in the sense that government bodies at the international level would be directly involved in regulating the post-war international economy. This, too, was an assault on the classical system because "free trade" was, in that system, the analog to an unregulated domestic economy. One observer, looking back on the effects of the system the delegates produced, has written:

> Between 1945 and 1973, when the regime of [international] financial controls remained in effect, the war-ravaged economies of Europe and Asia were rebuilt, and the developed world as a whole enjoyed annual economic growth rates exceeding four per cent, which translated into the virtual tripling of total output. (Cassidy 1998b)

Since the 1970s, much in this regard has changed. The ideology of "free trade" was a part of the Reagan/Thatcher laissez-faire agenda, and picking up where they left off, Democrat Bill Clinton campaigned more vigorously for unregulated international capitalism than any president since before the Great Depression. In their championing of "free trade," presidents Reagan, George Bush, and Clinton used the considerable authority and power of the U.S. government to dismantle the system of international controls established at Bretton Woods. Some regulations, such as those controlling the values of currencies, were dropped in the 1970s. Others, such as the regulation of capital flows across borders, were eliminated in the 1990s as developing countries come under pressure from the U.S. and other powerful capitalist nations to adopt their own "free trade" policies. It is not possible to know if these trends will continue, particularly after many experts blamed the recent collapse of the financial systems in several Asian countries on the lack of international controls over capital flows.

Though we cannot know now the long-term effects of this age of laissez-faire rhetoric, there is one measure that might help us to put into a sensible context the real, rather than the rhetorical, effects of government intervention in U.S. capitalism. That measure is the comparable rates of growth in the size of the U.S. economy during two periods. During the first of them, 1945-1970, when Keynesian ideas shaped domestic fiscal policy in the U.S. and the international system established in Bretton Woods was still in effect, the average real growth rate in our economy was about 3.5%. During the second period, 1970 to the present, by which time both domestic and international controls have been rolled back in significant ways, the annual real growth rate has been between 2-3%. Because so many elements determine growth rates in addition to government's role in the economy, we can safely extract but one conclusion from this comparison: the most sustained period of economic growth in U.S.

history occurred during the period in which both U.S. and international economic policies were most thoroughly Keynesian.

As a final word on Keynes and the international economy, despite what seems to be a strong connection between his policies and a sustained two-decade boom described above, there were much less desirable consequences of the international economy he helped to shape. The Bretton Woods agreement is, in our own time, most importantly embodied in the International Monetary Fund and the World Bank. For three decades, these two institutions have developed a policy of bullying the world's poor nations into making themselves into largely unregulated capitalist states. Deregulating the economies of poor countries has meant eliminating labor and environmental protections, "restructuring" government spending to starve social programs, and instituting an array of other reforms that serve the interests of corporations and Western governments. In Russia, since the IMF medicine has been administered, and as a measure of how well it has worked, life expectancy has plummeted to its lowest level in fifty years.[16] In Argentina, the IMF prescribed austerity measures that decimated employment and social programs so deeply that in 2001 the people overthrew the government that implemented the measures. More recently, the IMF and World Bank have been joined by the World Trade Organization, which also seeks to deregulate the global economy. All three of these organizations are dominated by the United States, and there is no surprise in our time that the U.S. uses its might to try to shape the rest of the world to serve its own interests.

It is hard to imagine this U.S. dominance as an outcome Keynes intended — he was more interested in stabilizing currency values and facilitating orderly trade. Yet, the domination of these three organizations by the U.S., and the other largest capitalist states, can be seen as an inevitable outcome of domestic or international regulatory agencies in the new global economy. As Marx put it, government officials in capitalist nations (or in the integrated capitalist world) tend to become the "executive committee" of the capitalist class. It seems clear in retrospect that Keynes, in ignoring Marx's ideas, held to a badly underdeveloped theory of politics in capitalist countries. Like most mainstream economists, Keynes assumed that good policy based on good analysis would win the day. In fact, in capitalism, the capitalists almost always win the day, and in large part because, as political economists have known all along, they have already won the state before the day begins. Despite all his contributions, Keynes would have made richer ones yet had he spent more time studying economists from the other end of the political economy spectrum, most notably Marx. Doing so might have helped him see more clearly how the dominating capitalists, and their executive committee, turn "good' economic analysis into yet another advantage they have on the playing field.

Conclusion

Keynes and his ideas are included in this book because he shared two important ways of thinking with political economists. For his study of economic life, no information was outside his purview. He was a thoroughly erudite man, a voracious reader and consummate conversationalist, and he believed that dependence on all the senses—what one had read, heard about, seen, could intuit, and even what one felt—was central to the work of any good economist. This is a far, far cry from the restrictive methodological stance that dominates mainstream economics. Unlike those who dominate mainstream economics, and who claim to be "making correct scientific judgments," Keynes never stopped giving his opinions to the day that he died. Keynes also shared with political economists the conclusion that unregulated capitalism is an unsustainable system, and for it to last over the long run its aggregate performance will have to be overseen by a strong government, ultimately more powerful than the most powerful corporations. In our view, Keynes' development of this argument has no worthy rival.

Suggestions for Further Reading

Alvin Hansen. *A Guide to Keynes.* New York: McGraw-Hill, 1953.

Robert Lekachman. *The Age of Keynes.* New York: Random House, 1966.

Guy Routh. *Unemployment: Economic Perspectives.* London: MacMillan, 1986.

Joseph Schumpeter. *Ten Great Economists,* London: Allen and Unwin, 1952.

Skidelski, Robert. *John Maynard Keynes: The Economist as Saviour, 1920-1937.* London: MacMillan, 1992. (This is part of an acclaimed and readable multivolume biography of Keynes, his life and work.)

5
Social Classes in U.S. Capitalism

INTRODUCTION

The Class System at Our University

The *Catalog* for Bucknell University, where we teach, is typical of such catalogs in that it contains a lofty "Mission Statement" telling the world that the university is dedicated to noble goals. Of these goals, the following are representative:

> To develop new experiences that will enable students to grow in moral sensitivity and in respect for other persons. To engage in institutional programs and practices that exemplify compassion, civility, and a sense of justice.

Only the most churlish person could criticize such goals for a university. And wonderful it would be for professors if students left our classrooms morally sensitive, respectful of others, compassionate, civil, and having a sense of justice. Wonderful, too, if professors were that way themselves!

These goals, alas, are pronounced against a jarring social reality ignored at most universities: *social class*. The undeniable existence of an array of social classes at universities, among the students and among those who work as faculty, staff, and administrators, is a constant reminder that some of us are accorded more respect than others. To us, it is hard to know what "sense of justice" a student might gain from an institution which bestows benefits and status in glaringly unequal ways.

Students will learn from dorm life the first week of classes that some are from very privileged backgrounds, some from merely privileged backgrounds, and some from considerably lower ones. Expensive cars and clothes, or the lack of them, and all the talk about one's family reveal the degree of social privilege each student has enjoyed. In turn, each student receives some added privilege simply by attending college: soon forgotten will be the more than 50% of the eighteen and nineteen year olds off campus, almost all of them from the lower half of the class system, who are not at universities but heading for low wage jobs or the military service.

Within the university, striking income inequality illuminates the class structure. This year (2002), Bucknell's president is being paid about $200,000, an income supplemented by over $30,000 in benefits and an elegant, sprawling home to live in. Between him and the faculty are a number of top administrators whose salaries range from about $100,000 to $150,000. Beneath them in this hierarchy of money and power are the faculty members whose average income is about $65,000; and below them are those called, in a perfect word for a class system, "support staff." Annually, they make between roughly $13,000 and $50,000, most of them falling in the lower ranges of this spread. Secretaries with decades of experience can make less than $30,000, or less than the value of the benefits paid to the president. For all the apparent reasons, the inequality of this income is matched quite closely by the varying amounts of power and status attached to each of the income strata.

All this relative privilege and power utterly contradicts the goal of exemplifying a sense of justice. Consider the effect of Bucknell's income inequality on the children of this university community. The higher salaries of leading administrators and faculty members unquestionably allow them to pass on to their children a number of advantages, such as better odds at attending the best schools; access to superior food, clothing, doctors and dentists; and a better environment in which to learn the linguistic styles and the cultural prejudices of other elites who will eventually hire them for better jobs. It is hard to imagine how a community could describe itself as just when it systematically allows a minority to pass significantly greater opportunities on to its children than the majority are able to pass on. No university community, or any other kind, which truly is committed to justice would construct a system of compensation that trickles down so unequally to the children in it. As the children might put it, and they tend to begin to understand these things at an early age, "That's not fair!"[17] Why then, this lofty language about justice in our *Catalog*? Is it simply a guise to attract unwary students, to pry lucre from their parents' pockets?

The answer is "no." Our university *Catalog* is not lying to the world – at least not beyond generating the half-truths that, like all vendors, it publicizes to attract its customers. Americans have worked mightily to explain away the system of social classes that shapes our lives and whose ugly consequences are routinely acknowledged in every other industrial society in the world. The myths of the "melting pot" and the "American Dream" figure prominently in Americans' denial of social class. The first of these suggests that once on U.S. shores, all people meld into a similar kind of being: American! And the second promises that anyone can make it to the top with a little guts and gumption – a notion that contests the very idea that class barriers exist.

Meanwhile, as history has unfolded, the structure of social classes brought here by Europeans has remained more or less intact. The highest social classes remain inhabited mostly by rich white men and their families, who are at the top because they dominate the economic order, and the political order along with it. At the bottom of the social order are disproportionate numbers of women, people of color, and white men who are considered unskilled and uneducated – precisely the people who were there in 1800.

Social Class in More General Terms

The system of social classes is interesting because of its complications, its layerings, and its changes over time. It is also consequential for what happens to any of us, whether we recognize it or not. In the United States, the subject of social class is more compelling yet because the directive to deny its existence gives a hint of the illicit to discussions about it.

The first part of this essay briefly reviews central ideas in the broad literature about social class. In the second part we will discuss the consequences of social classes, particularly the differential effects of social class on the physical and emotional health of people in modern capitalist societies. We will find in this section good evidence that the lower your social class, the more likely you will suffer from serious psychological and physiological disease, and the shorter your life is likely to be. What could be more consequential? In the last part of the essay we look briefly at the issue of "upward mobility" in capitalist societies, and challenge the popular myth that the road upward is available to most, if not all, and always fulfilling to those who make it.

Finally, before we turn to the theorists, we want to emphasize what this essay is *not* about. In isolating social class as a determinant of our behavior, we do not mean to ignore the other factors that mold and make us. We all know that race and sex are two other powerful shaping forces in our lives, and both of these act interdependently with social class. Black people in the United States, for example, make about 60% of the income of whites because ingrained and unrelenting racism has for all our modern history denied most blacks access to the best schools, neighborhoods, and jobs. Further, while the interdependence of race and gender are obvious and powerful determinants of whom we are and what happens to us, they do not stand alone. In this essay, we seek only to bring into a sharper focus one element among a number which shape us into the people we are becoming.[18]

SOCIAL CLASS: THEORIES AND PRINCIPAL CONSEQUENCES

The two predominant ways that people today think about social class come from Karl Marx, writing in the middle of the nineteenth century, and Max Weber, who wrote at the turn of that century. We will introduce their ideas on social class, along with those of Pierre Bourdieu, a recent interpreter of Weber. Our focus on these three writers means, of course, that we are not providing the broad survey that one might find in textbooks on social class. However, we will introduce all the important categories and dimensions of the current scholarly discussion of social class. Along the way, and at the end, we will mention a few other authors our readers might want to look at for greater depth and details.

Marx and Social Class

Marx developed his idea of social class in the midst of growing theorizing on the topic. The use of the word "class" to describe people's roles in a social hierarchy emerged in the early eighteenth century in the work of Daniel Defoe, an English political pamphleteer best known for writing *Robinson Crusoe*. Soon, theories of class found their way into French analyses of society, fueling the French Revolution and the overthrow of the French aristocracy in the late eighteenth century. The most influential writers in the British classical school of economics, Adam Smith and David Ricardo, both recognized that the different streams of income in capitalism—wages, profits, and rents—flowed into the households of separate groups, or classes of people: laborers, capitalists, and landowners. Ricardo was especially important in shaping modern conceptions of social class because he argued that conflict between the social classes was inevitable. His reasons need not deter us, except to note that he saw capitalists and the workers ever engaged in a struggle over the distribution of what was left to them after rents were paid to the landlords.

Marx was aware of these earlier French and English theories of social class and, typical of all his work, he built on such theories to develop his own. At least two things distinguished his ideas about social class from earlier ones.

First, they formed the center of a larger, more complex analysis of capitalism that continues to attract significant attention. And second, Marx and his frequent co-author, Frederick Engels, argued that class conflict would ultimately generate a revolution that would bring an end to capitalism.

In a brief section on social class in our earlier essay on Marx, we quoted economist Teresa Amott's comment that "Marx's original conceptions continue to define and shape the argument" about social class in capitalism. To refresh memories about that essay, in Marx's analysis the capitalist class (or bourgeoisie) rules in capitalism: it owns the firms that dominate the economic order, and this preeminence provides the money and power to rule the political order as well. We also described Marx's argument that the income and wealth of the capitalist class derive from "surplus value," that part of the workers' output that goes to the capitalists in profits rather than to the workers in wages or salaries. These wage workers, by far the majority, comprise the other major class in capitalism, and the continual struggle between capitalists and laborers over their wages and working conditions is the dynamic center of the system.

Marxists say that class position is defined by one's "relationship to the means of production" – the factories, equipment, and other productive assets used to produce goods and services. If you own these, or manage them in the very top positions in corporations, you are in the capitalist class. If you don't, you are in the proletariat. Marx was aware, and those who have extended his work were aware, that his two-part class system was a broad, abstract construct used as a way to see the most essential structural features of capitalism, as well as its likely direction. However, when Marx wrote about events of his own time, he would always introduce a host of highly specialized class groupings, including the dominant capitalists and their allies in struggle against an unruly amalgamation of working-class groups. What has happened to his theory of social class in the hands of later theorists?

Max Weber and Social Status

Max Weber was a German social theorist who lived from 1864 to 1920 and whose writings were central to the development of modern sociology. He constructed a carefully-reasoned and complex theory of social classes, in which he introduced several key terms such as "social class," "status hierarchies," and "lifestyle." Importantly, Weber replaced the idea of two classes endlessly struggling against each other with the image of social "stratification." This metaphor implied that classes are more like layers of rocks at a geologic site than the two warring classes of owners and workers in Marx's model. Weber's social geology is responsible for the current popular image, where the "upper class" rides atop a hierarchy of classes that descends to the "middle classes" and on down to the "underclass." Weber's theorizing about social class is currently more influential among U.S. academics than Marx, in part because radical views of U.S. society, from social scientists or anyone else, and whether they are right or wrong, have been marginalized for most of the past century.

Weber did not abandon Marx's position that employment, one's relationship to the economic order, mattered greatly in determining class position. Weber argued that a person's participation in the economic order, especially whether he or she was a capitalist owner, determined *social class,* and that played the dominant role in determining *life chances.* However, Weber wrote that a person's overall class standing also depended on what he called *social status,* how one's economic position, activities, and possessions are perceived by others in the community.

Dennis Gilbert, an author we have already cited, and will do so often in this chapter, has summarized Weber's ideas about how one's status is interdependent with one's economic class. Gilbert writes that:

> Because of class position, a person earns a certain income. That income permits a certain lifestyle, and people soon make friends with others who live the same way. As they interact with one another, they begin to conceive of themselves as a special type of people. They restrict interaction with outsiders who seem too different (that may be too poor, too uneducated, and too clumsy to live graciously enough for acceptance as worthy companions). Marriage partners are chosen from similar groups because once people follow a certain style of life, they find it difficult to be comfortable with people who live differently. Thus, the status group becomes an ingrown circle. It earns a position in the local community that entitles its members to social honor or prestige from inferiors. ...To preserve their advantages, high status groups attempt to monopolize those goods that symbolize their style of life—they [might] they band together to keep Jews or blacks out of prestigious country clubs or universities. (Gilbert 1998, 9)

As an example of the social exclusion Gilbert describes, the men who run the Masters Tournament at a fancy golf club in Georgia apparently see women as a threat to all that is hallowed at their club, and to this day do not allow them as members. It does not take much analysis to see clearly that the class system is rigidified by the exclusion of blacks, Jews, or women from plush golf courses always dominated by elite men.

We can now see that in the Weberian system, one's economic class is *objectively* determined, meaning that it is what you do in the economy, along with the power and benefits you get from it, rather than how others might value it. On the other hand, social status is *subjectively* determined, meaning that our views about where in the status hierarchy we abide, and the place where others might be, rest on a complex, shifting mosaic of attitudes. Weber knew of the interdependence between economic class and social status, and that the former always shaped the latter. Elite groups, such as the socially prominent families in a city, typically get their income and wealth from an economic and political order they dominate by owning factories, banks, and service companies. They translate this advantage into a lifestyle not affordable for most others, and they consider themselves better than others because the evidence seems so obviously that way to them. Finally, they use schooling and networking to protect their privilege into the future, making sure that their children will be more likely to dominate the economic and political order, and thus the world of status. A critical feature of status groups, Weber argued, is that they bond together to construct boundaries between themselves and others, and the higher the status of a group, the thicker are the walls that separate it from all the others.

Over the years, Weber's followers have gradually replaced his distinction between the economic basis of social class and the lifestyle basis of social status; they widely accept that the term "social class" includes both elements. This means, for example, that you can improve your "social standing" – another phrase for class position – either by getting a more highly paid job, or keeping the same job and moving into a more prestigious neighborhood. In most such cases, of course, higher pay will be the reason for moving to a more prestigious neighborhood. In other words, Weber modified and made more complex Marx's theory of social classes, but he retained the preeminent role that Marx assigned to one's place in the economic order.

Pierre Bourdieu: Class Position and Cultural Capital

In the 1960s, the French sociologist Pierre Bourdieu interviewed 1,200 French men and women about their living and spending habits, and collected the information in his work *Distinction: A Social Critique of the Judgment of Taste.* Bourdieu analyzed this data in terms of ideas about social class derived from those before him, especially Max Weber. However, Bourdieu added an extended discussion of what he called "personal capital," which proved useful in illuminating barriers between social classes. Personal capital can take several forms, including economic capital (income and/or wealth), educational capital (years of education and institutions attended), and social capital (the network of family and associations). All these "capitals" are implicit in the work of Weber and his followers, but Bourdieu enriched the old mix by focusing on what he called *cultural capital*. Douglas Holt, an interpreter of Bourdieu, has described cultural capital as being "fostered in…the social milieu of cultural elites." In simple terms, it is elite cultural know-how acquired by spending time in elite circles. Holt writes cultural capital includes the following crucial elements:

> [U]pbringing in families with well-educated parents whose occupations require cultural skills, interaction with peers from similar families, high levels of formal education at institutions that attract other cultural élites studying areas that emphasize critical abstract thinking and communication over the accumulation of particularized trade skills and knowledges, and refinement and reinforcement in occupations that emphasize symbolic production. (Holt 1999, 3)

Bourdieu focused on styles of consumption as manifestations of cultural capital, arguing that consumption was one way that cultural elites draw distinctions between themselves and others. For instance, in *Distinction,* Bourdieu discussed the different ways that social classes "consume" commercial films (Bourdieu 1984, 27ff). Although we will use a film as our example, it is easy enough to see how the consumption pattern of other cultural items, such as newspapers, literature, food, and clothing can also create distinctions. Even the language used to discuss cultural products purchased by elites can be inaccessible to non-elites, as an example will demonstrate.

Try to imagine yourself the daughter of parents with high school educations, your father a brick layer, your mom a homemaker, and yourself a college freshman. The mother of your assigned roommate is a professor and her father is an ambassador to a foreign country. Now, imagine spending a weekend with your friend at her parents' country home. At dinner, the subject of the film "Titanic" comes up, and someone at the table asks you what you think about it. You say that the film had fantastic special effects and an interesting dose of history that you didn't really know. Then, mom and dad weigh in with a few ideas about films, commenting on the director's choices, the twisted version of history the film portrays, and its odd casting. Finally, dad sighs with a dismissive gesture that the film was "overwhelmed by typical Hollywood sentimentality." A bit peeved by it all, mom dismisses all Hollywood films as being that way, and, additionally, always inferior to French films. Perhaps before dinner, you might have felt out of place because of the differences between your families' house and contents, cars, and lawns. After dinner, you might also realize you're in a world of *ideas* you didn't know existed.

As a guest at this country home, you might also have concluded that your own father possessed more useful knowledge than your friend's father, and that your mother had a much more coherent and comfortable sense of design than your friend's mother. You might well have been right on both counts. However, and this is the point, the people who control the world into which you are moving – the schools and job markets, for example – will likely share the cultural values of your friend's parents. In other words, different forms of cultural capital are neither better nor worse, inherently. They are, however, valued differently by social elites, and therefore they differ crucially in how they aid or retard one's ability to navigate the class system.

We can already guess which of our two first-year women will most likely be a cultural elite in the next generation. Clearly, the daughter of the professor and ambassador has already accumulated enough educational and social capital to have a great advantage over her roommate. By not living in a house with elite consumption items, and not learning the way in which such items are used and talked discussed, our working class student has already fallen far behind in accumulating cultural capital.

It is apparent that all these kinds of capital—economic, educational, social, and cultural—are more readily accessible to the children of the privileged than those of the middle and working classes. The decreasing access to social capital as one descends the class ladder substantially lessens the quantity and quality of choices one has in life. None of this is to say, of course, that we can know which of the two young women in our example will work her way highest up the social ladder and how life will be there. Our privileged student might fall into the grip of a destructive eating disorder while our bright and persevering working class student works her way to the top of a corporate ladder. Our argument is only that the richer your family, the greater your odds to accumulate crucial kinds of personal capital. We shall see some stunning consequences of these odds in a later discussion of social class and health.

Regenerating Social Class Privilege

The Children's Defense Fund (CDF), an advocacy research group, has published data that explain more directly how the children of the privileged acquire more personal capital than other children. In 1998, the CDF published a report entitled *Expenditures on Children by Families* (www.usda.gov/fcscnpp/using2.htm). It included the information summarized in Table 1 on expenditures on children by "husband-wife" families of varying incomes.

Table 1.

Annual Family Income	Average Expenditures on each child to Age 18
Under $34,700	$110,040
$34,700-58,300	$149,820
Over $58,300	$218,400

The numbers in Table 1 mean that parents in the top third of the income distribution spend about twice as much money on each child to age eighteen as parents in the lowest third. Thus, on average, richer kids get more and better food, clothing, health care, schooling, travel, and all the rest. And, directly or indirectly, these material advantages allow them to develop more economic and social capital. Taking the full extent of economic inequality in the U.S. into account, these differences can be staggering. In 1996, there were slightly over 10 million U.S. families whose average incomes were *over $100,000*, and we can only imagine how much more cultural capital is accumulated at that level, where all the food, clothing, and schooling are better yet.

Our argument, we want to emphasize, is that larger family incomes lead to greater accumulation of personal capital, including cultural capital, for children, and thus greater opportunities to become elites as adults. It is *not* that a larger family income necessarily leads to a more productive life or a better sense of well-being. In fact, economist Juliet Schor, in her engaging book *The Overspent American*, reports that 39% of people in U.S. families with incomes between $75,000 and $100,000, and 27% of those with incomes over $100,000, told interviewers they did not have enough money to buy all they needed (Schor 1999). We all know unhappy rich people, and people who gain contentment with modest means. Indeed, aside from extreme wealth compared to extreme deprivation, there is probably no way to know whether more money typically makes for a more satisfying life. Nevertheless, most people in our society would prefer more income than less, and few parents would turn away the opportunity to give their children better health care and education, or more cultural experiences.

Without question, cultural capital is one way—along with the other advantages of being richer—that social classes tend to "reproduce" themselves from one generation to the next. The best way to get into the most prestigious and privileged positions in the economy remains having prestigious and privileged parents.

A Final Advantage of Being Rich

Economic power does not just make the upper classes rich: it gives them unrivalled political power. Because the upper classes dominate the political order, the government shapes its economic policies to help them maintain and increase their social and economic advantage. As a prime example, consider the massive redistribution of income that has occurred in the past two decades. During this period, while the real income of most families in the U.S. has grown only modestly, the richest 5% of the families has increased its share of total income by hundreds of billions of dollars per year. Alice H. Amsden sums up key ways that public policy ensured this result:

> With so much money sloshing around [in the 1990s], contributions by business to politicians increased. With more campaign funding, deregulation resumed where Reagan left off. [The] effective federal tax rate for the top 1% of families fell from 69% in 1970 to about 40% in 1993, with plenty of loopholes remaining. Over the same period, the tax rate for the median family increased from 16% to 25%. Between 1950 and 2000, corporate taxes as a percentage of total tax receipts fell from 27% to 10% while [social security] taxes, mostly paid for by the middle class, jumped from 7% to 31%.... (Amsden 2002)

Amsden goes on to note that the Clinton administration allowed the accounting industry to relax auditing standards, freeing corporations to defraud workers and investors. The Reagan deregulation "revolution," continued by Clinton, unleashed a tidal wave of greed, exemplified by the fact that the ratio of CEO pay to average wages went from less than 100 to 1 to over 500 to 1. As money poured to the rich and the corporations they own, both tightened their grip on government. Marx's comment that capitalism turns the government into the "executive committee of the capitalist class" seems an apt description of the last twenty years of U.S. economic policy.

The Living Consequences of Social Class

Mainstream economists ignore social class principally because its existence conflicts directly with their benign view of capitalism. This basic prejudice leads economists to perceive themselves as "dispassionate experts" with the professional obligation to offer policy solutions for problems that arise in capitalism, rather than to consider the relative merits of the system itself. As a modern "scientific" economist might put it, "Our job is study *what is*, rather than *what ought to be*," without ever considering whether there *ought to be capitalism* as opposed to some other system. In this way of thinking, and especially in the United States, nasty aspects of capitalism—such as its inevitable ruin of the environment, gross inequality, its directive that we be as greedy as we know how to be, and its rigid and damaging hierarchy of classes—are necessarily kept out of sight.

Thus, mainstream economists assiduously avoid of the study of social class, for within that world of analysis are powerful challenges to the notion that capitalism is an essentially benign system that needs to be tinkered with rather than overhauled or replaced. What, then, are these powerful challenges?

Life Itself

Social class is a crucial indicator of whether one will live a long and healthy life. What evidence do we have to make so broad a claim? To begin with, consider the following statement about income and health in a recent The *New York Times* article:

> Scientists have known for decades that poverty translates into higher rates of illness and mortality. But an explosion of research is demonstrating that social class—as measured not just by income but also by education and other markers of relative status—is one of the most powerful predictors of health, more powerful than genetics, exposure to carcinogens, even smoking. What matters is not simply whether a person is rich or poor, college educated or not. Rather, risk for a wide variety of illnesses, including cardiovascular disease, diabetes, arthritis, infant mortality, many infectious diseases, and some types of cancer varies with relative wealth or poverty: the higher the rung on the socioeconomic ladder, the lower the risk. And this relationship holds even at the upper reaches of society, where it might seem that an abundance of resources would even things out. (Goode 1999)

This is the conclusion of an article that refers to 193 recent papers about socioeconomic status and health in scientific journals. A principal cause of this burst of interest among medical professionals was a study begun in the 1960s of 18,000 male civil servants in Britain. The researchers, who described themselves as "astonished," found that:

> Mortality rates varied continuously and precisely with the men's civil service grade: the higher the classification, the lower the rates of death, regardless of cause...A 25-year follow up of the subjects [in 1996]...found that the social class gradient persisted well past retirement, even among men into their late 80s. (Goode 1999)

Intrigued by these findings, the British researchers began a second study in 1985, in which they included both men and women from whom they collected more details, including information about the "amount of control people had" on the job. The researchers found that:

> Job control...varied inversely with employment grade: the higher the grade, the more control. And, the less control employees had, as defined either by their own or managers' ratings, the higher the employees' risk of developing coronary disease. Job control, in fact, accounted for about half the gradient in deaths from pay grade to pay grade. (Goode 1999)

This article also reported that, while blacks in the United States have lower life expectancies (for instance a 45-year-old black man can expect to live five years less than his white 45-year-old counterpart), studies accounting for social class difference showed that black and white men had about the same life expectancies. Some of these studies used such evidence as the fact that the richer your neighborhood the more likely "you can trust your neighbors" and the less likely you believe they are trying "to take advantage of you." These aspects of neighborhood life are analogous to loss of control on the job, in that people who cannot trust the safety of their own neighborhood have a good deal less control over their ability to protect themselves and their loved ones.

These findings are in some ways quite surprising, especially that even very small differences in job grade produced consistent and measurable differences in mortality. Yet their overall message about health and social class in capitalism has long been noted. As early as the mid-nineteenth century, Marx, Engels, and novelists such as Charles Dickens wrote extensively about the awful circumstances that limited the lives of the working classes. In *Capital*, Marx presented considerable data from British Parliamentary studies showing that the health and the life span of British workers depended importantly on what they did for a living and where they did it. In the United States, many scholars have studied this connection between social class and health and life, among them Vincente Navarro at Johns Hopkins.[19] In 1991, Professor Navarro explained why U.S. health researchers were just then discovering a relationship between health and social class that should have been apparent all along:

> The way in which the U.S. government collects health and vital statistics reflects [the fact that class is rarely discussed in the scientific and mainstream media]. The government collects statistics about mortality rates and causes of death by race, gender, and region, but not by class. The overwhelming majority of other developed capitalist countries do collect mortality statistics by class. (Navarro 1991)

As an example of Navarro's point, for some time it has been widely known that in the U.S. black men, on average, live shorter lives than do white men. This result, as is also widely known, can be traced to a mixture of socioeconomic class background and racism. However, if we control for income, we find that the longevity of black men is about the same as that of white men. However, as Navarro points out, because the U.S. government doesn't look at these matters in terms of social class, those who use government statistics must explain them all in terms of race.

Navarro describes a 1986 report on the relationship between social class and health care as "one of the few occasions" that the U.S. government reported on this relationship. The report broke people down into several categories, and listed their mortality rates for heart disease, per 10,000, as shown in Table 2.

Table 2.

Heart Disease Mortality Rates
per 10,000

Management/Professional	37
White Collar Workers	43
Service Workers	59
Craft Workers	69
Blue Collar Workers	86

As we travel down the hierarchy in Table 2, we descend into a world in which people have less and less control over their work. While it is difficult to precisely rank the amount of control held by what the government calls service, craft, and blue collar workers – and in many cases, these categories seem to overlap – the much higher rates of heart disease among these workers tells a chilling story.

Personal Capital and Access to Health Care

One explanation for this data on health and social class can be explained in terms of Pierre Bourdieu's idea of personal capital. Having more educational and cultural capital makes it easier to negotiate for one's self in public life. Knowing how to get health care when you need it is importantly a matter of reading skills, access to information and understanding what to do with it, and regular contact with others who have the same skills and have sought the same health care you seek. Then, of course, having more economic capital allows you more readily to pay for the care. Added to these limitations for wage earners relative to professionals is the fact that their work schedules are typically less flexible. It is easier for lawyers and dentists to arrange their schedules to include health care visits than for wage earners who work from nine to five, or worse in this regard, the swing shift in many modern work places. Further, most professionals have health insurance, while more and more wage earners don't; professionals typically have longer vacations; and professionals seek health care from other professionals, thus people like themselves who have the same linguistic habits and may be on the same wave length in other respects. Finally, because they have more education, income, and access, professionals are much more likely to participate in stress-reducing leisure activities at sports clubs, golf courses, and similar places where one can simultaneously work off the fat and have fun.

Social Class and Emotional Health

The evidence gathered by scholars over many years concerning mental health and social class is quite persuasive. Before we present the evidence, however, we want to make certain readers do not confuse our point. All of us know people from different social classes, and we can all cite instances where someone from the working class seems more satisfied with his or her life, and more emotionally sound, than someone who is rich and privileged. Here, our argument is comprised of generalizations with no power of prediction whatsoever about a single individual, or even a small group of individuals. We will be discussing qualitative aspects of the behavior of large groups of people, and these are always relatively imprecise and given to many conflicting interpretations. Nevertheless, we believe the data at this general level comprise a persuasive and powerful argument.

Scholars John Mirowski and Catherine Ross have produced an especially important study of the relationship between social class and mental health in their analysis of a broad survey done in Illinois in 1985 (Mirowski and Ross 1989). In the Illinois study, 809 people were interviewed in depth about their lives, their feelings, and the extent to which these could be identified as symptoms of depression. Mirowski and Ross broke down the data down into "deciles," ascending from the bottom 10% to the top 10%, where those in the bottom 10% had the least income and the least education, respectively. Their conclusion in this regard is straightforward enough: the less income you have, the more likely you are to be depressed; and the less education you have, the more likely you are to be depressed.

On the matter of "severe psychological distress," Mirowski and Ross wrote the following:

> Social factors account for a great deal of distress, but do they account for severe psychological distress? To address this second question, we defined extreme distress as a level of symptoms greater than that evidenced by 95% of the population. Approximately 61% of these people would qualify for a psychiatric diagnosis. If we split society into two halves, socioeconomically, better and worse, the worse half of society has 83.2% of all the severe distress. The advantaged half has only 16.2%. Stated another way, the odds of being severely distressed are 5.9 times greater in the worse half than in the better half. (Mirowski and Ross 1989, 17)

Mirowski and Ross give as major reasons for these outcomes the fact that rich people are more likely to detect mental illness in its earlier stages, more likely to know how to seek treatment, and better able to afford better treatment than their less advantaged counterparts in the class system. All these factors would produce statistical evidence that mental illness is less a burden for the rich than for all others, particularly the poor.

In this kind of research, we must be wary of the enormous practical difficulties that exist, such as defining mental illness, the limitations of interview data, and imperfect record keeping by hospitals and mental health workers. Nevertheless, we have reported the data from Mirowski and Ross because it is consistent with other studies in its general conclusion that the best way to avoid mental illness is to be born into the upper classes. We say "born into" because getting there by upward mobility can itself create mental distress, as we shall see.

The Central Role of "Control" in Health and Longevity

There are a number of factors other than one's social class that determine how healthy you are and how long you live. Diet, habits, and genetic makeup all have a great deal to do with well-being and longevity. And, within particular social groups, researchers have found that it matters greatly whether your family and community is nurturing when you are young, understanding and tolerant when you're older. It also matters whether you have stable and loving intimate relationships. Yet, when we take all these factors into account, statistically, they do not explain all the outcomes we can observe. Certain other aspects of our lives remain central determinants of how well we fare.[20] We are going to focus on one of these, the amount of control over one's work, because it is closely related to all definitions of social class, and because there have been quite a few recent studies about it. The issue of job control gathers attention in our society because the workplaces in the United States have been designed such that in most of them (as Marx once put it), "the hand is separated from the brain." In other words, managers design and control the work, while workers actually perform it.

This separation is importantly a consequence of the work of Frederick J. Taylor, the father of "scientific management" in the early part of the twentieth century. He convinced the owners of many of the largest firms to use techniques like time and motion studies to divide production processes into their simplest components. The goal was to establish workplaces where jobs were simple, mindless, and repetitive, and where workers were told what to do, when to do it, and how to do it. Thus, increasingly U.S. firms developed ways to produce goods and services where specific tasks were imagined and designed by a relatively small number of professionals, such as engineers and management specialists, and overseen by top officers, including financial specialists. The work of producing the goods or services, though, was mostly done by wage earners whose jobs were "deskilled" by the process. This production process gradually spread its way through the economy. Indeed, it became known as the "American Way" of production, or what we now call a "bottom line mentality."

What are the consequences of this lack of control over work, which is the basic fact of life for most employed adults in our society? Consider first this very general statement from Mirowski and Ross about control and well being:

> Of all the things that might explain the social patterns of distress, one stands as central: the sense of control over one's own life. Many studies in many sciences find the sense of control associated with lower distress. This sense reflects the reality of the individual's experiences, opportunities, and resources. It implies an attentive, active, and proactive approach to problems. ...[For] the large majority.... a greater sense of control would be psychologically beneficial. (Mirowski and Ross 1989, 167.)

It is certainly not hard to translate this assessment of control and well being into a system of social classes. For instance, Robert Karasek, an engineer at University of Southern California, and Tores Theorell, a physician and professor at Sweden's National Institute for Psychosocial Factors and Health, produced a study worth attention, *Healthy Work: Stress, Productivity, and the Reconstruction of Working Life*. Karasek and Theorell pay particular attention to what they call "decision latitude," a measure of the degree to which workers control their work. This concept implies that it is not the demands of your job that make it stressful, but the extent to which you determine what good or service you make, how you make it, and at what pace. Concerning, for example, the effect of control at the job site on blood pressure, Karasek and Theorell wrote:

> If an employer increases the demands on employees while concomitantly decreasing their decision latitude, the employees will experience rising blood pressures levels. Only some of them will react, and they will probably be the best workers – highly motivated and cooperative. Certainly the toll of badly designed jobs is high: our evidence builds a strong case that the work environment can become a biological prison that the average human being cannot endure without adverse physiological effects in the long run. (Karasek and Theorell 1990, 157)

Karasek and Theorell divided jobs on a grid in terms of two dimensions, "low/high psychological demand" and "low/high decision control." They found the breakdown summarized in Tables 3 and 4 consistent with their data on heart disease.

Table 3.

**Examples of jobs under the most stress
(high psychological demand/low control):**

---

sales clerk (female)	freight handler
waiter and waitress	garment stitcher
firefighter	mall worker
telephone operator	cashier
cook	

Table 4.

**Examples of jobs under the least stress
(low psychological demand/high control):**

---

sales clerk (male)	peddler
architect	auto repair worker
natural scientist	forester
dentist	skilled machinist

These findings are open to question – for instance, they present the surprising idea that male sales clerks have low-stress jobs while female sales clerks have high-stress ones. Yet as far as they go, these findings do not bode well for the health of workers in the next century, since the federal government predicts that some of the fastest growing job sectors in the U.S. economy into the next century will be cashiers, sales clerks, waitresses and waiters, and mall workers. Karasek and Theorell argued in their book that the United States was woefully behind other countries in studying the relationship between stress on the job and health. More recently, Professor Karasek, just back from a year advising the government of Norway on the issue, told a *Boston Globe* writer, Delores Kong, "The government used to fund large-scale occupational health studies but stopped about 20 years ago" (Kong 1999). Can our readers guess why this happened about 20 years ago?

A recent study done by Dr. Peter Schall, director of the Center of Social Epidemiology at the University of California at Irvine, confirms the data from Karasek and Theorell on job strain and hypertension (high blood pressure). According to Delores Kong:

[Dr. Schall] cites an automobile plant in California, where the assembly line is sped up so much that employees were timed spending 58 seconds out of every

60 seconds working. "Every second of every minute of every working hour is accounted for in plants like this," Schall said. ...[Schall and his colleagues] monitored the blood pressure of nearly 200 men for 24-hour periods. Those who had the highest job strain had on average a systolic blood pressure (the upper number) nearly 12 points higher and diastolic blood pressure nearly 10 points higher than those with the least strain.... Dr. Schall said, after looking at all possible causes of high blood pressure, job strain was found to be more important than smoking or salt in the diet. (Kong 1999)

This kind of data, like that on relative degrees of mental health, is qualitative, tentative, and subject to differing conclusions depending on the nature of the studies made, basic definitions, and research methodologies, to name the most obvious limitations. However, the experts increasingly agree that people who work at jobs over which they have little control, and at which they can use few of their skills, are affected in the same way as by a lack of control over their personal lives. Such work can depress them, make them sick, and take years off their lives.

These findings are particularly important in focusing on one's economic position in the world, one's "relationship to the means of production," as Marx put it, as crucial to one's well-being. The findings also support Marx's broad two-class structure, in that we have two such classes: the minority that controls work and the majority that labors at the beck and call of their bosses.

Precisely because the jobs at the top always pay much better and are the healthiest places to be, most everyone in the lower classes tries to get there. When those from the bottom half get to the upper half, it is considered an example of significant "upward mobility," and this event in someone's life is often known as realizing "The American Dream." This dream, which depends on the idea that anyone can pull himself or herself up "by the bootstraps," is presented as a powerful antidote to the damages wrought by the class system. If anyone can "make it" by trying hard enough, no matter how deprived life had been down below, the awful effects of work in the different social classes are presented as, somehow, justified. We need to look at this claim carefully.

SOCIAL CLASS AND THE AMERICAN DREAM

The claim that upward mobility allays the damages of the class system is actually composed of two related arguments. The first of these is that anyone can make it to the top with enough effort; and the second is that those who do make it are, in fact, delivered into the Promised Land. We will look at these separately.

How Much Mobility is There?

Though data on this important question is surprisingly sparse, Dennis Gilbert, in *The American Class Structure*, has produced what we consider the most comprehensive look at the trends between 1962 and 1990.[21] But, before we get to Gilbert's data, we need to discuss the limitations of all the figures on mobility. Two limitations have to do with gender and race. As Gilbert points out, almost all U.S. studies on mobility have focused on men. He shows that available data on women, as a group, demonstrate a similar mobility pattern to that of men, but its sparseness leaves the mobility of women a subject badly in need of study. The picture is also more complicated when it includes blacks. As we might expect, blacks have greater numbers in the lower class categories and less upward mobility than whites, but the rate of their upward mobility has steadily increased since 1960.

A third limitation of social mobility data is more fundamental. Some writers believe that factors other than social class are so influential as to outweigh it; most notably, they point to the influence of the media and of U.S. subcultures, arguing that these determine behavior and social position at least as much as social class does. For instance, recently some writers have pointed to the rapidly changing way by which status symbols emerge, confer their magic on this or that group of people, then are lost from sight. Because an all-encompassing media is the principal agent by which status is hyped and publicized, these writers see a weakening in the lasting power of status symbols and thus, to some degree, less rigidity in the class system. On the other hand, other scholars see our society as having genuine class boundaries. When we began our own research on these matters two decades ago we concluded that *significant* (which we define more precisely below) upward social mobility occurred for no more than 10% of the working population, a figure that, among studies on social mobility, is quite low.[22] Many readers of this early research, including some scholars and journalists, criticized how low our figure was; others, however, saw it is as quite reasonable.

In other words, scholarly studies on the ratio of upward mobility produce figures that range all over the place.[23] The researcher can literally select whatever ratio fits his or her agenda. Given this situation, we have chosen to use the work of Dennis Gilbert because, in our view, he gives the widest and the fairest reading of the literature on social mobility. He is aware of the limitations of these data and would be the first to advise accepting his own conclusions as tentative.

In his survey, Gilbert compared data from several studies over the years, and their different classifications made it necessary for him to compress them all into one set of categories. After doing that, he ended up with the following five-class system:[24]

- *Upper white collar* (professionals, managers, officials, non-retail sales)
- *Lower white collar* (proprietors, clerical workers, retail sales workers)
- *Upper manual* (craftsmen and foreman)
- *Lower manual* (unskilled, service workers, operatives, non-farm laborers)
- *Farm* (farm workers and farmers)

The figures below are about males only, and they indicate the percentage of all U.S. workers that ended up either above, the same or below the economic position held by their fathers. (This data relates to the period between 1982-1990, and the percentages are roughly similar to those in other studies done since the 1960s.)

Up:	44%
Stable:	36%
Down:	20%

As simple figures, these confirm the idea that there is a great deal of mobility in the U.S. economy, with almost half of the sons achieving a higher standing in the economy than their fathers. Most of this mobility, however, was the movement across one class barrier, such as the movement from lower to higher manual labor, or lower to higher white collar labor. Crossing a single class boundary is hardly the stuff of the American Dream, which promises a transformation from "rags to riches." Such success stories imply movement across several class barriers. What can we say about these bigger leaps?

We will define *significant upward mobility* as moving from the bottom of Gilbert's classification to the top, or the sons of lower manual laborers who ended up in upper white-collar work. An example would be the son of an unskilled laborer who became a doctor, or the son of a cashier who becomes a corporate executive. The following numbers express in percentage terms what kind of jobs were attained by the sons of men who were lower manual workers:

Upper white collar: 27%
Lower white collar: 11%
Upper manual: 25%
Lower manual: 37%

We can see that 27% actually made it to "the top," ending up with jobs as professionals, managers, officials, or non-retail sales workers. However, within these numbers, as Gilbert understands, there is a misleading simplification. Note that the data don't show us how many of these sons became, say, high status doctors and how many became lower status managers in small firms. This is one of those gaps in social mobility data that attest to our resistance to the idea of social classes: if we don't believe in them, why would have wanted to try to measure them? In any case, this gap means we can only guess at the real proportion who made the truly "big leap" upward, and in using Gilbert's ratio we are clearly inflating the figures for significant upward mobility.

More to the point, we can also see from this data, even as it inflates measures of mobility, that 62% of the lower manual workers *remained* manual workers. This means that, along with the mobility, there is for the sons of most manual labors a consignment to wage-earning, manual labor. It is also true, according to Gilbert, that about 60% of all those who are in upper white-collar jobs had fathers who were there.[25] It is hard to conclude from these data, however limited, anything other than this: *real structural barriers to upward mobility exist in the U.S., and the best pathway to success is not merit or hard work but being born to parents with socioeconomic privilege.*

Nevertheless, if we grant Gilbert his conclusion that about one quarter of U.S. workers experience significant upward social mobility, one might reasonably decide that, comparable to most societies over time, our system is remarkably "open." Before we draw that conclusion, however, we must ask ourselves this question: once they get to the top, what actually happens to the sons and daughters of factory operatives and service workers who became doctors, lawyers, and bosses?

Strangers in this Fine Place So Far From Home

What does happen, say, to a person from a working-class family who ends up at an elite university, then accumulates enough educational capital to land a job with a Wall Street firm dominated by fancy Ivy League types? That's an important question for two principal reasons. The first of these is that upward social mobility actually lessens the genuinely unfair constraints of social classes. Since the distribution of opportunities closely mirrors the distribution of income, and is thus greatly unequal, mobility allows at least some people to make their up way out of lower class standing. Second, upward mobility allows for more political stability than would be possible without it: if everyone in the bottom half was consigned there for life, particularly in a society claiming itself as free, rebellions would always be just beneath the surface of social life. Much depends, then, on whether upward mobility "works" as it is supposed to for those who achieve it.

It is a complicated question whether, in their own terms, upward mobility is mostly successful for the people who try achieve it, and the results of studies trying to answer it are mixed. However, there are some important conclusions that scholars have reached who have done the most influential studies. Consider, as a general statement, a dramatic claim from one of the most influential books written in the field, *Social Class and Mental Illness*: A *Community Study* by August Hollingshead and Fredrick Redlich. They conclude this about "social climbers," those upwardly mobile people who appear to have made their move "successfully":

> The climber may impress an observer as pleasant, successful, and very able if he is successful and appears well integrated. Only on longer acquaintance and after a deeper search does one become aware of the climber's conflicts and defenses. His deeper anxieties become manifested when his mobility drive becomes blocked; then his defenses do not function properly...When these social climbers were rejected by those who "are there" socially, their reactions were characterized by severe anxiety, depression, sometimes by antisocial acting out, and in ...extreme cases by suicidal attempts.... (Hollingshead and Redlich 1957, 368)

The tone and the overall conclusion of this quote are more important to us than its specific claims, because they signal that the literature on upward mobility is always in part about the stressfulness, called "status dissonance," that comes with it for so many who make the trip. One body of research that encompasses all the relevant issues about upward mobility focuses on essays by college professors who have working class backgrounds. By going from the lower or upper manual classes to becoming a college professor, such people have clearly made a substantial upward movement from their family backgrounds. In the books from which we will draw examples, there are dozens of different voices, and they all tell different stories. Some of these professors, for instance, expressed relief at having been lifted up from the drudgery of the wage work; others found pleasure at having a foot in two worlds; while still others found having their feet in two worlds wrenching and painful. Four studies that make up part of this research, each with a different focus from the others, are: Ryan and Sackrey 1984, 1996; Tokarczyk and Fay 1993; and Dews and Law 1995.

While all these voices were unique, there were unmistakable dominant themes, of which one can find examples in virtually all the essays. One theme was a genuine feeling of alienation from professional (often in these essays called "middle-class") life. The first voice here expresses this alienation as anger about colleagues, most of whom came from middle or upper class backgrounds:

> My friends have been a handful of fellow outsiders who share my contempt for the rest of "them." I feel quite unapologetic about these prejudices. I feel "they" are all deeply worthy of contempt. They parade a sense of inflated self-importance; take pleasure in feeling smarter than students; pretend they contribute meaningfully to GNP; dance for favors; create parochial empires; cower before symbols of authority; wallow in bogus professionalism; and submerge themselves in their narrow expertise, which, for many, is their ticket to a legitimate place in the academy. The tone and the anger in what I've written above give some indication of the depth of my alienation. (Ryan and Sackrey 1996, 261-2)

Another voice from these collections carried a second theme, mixing recognition of the durability of one's class origin with hopefulness that the conflicts that come from class mobility can be mitigated:

> How can working-class academics begin to integrate the divided or split sense of self that arises from belonging (yet in some fundamental ways, not belonging) to two distinct class cultures? As members of a transition class, it is likely that working-class academics will always feel marginal to some degree. However, if this outsider status is to become a source of empowerment rather than a source of internal conflict, it is imperative that such faculty begin to validate the working—and middle—class parts of themselves. To do so requires that they recognize and confront the ways in which they have internalized the classism of the larger society and, thus, their own oppression. This process is essential if working-class academics are to reclaim their power and develop an authentic or integrated sense of self. (Tokarczyk and Fay 1993, 54)

Another of these professors sounded a third theme that resonated in all the essays, about how long the path from home had become. She reflects on these matters by recalling the time when her parents were about to drive her back to her studies at Dartmouth, but her father was called back to duty at a paper mill.

> My father left [for the mill] a bit earlier…and as my mother began the drive out of town with me in the passenger seat, I remember being struck with the feeling that my father was out there somewhere, driving too, but on a very different road. With the greatest clarity I have ever experienced about the question of mobility, I saw myself on the road to my life of bright and interesting friends, a glut of culture and ideas, comfort and privilege. My father was on the road he took every day to the paper mill. Huge and noisy and noxious, the mill was where my father spent lonely, dirty days among men who shared none of his interest in reading about ideas. (Dews and Law 1995, 157-58)

Alienation, anger, the unending reminder that your parents went down a different road, the unmistakable power of social class to stick with you all the way down your own path, mixed in with hopefulness and willingness to struggle for legitimacy—these are the themes common to the literature on upward mobility. You might get to another place, but once there, you need to figure out how to deal with the fact that, unlike most people, you have a dual-class experience. Therefore, whatever else might happen, whether you are happy for most of your days or miserably angry at the pretensions of life at the "higher reaches," you must construct a way to negotiate a new terrain. Going from the working classes to the more prestigious professions is literally to move from one neighborhood to another one. At first, people in that new world might not even notice you; or, worse, they might despise you and all your trappings. Upward mobility puts you in a world in which those already there have likely accumulated more of Bourdieu's personal capital than you have. They will have a greater ease with the neighborhood, and a built-in savvy about how to negotiate the terrain.

The upward traveler must, therefore, develop a strategy to survive. The literature on upward mobility is in agreement on this point, without exception. These strategies range from assimilation (trying to be like them), to separation (trying to keep your job while staying to the side), to war (fighting them tooth and nail until they fire you). The absolute necessity of such strategies makes our essential point that social class is, however ambiguous and hard to tie down, a powerful shaping mechanism in our lives. Social classes exist because of real differences in our work, income, education, habits, and all the rest. To cross class barriers, one must learn to navigate in enemy territory and, perhaps as a precaution, wear a helmet.[26]

The alleged "freedom" of U.S. capitalism presumes some semblance of equality of opportunity: every Jack and Jill must have an equal chance to hit the big time. However, that kind of equality can only exist in a society in which *most* people have the opportunity to move upward significantly, and in which *most* of those who do find the trip worth the effort. Neither of these two conditions seems to exist in the U.S. Most people stay where they started, bossed around by the same kind of people who bossed around their parents. And, if they do move up, they go to a new neighborhood in which they are at the bottom, often despised, isolated, or misunderstood. The fact of social classes makes the American Dream a particularly deceitful myth.

CONCLUSION

We hope that readers will come away from this chapter considering the likelihood that social classes exist and play a crucial role in determining who we are; that most people inherit the class position of their parents and stay there; and that numerical representations of social class, such as by income levels, badly understate the overall effects of the class system. On this last point, if we say, for instance, that the top 10% of the income classes has about four to five times as much income as the bottom 10%, the numbers understate our point. Access to four or five times as much income as the next person gives you multiple advantages beyond the income, including especially the kinds of personal capital we have described. Being at the top of the income system means more of life itself: healthier lungs, a stronger heart, straighter and whiter teeth, and more things about which to smile.

Given that critical dimensions of social class cannot be measured precisely, if at all, it is no surprise that mainstream economists simply ignore it, leaving the subject for sociologists or other "soft" scientists to study. Yet in the work of political economists such as Marx and Veblen, and in less radical social policies aimed at "civilizing" capitalism, such as those developed in Sweden, the idea of social class is central. We agree that the issue belongs at the forefront of any discussion of capitalism.

Suggestions for Further Reading

Bourdieu, Pierre. *Distinction: A Social Critique of the Judgment of Taste.* Cambridge, Mass.: Harvard University Press, 1984.

Dahrendorf, Ralf. *Life Chances.* Chicago: University of Chicago Press, 1979.

Domhoff, William. *Who Rules America?* 4th Edition. New York: McGraw-Hill, 2002.

Fussell, Paul. *Class.* New York: Ballantine, 1983.

Gerth, H. H., and C. Wright Mills, eds. *From Max Weber: Essays in Sociology.* New York: Oxford University, 1946.

Gilbert, Dennis. *The American Class Structure in an Age of Growing Inequality.* 5th Edition. Belmont, Calif.: Wadsworth, 1998.

Kadi, Joanna. *Thinking Class: Sketches from a Cultural Worker.* Boston: South End Press, 1996.

Karasek, Robert, and Tores Theorell. *Healthy Work: Stress, Productivity, and the Reconstitution of Working Life.* New York: Basic Books, 1990.

Vanneman, Reeve, and Lynn Weber Cannon. *The American Perception of Class.* Philadelphia: Temple University Press, 1983.

Zaeig, Michael. *The Working Class Majority: America's Best Kept Secret.* Ithaca, N.Y.: ILR Press, 2000.

6
John Kenneth Galbraith and the Theory
of Social Balance

The ideas of John Kenneth Galbraith, so well known around the world from his many books and articles, and his more than half-century in U.S. public life, are surprisingly little known inside the mainstream of economics. Economist Ron Stanfield has called Galbraith "the most famous economist of the last half-century." Nonetheless, Stanfield notes, "he also represents a very obscure American institutionalist tradition. This paradox I cannot resolve for the reader... The Galbraithian Paradox puzzles me" (Stanfield 1996).[27]

Neither will we try explaining the marginal effect Galbraith has had on his own discipline, despite his wide renown. Instead, we will shift that question to our readers. After you read this essay, and perhaps more of Galbraith's work, ask yourself why you are unlikely to hear his ideas in a mainstream economics course. But, for now, who is this economist whose influence in the world is so oddly distributed?

THE MYRIAD WORLDS OF JOHN KENNETH GALBRAITH

Galbraith has said that Keynes, Marx and Veblen were the economists who most influenced his own thinking. We shall see that, like Marx and Veblen, Galbraith worked mostly outside the confines of mainstream economics. Now in his early nineties and still writing and giving interviews, Galbraith has been a prominent social critic or public servant for an astonishing *six* decades. He taught economics for forty years, mostly at Harvard University, starting in the 1930s. During the first two years of the Second World War, Galbraith led the federal Office of Price Administration, a position that gave him the immense power to determine which U.S. companies could raise which prices. He was an ambassador to India during the John F. Kennedy administration in the early 1960s. He wrote speeches for, and advised, prominent Democrats including Adlai Stevenson, the party's presidential candidate in 1952 and 1956, Presidents Kennedy and Lyndon Johnson, and Eugene McCarthy, a U.S. Senator who challenged Johnson for the Democratic presidential nomination in 1968.

Mostly, however, Galbraith is known for books and writings covering an immensely broad range of genres and issues. He has written terse theoretical works, articles about economics for *Fortune Magazine* (between 1942 and 1947), twenty highly readable books analyzing the economics and politics of modern capitalist societies, three memoirs, and two novels. He co-authored a book on Indian painting, wrote and narrated a thirteen-part PBS series on the history of economic ideas, and produced countless shorter pieces for academic journals and the press. All his analytical books have typically focused attention on three matters: (1) the operations and effects on economic and political life of the giant corporations that dominate the world economy; (2) the failure of mainstream economics to incorporate adequately the effects of these large firms into its analyses of capitalism; and (3) the issue of whether the central value in mainstream economics – that "more is better than less" – is a reasonable guide to social policy.

An especially prominent feature of Galbraith's writing and political activities is that he puts them forward as an unapologetic liberal, always arguing from the perspective that public policy needs to countervail the immense powers of huge corporations and, more generally, that an unregulated capitalist economy is chaos in-the-making. This open advocacy for a broad-reaching government sector separates him from mainstream economics, whose practitioners put forward the pretense of being "scientific," despite their typical belief that capitalist economies work best with minimal "government intervention," and that more is better than less. We will say more on this contradiction shortly.

In the first two decades of Galbraith's prominence as a writer, until about the late 1970s, mainstream economists frequently responded in print, or at conferences, to his critique of their own explanations of the economic order. However, since then, as most of them have retreated into a much narrower theoretical world than the one that engages Galbraith, they have increasingly ignored him. Thus, the irony that Galbraith's ideas are known and respected worldwide but largely ignored by most of the members of his own profession. Yet political economists, and many others outside the academic world, continue to find much of his work – above all his theory of social balance – relevant and important. To that interesting set of ideas, we now turn.

THE THEORY OF SOCIAL BALANCE DESCRIBED

In his 1958 book *The Affluent Society*, Galbraith argued that the slavish commitment of people in advanced capitalist societies to private goods at the expense of public services – such as schools, roads, efficient government, clean air and water, beautiful cities – could bring them to ruin. He called this analysis of private and public spending the "theory of social balance," and he stated its essential meaning in a well-known passage, as follows:

> The family which takes its mauve and cerise, air-conditioned, power-steered, and power-braked automobile out for a tour passes through cities that are badly paved, made hideous by litter, blighted buildings, billboards and posts for wires that should long since have been put underground. They pass on into a countryside that has been rendered largely invisible by commercial art. . . . They picnic on exquisitely packaged food from a portable icebox by a polluted stream and go on to spend the night at a park which is a menace to public health and morals. Just before dozing off on an air mattress, beneath a nylon tent, amid the stench of decaying refuse, they may reflect vaguely on the curious unevenness of their blessings. Is this, indeed, the American genius? (Galbraith 1958, 253)

What is the larger, structural, context of this florid, in some ways angry and frustrated, statement? Here is how Galbraith describes that larger structure:

> [The] disparity between our flow of private and public goods and services is no matter of subjective judgment. On the contrary, it is the source of the most extensive comment, which only stops short of the direct contrast being made here. In the years following World War II, the papers of any major city – those of New York were an excellent example – told daily of the shortages and shortcomings in the elementary municipal and metropolitan services. The schools were old and overcrowded. The police force was under strength and underpaid. The parks and playgrounds were insufficient. Streets and empty lots were filthy, and the sanitation staff was under-equipped and in need of men. Access to the city by those who work there was uncertain and painful and becoming

more so. Internal transportation was overcrowded, unhealthful, and dirty. So was the air. Parking on the streets had to be prohibited, and there was no space elsewhere. (Galbraith 1958, 252)

And, a bit later in his text, Galbraith argues that:

.... Every increase in the consumption of private goods will normally mean some facilitation or protective step by the [public sector]. [If] these [public] services are not forthcoming, the consequences will be in some degree ill. It will be convenient to have a term which suggests a satisfactory relationship between the supply of privately produced goods and services and those of the state, and we may call it *social balance*.

The problem of social balance is ubiquitous, and frequently it is obtrusive.... An increase in the consumption of automobiles requires a facilitating supply of streets, highways, traffic control, and parking space. The protective services of the police and the highway patrols must also be available, as must those of the hospitals. Although the need for balance here is extraordinarily clear, our use of privately produced vehicles has, on occasion, gone far out of line with the supply of the related public services. The result has been hideous road congestion, an annual massacre of impressive proportions, and chronic colitis in the cities. (Galbraith 1958, 255, emphasis added)

Galbraith went on to cite other examples, the particularly prophetic one that there was delinquency everywhere because the growing absence of parents – more of them working to feed their consumption habits – meant that children, "in effect, become the charge of the community for an appreciable part of the time. [And] if the services of the community do not keep pace, this will be another source of disorder." These and other examples together embodied the theory that consumer oriented societies will inevitably produce "private opulence and public squalor," as Galbraith put in one of his more memorable phrases. Why does this happen?

THE DEPENDENCE EFFECT

We begin with the "private opulence," whereby individuals shower themselves with more goods than are good for them and for society. How does this come about? Galbraith's answer focuses importantly on what he called the "Dependence Effect," explained as follows:

> As a society becomes increasingly affluent, wants are increasingly created by the process by which they are satisfied. This may operate passively. Increases in consumption, the counterpart of increases in production, act by suggestion or emulation to create wants. Or producers may proceed actively to create wants through advertising and salesmanship. *Wants thus come to depend on output. In technical terms it can no longer be assumed that welfare is greater at an all-around higher level of production than at a lower one. It may be the same.* The higher level of production has, merely, a higher level of want creation necessitating a higher level of want satisfaction. There will be frequent occasion to refer to the way wants depend on the process by which they are satisfied. It will be convenient to call it the *Dependence Effect*. (Galbraith 1958, 158, emphasis added)

The point here is that in high consumption societies, wants come to depend on output, and for two major reasons that we now turn to.

Veblen's Pecuniary Emulation, Revisited

The first reason wants come "to depend on output" is that increases in output will generate spreading consumer envy wherever new products, or multiple units of other products, come to rest in a private household or driveway, become the latest fashion styles, or otherwise gain the attention of consumers. As we discussed in another essay in this volume, social critic Thorstein Veblen called this process "pecuniary emulation" and considered it a consequence of our desire to mimic the habits of those with a higher social ranking. This is an easy idea to remember because now everyone calls it "keeping up with the Joneses," and of course because we all do it. For instance, ten years ago university students would not be bothered by lack of access to "Power Point," or to a CD player, both now regarded by a growing number as utterly essential. Similarly, most U.S. households now view air-conditioning and dishwashers, once "luxuries," as necessities.

The Dependence Effect and the Advertising Blitz

The second cause of the Dependence Effect is the enormous and corrosive influence of advertising, or, as Galbraith puts it more gently, "...producers may proceed actively to create wants through advertising and salesmanship." Modern U.S. society is abuzz, ever more loudly, with the noise of advertising. Indeed, as we point out in our chapter on economic methodology, one estimate is that adults in our society are bombarded with over 3,000 ads per day.[28] For an idea of the level of this intensity, consider a few quotes from an article that appeared last year in the *Washington Post*:

As the U.S. economy continues to roar and traditional commercial spots on television, radio and even billboards are booked and/or too expensive, companies are seeking ever more novel places to promote their goods and services. Parking meters, elevators, restaurant restrooms, portable toilets, golf course locker rooms – plus the handles of golf clubs and baseball bats – have all become eligible targets....

A combination of factors is spurring advertising's aggressive movement into virtually every facet of daily life. The healthy economy continues to give companies both money and incentive to advertise. Yet, at the same time, many advertisers believe the traditional means of advertising have become less effective....particularly [in reaching] 20- to 30-year-olds. (Quoted in Mayer 2000)

This article provides a number of intriguing examples of places where advertising is, literally, penetrating the collective consciousness: television monitors that run short loops of programming in gasoline stations, convenience stores, elevators, and train platforms; and ads on cocktail napkins and glasses at bars, in restrooms above urinals and inside stall walls, on turnpike coupons and portable toilets, and on ATMs. Other bright ideas, so far rejected by producers, have been to place stickers on melons advertising bras and on bananas advertising condoms.

No less frenzied, and likely more deleterious, is the increasing number of ads aimed at children. *Business Week*, hardly a chronicle of social criticism, discussed this trend in a 1997 article. Kid-centered ad campaigns, it argued:

... represent a quantitative and qualitative change in the marketing aimed at children.... [V]irtually no space is free of logos. And traditional ads have more venues than ever, with a gaggle of new magazines, dozens of Web sites, and entire TV channels aimed at kids. From 1993 to 1996, alone, advertising in kid-specific media grew more than 50%, to $1.5 billion, according to Competitive Media Reporting.

The cumulative effect of initiating our children into a consumerist ethos at an ever earlier age may be profound. As kids drink in the world around them, many of their cultural encounters – from books to movies to TV– have become little more than sales pitches devoid of any moral beyond a plea for a purchase.... Instead of transmitting a sense of who we are and what we hold important, today's marketing-driven culture is instilling in them the sense that little exists without a sales pitch attached and that self-worth is something you buy at a shopping mall. (Leonhart and Kerwin 1997)

A Slight Digression:
The Dependence Effect and Mainstream Economics

A discussion of the corporate creation of demand inside the heads of toddlers is a good place to digress briefly and relate Galbraith's concept of the Dependence Effect to mainstream economics. In fact, the idea is a straight-forward challenge to the central article of faith in mainstream economics that more output always makes people better off. Mainstream *micro*-economists typically presume that, given the resource base, firms in competitive markets will produce the greatest possible output for "rational" consumers, who will be best off by getting the most products at the cheapest prices and will choose these products according to their pre-determined "preferences." In *macro*-economics, the central article of faith is that a growing GDP is good and grand (despite what it might be doing to the forests, lakes, streams, moun-tains, and seas that will be maimed a bit with each increase in output).

This idea that more output automatically produces more welfare became the national religion – and is now becoming a world religion – by virtue of what Galbraith termed the "growth lobby." Conservative political leaders are members of the lobby because a growing economy provides greater revenue, profits, and economic power for the big firms that are their principal sup-porters, hefty defense budgets that most conservatives support, and (especial-ly important) because growth affirms the conservative's central idea that cap-italism is the best of all possible economic systems. Liberal politicians join the lobby because they, too, get generous support from corporations, and because more output also means more taxes for more public services. Further, until recently, they had adopted Keynesian growth policies as the best way to create employment for, and increase the incomes of, the lower classes in capitalist societies. Politicians from both these camps also get crucial support from mainstream economists who use complex models to make their case, models put forward as "science" but that always carrying the crucial assumption that more is better than less. The fact that millions of their listeners are captive audiences of college students in their formative years helps to inculcate each generation with the religion.

Yet, despite the overwhelming adoption of the mainstream notion that more output means higher standards of living, in *The Affluent Society* Galbraith raised a question that continues to be fresh and challenging: How much extra welfare do we get from an additional 1% of GDP if it represents goods we did not know about last year (or even last week), *and* if their pro-duction and consumption spoil the environment in which we use them? We will not pursue this Galbraithian critique here except to suggest that, however astute, his critique turned out to have very little impact on mainstream thinking.

The Dependence Effect and the Big Firms

Why are the big firms compelled to continue turning up the volume of advertising? To begin with, in industries dominated by a few firms (what economists call "oligopolies"), price competition is generally replaced by product differentiation as the major way that firms distinguish their own output. This dimension makes it mandatory that, for example, consumers see Post Toasties as altogether different from Wheaties. In the global economy, increasingly companies seek customers everywhere, and so must scream out their slogans loudly enough to be heard all over the planet. This feature of capitalism has not been lost on any economist who has studied it, whether in or out of the mainstream. What Galbraith and other political economists add to the mix is how this process is increasingly orchestrated by gigantic firms operating on a world scale.

In another of his major works, *The New Industrial State*, where Galbraith gave careful attention to these big firms that dominate the modern economic and political life, he called them the "planning system" (Galbraith 1967). He argued that the big firms themselves are under the control of a host of professionals – technicians, engineers, production, distribution, and sales executives, accountants, lawyers, economists, and others – whom Galbraith called the "technostructure." Circling around these mammoth suns are millions of smaller planets, the more or less competitive firms that make up the rest of the economy, and in some ways fit the description given them in mainstream microeconomics. Galbraith noted the broadly *anti-democratic* influence of the planning system on government at every level, with the big firms spending whatever it takes to get government officials to do their bidding. So it is, too, with their necessarily growing influence abroad: as the tentacles of the companies they control reach ever further into an ever more globalized world, the technostructure broadens its influence on the activities of people everywhere.[29]

The argument about big firms in *NIS* is, of course, thoroughly compatible with the theory of social balance. Most centrally, in order to shape consumer wants these big firms can afford a well-paid cadre of skilled artists, designers, marketing specialists, psychologists, and others, to design and to impose their message. As examples of the scale of this sales effort, in 2000 the two largest corporate advertisers in the U.S., Proctor & Gamble and General Motors

(GM), each spent over $2.5 *billion* for ads, and the top twenty spent over $20 billion to try to cajole you, me, and the rest of the population to buy their products (*Advertising Age*, Sept. 2000).[30]

In a later book, *The Anatomy of Power,* Galbraith developed a useful structural model to describe how corporations, or any modern organizations, wield power in the contemporary world. Organizations accumulate and use two different kinds of power, according to Galbraith, "compensatory" and "conditioned," to get their will done. Regarding firms, the first of these is simply paying for things, particularly labor power and materials. The second, *conditioned* power, is the ability of the large corporations to use persuasion through public relations and advertising to affect the views of the citizenry, and lobbying to affect the views of politicians, about the general beneficence of corporate activity. Of course, compensatory and conditioned power comes together in the capitalist firm's "power of the sack," its ability to hire and fire workers at will. This immense power means that those who work for capitalist firms – most of us – are conditioned to think the corporate way, at least in public ... or else (Galbraith 1982). The now omnipresent laissez-faire ideology attests to the power of the capitalist class to "condition" the rest of us to believe along with a General Motors CEO, Charles Wilson, who stated in the 1950s that "What's good for General Motors is good for America."[31]

Big firms must condition consumers with ad campaigns because the bigger the corporation the greater are the stakes of not selling its output. Consider, for example, a company like GM. Assume, for instance, it produces 10,000 cars a week that cost $10,000 each to produce, a total expenditure of $100 million to buy labor, materials, other inputs, and to pay interest on the loans borrowed to finance capital expansions. Those costs of $100 million explain why consumer demand for these cars *must* be created.[32] And, that is why GM is the nation's second-largest advertiser. Smaller firms also need to advertise, and from their perspectives the stakes are the same: convince the public to buy the output or fold the tent. However, the smaller the firm the fewer funds it has available for advertising, another reason why the larger firms end up dominating, absorbing, or driving out of business their smaller rivals.

To Galbraith, then, the effects of pecuniary emulation, along with the unceasing imperative that the dominating firms sell their products, constitute what he calls the "Dependence Effect." Consumers develop a dependence bordering on addiction for the products generated by these firms. Of course, we should remember that all this producing, advertising, and emulating mostly takes place in the *private* sphere of the economy, and this growing private sector inevitably creates a need for goods in the *public* sphere. But, according to the theory of social balance, the supply of goods forthcoming in the public sector will always lag behind, leaving pollution, congestion, poor schooling, and all the rest in its wake. Why is that true, according to Galbraith?

THE PUBLIC SECTOR AS "INFERIOR"

In *The Affluent Society*, Galbraith makes the following argument for why the public sector inevitably lags behind the production and consumption of private goods:

> [The consumer] is subject to the forces of advertising and emulation by which production creates its own demand. Advertising operates exclusively, and emulation mainly, on behalf of privately produced goods and services. Since management and emulative effects operate on behalf of private production, public services will have an inherent tendency to lag behind. Automobile demand which is expensively synthesized will inevitably have a much larger claim on income than parks or public health or even roads where no such influence operates. The engines of mass communication, in their highest state of development, assail the eyes and ears of the community on behalf of more beer but not of more schools....
>
> The competition is especially unequal for new products and services. Every corner of the public psyche is canvassed by some of the nation's most talented citizens to see if the desire for some merchantable product can be cultivated. No similar process operates on behalf of the nonmerchantable services of the state.... The scientist or engineer or advertising man who devotes himself to developing a new carburetor, cleanser, or depilatory for which the public recognizes no need and will feel none until an advertising campaign arouses it, is one of the valued members of the our society. A politician or a public servant who dreams up a new public service is a wastrel. Few public offenses are more reprehensible. (Galbraith 1958, 260-1)

And, later Galbraith adds this:

> In this discussion [about the proper role of government] a certain mystique was attributed to the satisfaction of privately supplied wants. A community

decision to have a new school means that the individual surrenders the necessary amount, willy-nilly, in his taxes. But if he is left with that income, he is a
free man. He can decide between a better car or a television set. This was
advanced with some solemnity as an argument for the TV set. The difficulty is
that this argument leaves the community with no way of preferring the school.
All private wants, where the individual can choose, are inherently superior to
all public desires which must be paid for by taxation and with an inevitable
component of compulsion.... (Galbraith 1958, 268)

In sum, a social imbalance arises from an increase in the production and
consumption of private goods that is not matched by the public services
required by their use and where "all private wants . . . are inherently superior
to all public desires." The tendency becomes an imperative in capitalist societies that are dominated by giant firms because of their great need to sell their
products and because of the enormous sums of money they use to market
them. Last of all, it leads down the road to "private opulence and public
squalor." Is this a "good" theory, in that it might help us to understand and
improve our own world? We turn now to that question.

ASSESSING THE THEORY OF SOCIAL BALANCE: GALBRAITH'S VIEW

In a special edition of *The Affluent Society* published in 1998 to commemo-
rate the fortieth anniversary of its publication, Galbraith made very few
changes, letting the book stand on its own. In an "Introduction" to this edition, he wrote the following:

On two matters this book was right, and before its time.... [One of them is
that] forty years ago I stressed the compelling difference between public and
private living standards. We had expensive radio and television and poor
schools, clean houses and filthy streets, weak public services combined with
deep concern for what the government spent. Public outlays were a bad and
burdensome thing; affluent private expenditure was an economically con-
structive force.

My case is still strong. The government does spend money readily on
weaponry of questionable need and on what has come to be called corporate
welfare. Otherwise there is still persistent and powerful pressure for restraint
on public outlay. In consequence, we are now more than ever affluent in our
private consumption; the inadequacy of our schools, libraries, public recre-

ation facilities, health care, even law enforcement, is a matter of daily comment. The private sector of our economy has gained enormously in role and reward and therewith in political voice and strength. No similar political support is accorded the public sector, the weaponry and corporate welfare as ever apart. In civilized performance it has lagged even further behind the private sector,

So, Galbraith agrees with Galbraith, and for someone as self-confident as he has always been that cannot be a surprise. What's the evidence for his continuing advocacy of his theory of social balance? The first part of our response to this question concerns the public's attitude about government, and the second part concerns a substantial body of evidence from *real* scientists, rather than from economists, that Galbraith was right all along. We take these up in turn.

THE PUBLIC SECTOR AS ENEMY OF THE PEOPLE: 1958 AND NOW
In 1958, close to the end of *TAS*, Galbraith expressed hopes for a better social balance coming from a growing "New Class" of mostly educated people. He believed that this "new class" would see the problem clearly and fight politically for adequate public services and against the overpowering need of the giant firms to blind us with ads and bury us with products. This hope led him to call for broader and deeper education, as "our hope for survival, security, and contentment" (Galbraith 1958, 355). For myriad reasons, particularly a complex restructuring of the U.S. economic and political system and the abiding mistrust of government that has characterized most of our nation's history – reasons far too complex to take up here – this anti-government mood has persisted and has actually deepened since the late 1950s. Galbraith's hopes for a "new class" to bring us to our senses, in his terms, were dashed utterly.

So ingrained now is the sentiment against government in the U.S. that for about two decades it has been virtually *impossible* in the U.S. to get elected to public office by campaigning for higher taxes, at any level of government. The push to demonize government received great momentum with the election of Ronald Reagan in 1980, who championed tax cuts for the wealthy and a rollback of federal regulations of the economy. He, and the events of the time, succeeded in legitimating to a large segment of the population the dream of a return to the "good old days" before the New Deal social welfare programs of the 1930s. By 1999, according to a Gallup poll, only about a third of the public had solid confidence in the federal government and almost a third had "little or no" confidence (Gallup Organization 1999).

In part reflecting this deeply ingrained suspicion of government, in 2000 U.S. citizens, with a mighty push from the U.S. Supreme Court, put into the White House George W. Bush. Bush campaigned on a promise to limit government "interference" in the economy, and his major initial efforts were to reduce taxes, especially for rich people, and to declare war on environmental regulations, particularly those concerning the oil, mining, and utility industries. The public protest to the Bush economic policies was muted, but with the attacks on September 11, 2001 on New York and the Pentagon, there is a gathering body of criticism about our reflexive antagonism to government. Since September 11, there has been clamoring for more federal government action regarding national security, and corporations are clamoring for more tax breaks. The friendly ear that the Bush administration has lent to corporations in this regard, and especially his and others' claim that these proposals to cut business taxes are part of an overall plan for "national security," is fooling few outside the White House. Perhaps the public's view about less government is changing and citizens will press for a broader government presence in our lives. However, aside from expanding the government's roles in national security, the federal government remains controlled by people who beat loudly the drums for laissez-faire.

What can we say about this failure of Galbraith's theory to influence public policy and spending patterns in both the public and private sectors? Most fundamentally, we would say that the failure of an idea (or the typical complex of ideas that makes up a theory) to influence public opinion or policy does not mean that it is *wrong*. The "theory" that blacks, Native Americans, and women are less capable than white men in organizing and directing social life has been, to use Galbraith's term, "conditioned" by those in power – mostly white men – throughout most of our history. The social policies that emerged from this mistaken idea about human capabilities have been enormously costly to us as a society, particularly to most black people, Native Americans, and women. In other words, the truth of the matter – that the ability for leadership is determined by things other than one's sex and skin color – was a dormant one, bound to be discovered, but still ignored for centuries. In an analogous sense, we believe that Galbraith's theory of social balance is also a dormant truth about our form of capitalism, one bound to be discovered. We shall now explain why we think that to be the case.

THE SOCIAL BALANCE AND PUBLIC SERVICES

In a recent collection of essays written about Galbraith's ideas, Robert Reich, a professor of public policy and Bill Clinton's Secretary of Labor from 1992-1996, wrote a brief lament about public services forty years after *The Affluent Society* was published. As a liberal, he provided a familiar litany about their decline:

> [By] some estimates, two thirds of our elementary and secondary schools are in disrepair, and too few of them are providing our children with adequate education. Comfortable movement along public roadways and over bridges now requires the most sophisticated of automobile shock absorbers. Public recreational facilities are fast disappearing. More than one in five of the nation's children lives in poverty – lacking adequate housing, clothing, and nutrition. An ever-growing number of and percentage of Americans have no access to health care. Publicly supported basic research is on the wane. After rising through the 1960s and 1970s, federal investments in education, infra-structure, and research as shares of GDP have continued to fall over the last three administrations. They represented...sixteen per cent in 1998, lower than at any time since 1962. (Reich 1999, 89)

Like many other liberals, in the Galbraithian sense that a broader and more efficient public sector will allow us better to enjoy our private riches, Reich sees freedoms lost in bad schooling, poverty, and sick kids without recourse to good health care. It is not simply the inability to choose health care that is costly to freedom, but freedom also implies the ability to choose a society where one's own health is protected because *everyone else* has ready access to quality health care. Particularly troubling is that in the "affluent soci-ety" all this squalor is unnecessary, as in Reich's estimate that two-thirds of all public schools are in disrepair while almost all of us are buying things we don't need.

An inherent problem with our views about the need for, and the quality of, government services is that none of us can actually *prove* our case. While a liberal might see a crumbling transportation system (exemplified by a recent report from the state of Pennsylvania that about one-third of all its bridges needs repairs), conservatives might see a wondrous system of highways avail-able to all, and the freedom to drive anywhere as one of the great benefits of our kind of society. Nevertheless, as we have seen from the introduction to a recent edition of *The Affluent Society*, Galbraith continues to see certain elements of social imbalance about which, in the terms of his argument, there can be little ambiguity. As an example, consider first one involving the ongoing culprit, the private automobile, as described in *Parade Magazine*:

> Most auto accidents occur while we're driving to and from work, not late at night. And, that's not encouraging, because key commuter arteries are getting worse around the nation. In the last 30 years, there has been a 131% increase in vehicle miles traveled, while our highway capacity has grown by only 5.7%.... For example, planners in the '70s recommended building 14 new highways in the Washington, D.C. region to accommodate future demand. Because of public resistance, only two of the 14 were built, and now the area trails only L.A. for highway congestion despite being No. 2 in use of public transportation. (*Parade Magazine*, Feb. 25, 2001)

What characterizes this situation as a social imbalance is not, as *Parade Magazine* would have it, that there are too few roads in the D.C. area and elsewhere, because building more highways will simply attract more cars. And, an imbalance will continue to exist until a mass transportation system emerges in Washington that will begin substituting train riders on public transportation for drivers in private vehicles.

Our second example concerns food. A recent article by *New York Times* reporter, Greg Winter ("Contaminated Food Makes Millions Ill Despite Advances," March 18, 2001), claims that people in the U.S. are twice as likely now as just seven years ago to get sick from eating contaminated food. A particular problem concerns imported foods, and as a pristine example of the social imbalance, here is why:

> With imported foods, the FDA [Federal Food and Drug Administration] is at a particular disadvantage. In the last four years alone, the number of foreign food items increased by 50 percent, from 2.7 million items in 1997 to 4.1 million last year. The responsibility of examining that avalanche falls to a cadre of just 113 federal food inspectors, and the force has grown by only 3 workers since 1997. As a result, the FDA *inspects less than 1 percent* of all imported foods, according to the General Accounting Office. (Winter 2001, emphasis added)

This gridlock in the nation's capital and the tidal wave of uninspected foreign foods seem clear enough evidence of a social imbalance, and it is unclear

how the anti-government majority might explain such squalor in public services as a net addition to personal freedom. Yet, even with such examples as
these, conservatives and liberals are likely never to agree about the overall
quality of public services; that is, Galbraith and his followers still don't have
the smoking gun of proof that our public services are "squalid." The best we
can offer is for our readers to test the theory of social balance, as it relates to
public services, by looking closely at the cities and towns where they live. Are
the malls, the cars, the homes, the driveways, and the lawns usually cared for
better than the schools, roads, hospitals, and the children of the poor?

SOCIAL BALANCE AND THE ENVIRONMENT

Increasingly, scientists are concluding that environmental degradation threatens us all, rich and poor alike, and our different views in this regard cannot so
readily be dismissed as a matter of judgment. Further, governments are typically responsible for trying to protect the environment. In the U.S. that effort
is a complex matrix of federal, state, and local regulations defining what any
of us, and especially firms, can emit into the air and water. There are other
aspects of the environment, in particular its aesthetic qualities and how it
nurtures all living things, for which the government is also ultimately responsible. Who, for instance, would trust the habitats for birds or for other beasts
to, say, Exxon or Dow Chemical Company? Yet, despite this matrix of laws,
parts of which all capitalists resist as "intrusions in free enterprise," there is an
enormous and growing body of evidence that high levels of production and
consumption in the developed world, and the lack of adequate environmental controls in much of the developing world, threaten the planet.

To state our case in the most general terms, we will cite first the voices of
the heads of the two most prestigious scientific associations in the world, Sir
Michael Atiyah, president of the Royal Society of London, and Dr. Frank
Press, president of the U.S. National Academy of Sciences. In a 1992 joint
statement, "Population Growth, Resource Consumption and a Sustainable
World," they wrote that:

> [I]f population growth and patterns of human activities remain unchanged ...
> science and technology may not be able to prevent either irreversible degrada-
> tion of the environment or continued poverty for much of the world.... The
> future of our planet is in the balance.... Sustainable development can be
> achieved, but only if irreversible degradation of the environment can be halt-

ed in time. The next 30 years may be crucial.[33] (*Rachel's Environmental and Health Weekly* #699, Sept. 23, 1999. Hereafter referred to as *Rachel's*.)

What do these two eminent scientists mean by these sweeping, frightening comments?

Below we provide examples that we find compelling in terms of the theory of social balance. We chose these examples both for their dramatic effect and moral implications, and because we find them to be information all citizens should consider carefully. Our best advice to our readers is to extend their consideration of these claims by moving from our sources to a broader reading.

Children (1)

As a beginning, consider comments by biologist Sandra Steingraber, concerning breast milk:

> *Of all human food, breast milk is now the most contaminated.* Because it is one rung up on the food chain higher than the food we adults eat, the trace amounts of toxic residues carried into mothers' bodies become even more concentrated in the milk their breasts produce. To be specific, it's about 10 to 100 times more contaminated with dioxins [described below] than the next highest level of stuff on the human food chain, which are animal-derived fats in dairy, meat, eggs, and fish. This is why a breast-fed infant receives its so-called 'safe' lifetime limit of dioxin in the first six months of drinking breast milk. Study after study also shows that the concentration of carcinogens in human breast milk declines steadily as nursing continues. Thus the protective effect of breast feeding on the mother appears to be a direct result of downloading a lifelong burden of carcinogens from her breasts into the tiny body of her infant.... [A principle source of dioxin], Polyvinyl Chloride (PVC), ... is found in medical products, toys, food packaging, and vinyl siding. [Frequently, these products] are shoveled into incinerators [that] are de facto laboratories for dioxin manufacture, and PVC is the main ingredient in this process. The dioxin created by the burning of PVC drifts from the stacks of these incinerators, attaches to dust particles in the atmosphere, and eventually sifts down to Earth as either dry deposition or in rain drops. This deposition then coats crops and other plants, which are eaten by cows, chickens, and hogs. Or, alternatively, it's rained into rivers and lakes and insinuates itself into the flesh of fish. As a breast-feeding mother, I take these molecules into my body and dis-

till them in my breast tissue.... [And through other biologic processes] this milk springs from grape-like lobes and flows down long tubules into the nipple, which is a kind of sieve, and into the back of the throat of the breast-feeder. My daughter." (*Rachel's* #658, July 8, 1999, emphasis added)

Dioxin, increasingly seen by many scientists as an expanding threat to living things, is a product of both incineration and some other industrial processes. It does not degrade easily, is cumulative, and is stored in fat cells in the body. And, because we live in a world in which dioxin is now widely distributed in the water, the soil, and in our bodies, we are accumulating it constantly. The federal Agency for Toxic Substances and Disease Registry in Atlanta concluded that the typical dioxin accumulation in people in the U.S. is presently between three and six times what it believes to be a "safe" level.[34]

On the matter of chemicals in women's breast milk, Canadian scientists Frances Labreche and Mark Goldberg, along with many scientists all over the world, have been working to determine if there is a causal relationship between such chemicals and the widening incidence of breast cancer. Central to this research, as they point out, is the astounding fact that the breasts of *all women in industrialized countries* harbor at least eighteen different chemicals that come from the production of industrial and consumption products, several of them known carcinogens in certain concentrations. It is hard to fathom this kind of information if you are a not a scientist in the field, but it remains nonetheless an extraordinary comment on the insidious nature of modern industrial production.

The known deleterious effects on living creatures from so many industrial chemicals makes it striking that we allow the production and distribution of roughly 3,000 of these industrial chemicals without their having ever been subjected to analysis by the EPA to determine their toxicity to living things. The two barriers to our knowing, of course, are the considerable funds the EPA would have to expend to find out, and the ongoing resistance of the chemical industry to "outside interference" by government.

Children (2)

As a second example regarding children, consider the food they eat. Marian Burros, writing in the *New York Times*, reported that:

Using U.S. Department of Agriculture statistics based on 27,000 food samples from 1994 to 1997, *Consumer Reports* (the magazine of the Consumer Union) looked at foods children are mostly likely to eat. *Almost all the foods tested for pesticide residues were within legal limits, but were frequently well above the levels the EPA says are safe for young children.* According to the Consumer Union *Report*, even one serving of some fruits and vegetables can exceed safe daily limits for young children.... Methyl parathion [the pesticide ingredient] accounts for most of the total toxicity on the foods that were analyzed, particularly peaches, frozen and canned green beans, pears and apples. *Last year EPA said that methyl parathion posed an 'unacceptable risk' but that it had not taken any action to ban it or reduce its use.* Organophosphates [such as methyl parathion] are neurological poisons and work the same on humans as they do on insects. (Quoted in *Rachel's* #660, July 22, 1999, emphasis added)

John H. Cushman, writing in the *The New York Times*, September 29, 1997 ("U.S. Reshaping Cancer Strategy As Incidence in Children Rises"), reports that an increase in the incidence of cancer among children nation-wide, "may be tied to new chemicals in the environment." Cushman stated that that between 1973 and 1994 one form of leukemia had risen 27% among children, and brain cancer had risen nearly 40% (Cushman 1997).

Children (3)

New York Times columnist Bob Herbert wrote this about a report from the American Lung Association on ground level ozone:

A series of well-documented scientific and medical studies have linked [ground level] ozone and particular matter [from such sources as truck exhausts, gasoline powered lawn mowers, and unpaved roads] to decreases in lung function and other forms of respiratory distress in children and adults, to increases in emergency-room visits and hospital admissions and to increases in mortality. According to the American Lung Association, children playing outdoors in ozone levels 33% percent below the current standard have experienced as much as a 20% loss of lung function. The problem is worsened by the fact that ozone levels tend to be highest on warm, sunny days – the very days on which kids are most likely to be playing outside. (Herbert 1997)

The national organization Environmental Defense, whose Web site is an exceptionally valuable source of information about pollution in the U.S., reported on an "asthma epidemic," most of whose victims will be children, with a headline that read, "Asthma Cases Are Projected To Double by 2020, Hitting 1 in 5 Families." Environmental Defense summarized the report this way:

The nation is in the grip of a rapidly growing asthma epidemic whose victims will more than double by 2020, according to a recently released study by the Pew Environmental Health Commission at the Johns Hopkins School of Public Health. Asthma is a chronic disease whose causes are largely unknown, but genetic predisposition *and environmental triggers* in both indoor and outdoor air are known contributors to asthma's developmental severity. The Johns Hopkins researchers concluded that new cases of asthma among Americans are increasing so rapidly that by the time another generation of children is born, asthma will strike 29 million Americans. (See http://www.environmentaldefense.org/home.cfm, emphasis added)

The point of these examples involving children is that, to the extent that the scientific assessments are true, they are woeful examples of the failure of government to provide a crucial public good – clean air and water – that would protect the welfare of the most vulnerable and most innocent among us. This damaging, unchecked pollution comes, of course, from the production and consumption of goods and services. And, it is our pleasure from them that blinds us to Galbraith's point that we quoted earlier:

Advertising operates exclusively, and emulation mainly, on behalf of privately produced goods and services.... [And] every increase in the consumption of private goods will normally mean some facilitation or protective step by the [public sector]. [If] these [public] services are not forthcoming, the consequences will be in some degree ill.

Children are the "ill" in this case, a social imbalance of the grimmest form.

Fish
According to Peter Montague:

The world's fishing fleet has doubled since 1970. New fishing gear (global positioning system receivers, fish finders, and new kinds of trawls and nets) have made it possible to sweep the oceans like a vacuum cleaner, sucking up nearly everything that lives. A recent report from the Marine Conservation Biology Institute in Redmond, Washington, says modern fishing is comparable to forest clear cutting – except that the wreckage caused by modern "factory trawlers" is hidden from view. As a result of new fishing technologies, 13 of the world's 17 major fisheries are depleted or in steep decline. For fish and for fishing, the future looks grim. (*Rachel's* #587, February 26, 1998. See also *Rachel's* #659, July 5, 1999.)

Because the shallow fishing beds are being exhausted, fishing companies are using military technology to develop ways to fish as deep as a mile. Tyson's, the chicken giant, has expanded into fishing and its several huge ships sink nylon nets that sweep the ocean's bottom to gather up to 400 tons of fish at a time. Unwanted creatures, like seals, sea lions, and fish with no markets, are called "bycatch" and are ground up and thrown back into the sea. This grinding amounted to almost 4 billion pounds of fish in 1997, in the northeast Atlantic alone. Deep-sea fishing threatens a gradual depletion of the bottom dwelling species, as well as the loss of much of the other life at the ocean's bottom that sustains all above it. How *incredible* that, within a few decades, we humans would eat the fish at such a rate that they might face extinction! Other studies, of New York Coastal waters, have found as many as 40% of shellfish infected with viruses with human origins.

Apparently, many of us share with the fish the perils of swimming in the ocean. On January 24, 1999, the National Desk of the *New York Times* ("As Oceans Warm, Problems From Viruses and Bacteria Mount") reported on a study showing that *almost 25%* of people who swim, windsurf, or boat in the water along Florida beaches pick up viruses from 1.6 million septic tanks releasing sewage into Florida's coastal waters. The viral diseases included ear, eye, throat, respiratory and gastrointestinal infections, along with more serious ailments like heart disease, meningitis and hepatitis. And, how *bizarre* – there is no better word – that for health's sake we should give up frolicking on Florida's beaches because we refuse to pay the taxes necessary for sewage treatment plants. Is there a more insightful explanation for these kinds of anomalies than the theory of social balance?

RUINING THE WHOLE PLANET: GLOBAL WARMING

Last, in this exemplary tip of a huge iceberg, there is the problem of global warming, perhaps the direst threat of them all over the long haul. It is caused by the "greenhouse effect" of sunlight striking the planet, turning into heat, and then being trapped by "greenhouse" gases. These gases, primarily water vapor, carbon dioxide, and methane, allow the sunlight in, but do not allow all the resulting heat to escape, thus causing "global warming." After a few years of trying to deny the problem, a growing number of major corporations now admit that it is real and it is really threatening. Bette Hileman, writing in the American Chemical Society's *Chemical and Engineering News*, gives the details this way:

> The Earth's average temperature has been rising for at least 100 years, but in recent decades the rate of increase has speeded up. Eleven of the past 16 years have been the hottest of the century. The average global temperature in 1998 was higher than it had been at any other time during the previous 1000 years. The polar regions of the planet are heating up much more rapidly than the average. The carbon dioxide is thrown into the air mainly by burning fossil fuels, deforestation, and methane from growing cattle and rice, and landfilling garbage. Increasingly, the carbon dioxide comes from vehicular pollution, and with 5% of the world's population, we in the U.S. are responsible for about 20% of the whole world's production. If left unattended, global warming will cause immense relocations in the developed world and be absolutely cata-strophic for billions of people in developing countries, particularly from flooding, crop loss, and violent weather. (*Rachel's* #664, August 19, 1999)

Other indications of global warming are changes in the weather. Annual rain and snow fall over the continental U.S. has increased about 10% during the last century, increasingly in the form of big storms. As an example, days with rainfalls of over two inches in the U.S. have also increased by about 10% during the past century, trends shared by Canada, Japan, Russia, China, and Australia. Intense storms over the North Atlantic and North Pacific have doubled during the past century. And, Britain's Hadley Centre for Climate Change, using billions of calculations from the world's largest supercomputer in Berkshire, concluded, among other horrific predictions, that current trends of emissions from burning fossil fuels (mostly by vehi-cles), "will turn parts of the Amazon rain forest ... into deserts by 2050, threatening the world with an unstoppable greenhouse effect" (Brown 1998). Global warming and our collective reaction to it, reflects well all that Galbraith has written about social balance. As we stated above, the public's longstanding lack of confidence in government helped in 2000 to elect George W. Bush, who campaigned in large part against government and for the expansion of all aspects of the private sector (via lower taxes and fewer regulations). Bush's first decision concerning the environment was to go back on a campaign promise to press for reducing the emissions of coal burning utilities that are, along with vehicle emissions, a principal cause of global warming. A companion to this decision was his administration's abandonment of the international treaty on global warming known as the "Kyoto Protocol," despite the fact that our 5% of the world's population is responsible for emitting 20% of its carbon dioxide (the principal pollutant leading to global warming). This policy on global warming, which has stunned and enraged most of the rest of the developed world, is part of an overall administration plan that Bush has stated must not include any environmental regulations that would weaken the American economy. As he put in April, 2001, in defending his decision to abandon the Kyoto Protocol, "We will not do anything that harms our economy, because first things first are the people who live in America" (Andrews 2001). Soon after his pronouncements on global warming, Bush decided to ignore the advice of the American Academy of Sciences, and his own EPA, to lower by a factor of ten the acceptable level of arsenic in drinking water. In these two cases, it is clear that the president was responding, not unwillingly, to immense pressure from a handful of oil, gas, and mining corporations. The Bush administration's vision of our future will lead it to give the private sector every advantage to expand, relative to the public sector. No doubt, if Galbraith is the sort to have nightmares, George W. Bush will be an actor in his worst ones. Thus, in the end, the ultimate irony is that the one public good that we most desperately need, the protection of the environment, is in many of its dimensions not available to any of us, regardless of our income, status, or location. Even the richest of the rich in our society have children breathing fouled urban air and eating peaches, apples and pears whose sweetness disguises the bitter poisons many of them harbor inside. One is left with such questions as this one: How hot does the planet have to get before we begin to see the hottest consumer products as a problem for all of us rather than a solution for those who buy them?

CONCLUSION

We conclude this essay on Galbraith's theory of social balance by saying that we believe it an indispensable guide to understanding the kind of capitalism that has developed in the United States. In his theory, and in his other works, Galbraith points to the unyielding and growing power of corporations to shape our wants, even to the point of taking the lowest road of them all – trying to shape toddlers into insatiable consumers. A central marker of this growing corporate influence in our lives is that the number of messages we must endure, urging us to buy private goods, has increased to *thousands per day*. While we hear this cacophony of corporate pleas that we buy consumer goods, these same voices tell us little about the desirability of public goods except that the government sector is too big, too inefficient, and that our very freedom depends upon its being reduced even more. Joining the corporate choir are the voices of politicians, most in office only because of corporate donations. This perplexing, perhaps insoluble, problem confirms Galbraith's claim, emerging first in the work of Karl Marx, that the corporate capitalist class largely fashions the actions of government. For us, the most compelling evidence leading us to see Galbraith's theory as crucial in explaining our world is that growing production and consumption levels in the U.S. have already led to the contamination of breast milk suckled by our children, the sickening of some of these children and some of the rest of us from a spewing of chemicals most of which have health effects we know nothing about, and the filling of the atmosphere with enough carbon dioxide to render the planet, in the long run, uninhabitable.

Along the way in this essay, we have mentioned, but not developed, the other side of the story, the conservative critique of Galbraith's theory. In this critique, the bedrock presumption is that government is at best a necessary evil; that with every reduction in taxes and public services, our freedom is expanded; that the booming economy during the last two decades proves the case, if nothing else does; that dominance by the U.S. of world economic and political affairs attests mightily to the powers unleashed in the absence of an intruding, inefficient government; and that the alleged squalor in public services seen by liberals like Galbraith is caused by a blindness about what constitutes true freedom and liberty.

Each of us, of course, ultimately will judge which of these two assessments best describes the world we experience. Are we a freer people as our economy expands; is more always better than less? Are we always better off when taxes come down and public services are cut? If your community has more cars in family garages, are you likely to enjoy more "consumer welfare" than if you and your neighbors had fewer cars but your city had ambient air that was healthy for you, or for your children? Is their a richer and deeper meaning to "freedom" and "liberty" than the ability to buy anything you want, no matter the consequences to your neighbors, the world community, and the planet itself? Or, as Galbraith would have it, are we in a lemming-like march to the abyss, done in by a love affair with consumer goods?

Suggestions for Further Reading

Bowles, Samuel, Richard Edwards and William G. Shepherd. *Unconventional Wisdom: Essays on Economics in Honor of John Kenneth Galbraith.* Boston: Houghton Mifflin, 1989.

Hessions, Charles H. *John Kenneth Galbraith & His Critics.* New York: New American Library, 1972.

Motague, Peter, ed. *Rachel's Environment and Health Weekly.* Annapolis, MD: Environmental Research Foundation. You can receive this newsletter free and online by sending an email to: listserve@rachel.org, with the words, SUBSCRIBE RACHEL-WEEKLY [YOUR NAME] in the message.

Okoi, Loren J. *Galbraith, Harrington, Heilbroner: Economics and Dissent in an Age of Optimism.* Princeton, N.J.: Princeton University Press, 1988.

Williams, Andrea, ed. *The Essential Galbraith.* Boston: Houghton-Mifflin, 2001.

7
U.S. Monopoly Capitalism: An Irrational System?

INTRODUCTION

Is U.S. capitalism an "irrational" system? Despite its having chased all competitors from the economic playing field, and despite its global political domination, could the system be described in such negative terms? Two Marxists, Paul Baran and Paul Sweezy, thought so. In 1966, they offered a famous explanation of their conclusion in a book entitled *Monopoly Capital: An Essay on the American Economic and Social Order*. In the final chapter to this book, called "The Irrational System," Baran and Sweezy argued that the giant firms that dominate our economy were in a permanent war with their employees, customers, and the entire society.

Baran and Sweezy were working to update Marx's work by looking at the huge multinational firms whose dominating power Marx saw on the horizon. Both Adam Smith and Marx had developed their ideas during a time when capitalism was considerably more competitive than it is now. Smith had warned his readers in *The Wealth of Nations* that the "joint stock" companies (corporations) emerging in Britain threatened the atomistic competition he championed. The big firms he warned against were still consolidating power when Marx wrote almost a century later. Thus, it was left to contemporary Marxists to study and theorize about giant firms in their developed states.

None of these Marxists produced a richer analysis then Baran and Sweezy in *Monopoly Capital*. As they stated their central theme:

> We must recognize that competition, which was the predominant form of
> market relations in nineteenth-century Britain, has ceased to occupy that posi-

tion, not only in Britain but everywhere else in the capitalist world. Today the typical economic unit in the capitalist world is not the small firm producing a negligible fraction of a homogeneous output for an anonymous market but a large-scale enterprise producing a significant share of the output of an industry, or even several industries, and able to control its prices, the volume of its production, and the types and amounts of its investments. The typical economic unit, in other words, has the attributes that were once thought to be possessed only by monopolies. (Baran and Sweezy 1966, 6)

Baran and Sweezy saw that although many industries go through a competitive phase, most become stable oligopolies – markets dominated by a few sellers. The result is that, as Marx predicted, for the last century most industries have been dominated by a few huge multinational firms. Each has substantial market power and vast economies of scale that allow it to make products at relatively low per-unit costs. To compete with a giant firm, as the owners of all small firms know, promises a predictable fate: in general, small fish will be gobbled up by the big ones, or will fail to swim at all in the low-cost world the big firms create. The gargantuan size of these big fish is demonstrated aptly in Figure 1.

Figure 1. **Mega-Corporations that Dominate the World Economy: Some Revealing Data**

- Fifty-one of the world's top 100 economies are corporations (the other 49 are countries).

- The combined sales of the world's top 200 corporations are greater than the combined economies of 182 countries, accounting for well over 25% of global GDP.

- Royal Dutch Shell's revenues are greater than Venezuela's Gross Domestic Product. Using this measurement, Wal-Mart is bigger than Indonesia. General Motors is roughly the same size as Ireland, New Zealand and Hungary combined.

- But the top 200 corporations have been net job destroyers in recent years. While they account for 27.5 percent of world output, they employ less than a one percent of the world's people. Thus their massive size and productivity does not necessarily translate into job creation.

- Ninety-nine of the 100 largest transnational corporations are from the industrialized countries.

Source: Corporate Watch (www.corpwatch.org), 2002.

When new competitors try to enter an industry, they face significant barriers. Consider, for instance, the formidable costs that would face anyone who wanted to produce automobiles for a profit. How much do you think it would cost to build a modern automobile plant that would compete with existing giants? Depending on the size, the cost could be in the hundreds of millions of dollars. It simply is not feasible for almost any person or small firm to put up this kind of money. Indeed, Marx saw the increasing complexity and cost of machinery as the principal reason that owners of small firms would ultimately be "hurled into the proletariat."

Age, size, and reputation confer other advantages on established firms that become barriers to new ones. Customers of an existing firm are familiar with its product, and often have significant brand name loyalty, which makes it difficult for new competitors to vie for business. And established firms may have long-term contracts with large buyers. How much do you think it would cost our new automobile magnate to establish brand name identity, loyalty, and the sales necessary just to pay for the factory? Currently, automobile firms spend in the *billions* of dollars *every year* to persuade you and me that buying their product will lead to adventures, make us cool, and even improve our love lives.

Another source of these firms' power is their ties with government. Whenever new competition from foreigners appears on the scene, firms do whatever they can to reduce that competition. When U.S. automakers faced competition from Japanese car producers in the 1980s, the U.S. firms did what the big firms always do in a pinch: they went crying to the government for help. Rather than build the smaller, better cars being imported, the firms coerced the government into putting a big import fee on Japanese cars. This move protected the price position of the auto giants, and cost Americans who bought any car during most of the 1980s about $1,000 extra.

Finally, large firms work together to eliminate competition. For instance, in markets where a handful of firms dominates, they avoid price competition by engaging in such forms of tacit collusion as price leadership, where one industry leader sets prices and the other firms follow suit.

Because of all these formidable barriers to the entry of competitors, the giant, dominating firms behave as if they were a single firm. In fact, they act like monopolies, and that is why Baran and Sweezy used the term "monopoly capitalism" to apply to modern capitalist economies like the U.S. economy.

In addition to describing the behavior of corporations, Baran and Sweezy wrote about the expansion of government since Marx's time. They pointed to rises in military spending and the development of a social welfare state in the

1930s and 1960s. During these two decades, in response to the worst excesses of capitalism and to quell worker unrest, U.S. politicians created a number of social programs. The social security program, minimum wage and unemployment compensation laws, the Wagner Act giving workers the right to form unions, tax laws helping the middle and working classes to buy homes – all of these are prominent examples of social welfare programs that did not exist in Marx's time. (Interestingly, in *The Communist Manifesto* in 1848, Marx and Engels advocated a similar array of social welfare programs for workers along with some more dramatic steps.)

Baran and Sweezy also analyzed the actions of governments after the Great Depression to insure that businesses remained profitable: the goal was to avoid an investment slump that might cause another depression. For example, recently, Joseph Stiglitz, an economic advisor to Bill Clinton, World Bank economist, and Nobel Prize winner, has written about suspect government measures to boost aluminum prices. These were driven by Paul O'Neill, who, before becoming U.S. Treasury Secretary, was the CEO of Alcoa, the largest aluminum producer in the world. According to Stiglitz:

> Seven years [before he became Treasury Secretary], [O'Neill] had asked for [and got] government help in stopping market forces from operating because they were leading to a worldwide decline in aluminum prices. The aluminum industry concluded that the best way to restore "stability" to the market (meaning high prices and corporate profits) was an international cartel. This cartel put the ordinary workings of competitive markets aside: each member country was assigned a fixed output. (Stiglitz 2002)

This example has all elements of the monopoly capital drama: big government, big business, an international cartel, all brought together by an industrial-mogul-turned-government-official. But while these examples are recent, they reflect an old alliance between government and capitalists. As we noted in Chapter 2, Marx and Engels described government as "the executive committee of the bourgeoisie" in the *Communist Manifesto*.

In general, Baran and Sweezy criticized monopoly capitalism because they thought that the huge firms that dominate it collude, merge and stifle innovation, generating rising profits in the process. But these rising profits cannot always find outlets, leading to waste and even economic crises. And finally, monopoly capitalism, like other forms of capitalism, invariably exploits labor in its pursuit of profit.

For Baran and Sweezy, the giant multinationals that now run the world formed the center of an analysis of capitalism, so that is where we begin. How do these firms exert their power, and what are the consequences?

THE BEHAVIOR OF GIANT FIRMS IN MONOPOLY CAPITALISM

Baran and Sweezy argued that U.S. society is fundamentally organized to maximize the profits of a few vast corporations. To them, this meant that our society is structured to "maintain scarcity in the midst of potential plenty" (Baran and Sweezy 1966, 337). For example, in the U.S., one of the wealthiest countries in the world, millions live in abysmal poverty despite the vast wealth that exists for the few. In underdeveloped countries, hundreds of millions of people suffer from disease and starvation even though there is enough food in the world for everyone and enough medicine to cure much existing disease. Baran and Sweezy, and most other political economists, see this inequality as an inevitable outcome of monopoly capital.

Baran and Sweezy argued that inequality was an essential result of capitalists' business strategies. Capitalists aimed to lower their production costs, but instead of passing the savings on to workers or consumers, they kept the savings for themselves as increased profits. Considering capitalism's capacity for production, innovation, and cost-cutting, Baran and Sweezy wrote:

> On the face of it this would seem to be an argument for monopoly capitalism's being considered a rational and progressive system. And if its cost-reducing proclivities could somehow be disentangled from monopoly pricing and a way could be found to utilize the fruits of increasing productivity for the benefit of society as a whole, the argument would indeed be a powerful one. But of course this is just what cannot be done. The whole motivation of cost reduction is to increase profits, and the monopolistic structure of markets enables the corporations to appropriate the lion's share of the fruits of increasing productivity directly in the form of higher profits. This means that under monopoly capitalism, declining costs imply continuously widening profit margins. (Baran and Sweezy 1966, 71)

Baran and Sweezy are talking about the long run tendency of the economy because in recessions, for example, profit margins fall, as do those of firms that can't compete in good or bad times. But the tendency of profit margins to increase over longer periods of time is a crucial characteristic of monopoly capital. While Marx believed that the more competitive form of capitalism that existed in his time would generate a declining rate of profit, Baran and Sweezy argued that under conditions of monopoly capitalism, the opposite would be true.

As an example of their point, Bill Gates boasted during anti-trust hearings that Microsoft had lowered the price of Windows and should not be prosecuted as a monopolist. What he neglected to mention was that costs had fallen so low that in 1997 Microsoft had the highest profit rate in the economy, with gross profit margins reaching 90 percent (Cassidy 1998a). Not only did Microsoft fail to match cost decreases with price decreases, but the firm even used its monopoly position to extract revenues from computer manufacturers that did not use the Microsoft Windows operating system. Microsoft charged computer manufacturers a per-processor fee on machines that installed other operating systems. They were able to do this because the computer manufacturers wanted to be able to sell Windows to the majority of their customers who "wanted" it; Microsoft took advantage of this need, and coerced them into paying for a copy of Windows for every processor they sold, whether Windows was installed on the machine or not! Similarly, The Gap, like most clothing manufacturers today, has taken to using sweatshop laborers in the Third World to make its clothes. Despite the lower wages The Gap now pays, the prices of its clothes have remained high. So firms like Microsoft and The Gap do indeed reduce costs, but they rarely pass on cost savings to consumers.

Why do firms go to such lengths to maximize profits? For one thing, profits are necessary for the *"accumulation of capital"* – the cycle of making profits to reinvest in capital goods in order to make more profits in the future. Accumulation is crucial for firms if they are to dominate markets and find new areas for investment. Capitalists also need profits because they generate the dividends and higher stock prices coveted by stockholders. And CEOs and upper management are only too happy to pursue profits and growth (capital accumulation) on behalf of stockholders because most CEOs receive a huge percentage of their pay in the form of stock options. Indeed, the incentive of CEOs to inflate stock prices for their own benefit was behind the Enron, WorldCom, and many other corporate scandals in 2001 and 2002.

Like any gambler, a CEO or investor likes nothing more than a sure thing. Thus a primary goal of multinational corporations is to rig markets in their favor. They collude to avoid price competition, buy out or merge with competitors, and they move into new markets, but only once it is clear that the markets are profitable. We will explore the implications of these strategies below.

Tacit Collusion and Price Leadership

In any mature industry with monopoly power, there is virtually no price competition. Big corporations are reluctant to lower prices because that could spark a price war that would cost all the firms in the market. When prices increase, they tend to be matched because this can result in greater profits for the industry as a whole. If a company increases price because it thinks it is in the interest of the whole industry, it will then wait to see if others follow suit. If they don't the leading firm will rescind the price change. As Baran and Sweezy described this kind of behavior, "it becomes relatively easy for the group as a whole to feel its way toward the price which maximizes the industry's profit" (Baran and Sweezy 1966, 61). In this manner—avoiding price cuts but matching most price increases—an industry can arrive at the price that a monopolist would charge, and that is why oligopolies end up pricing like monopolies. Baran and Sweezy noted that this behavior also "introduces a significant upward bias into the general price level", and they (correctly) predicted continuous inflation during the era of monopoly capitalism (Baran and Sweezy 1966, 62-3). For example, for the three decades prior to the oil price shocks of the 1970s, General Motors was the price leader in the auto industry, setting prices on models that were then matched by Ford and Chrysler. During this period it was not uncommon for automobile price increases to be three times the overall inflation level.

Often, we do see price competition when firms are fending off a foreign competitor or in less mature industries when firms are jockeying for market share. But most industries dominated by big firms settle into a stable, oligopolistic structure with little price competition. William Shepherd, who has been charting the operations of U.S. oligopolies for decades, recently published a study confirming that today, "cooperation in price setting *is* extensive" (Shepherd 1997, 262). To give one recent example (among the many hundreds of instances we know of), from 1954 to 1994, the leading Ivy League colleges conspired to fix the scholarships offered to students who applied to several schools. Admissions officers met to decide exactly what amount to offer each student, thereby preventing students from seeking tuition discounts and preventing colleges from offering more generous scholarships to lure top students away from competing schools.

Buyouts and mergers

Even better than colluding with competitors is buying them out or absorbing them to lessen competition. Four of the last five decades have featured merger waves of increasing magnitude. As Table 1 shows, the last few years of the 1990s saw a wave of massive mergers as firms attempted to (a) lessen competition (a horizontal merger), (b) explore profitable new areas by buying into them (especially businesses with some overlap where there may be "synergies"), or (c) gain greater control over their costs of production by absorbing a supplier (a vertical merger). Mergers that lessen competition, like the one that formed Exxon-Mobil, could be prevented by the government under anti-trust laws, but successive U.S. presidents since 1980—Reagan, the two Bushes, and Clinton—have instructed the anti-trust division of the Justice Department to approve virtually all the mergers that firms have applied to undertake. This policy, which accepts jockeying between a few global giants as sufficient for a "competitive" economy, has allowed corporate behemoths to gain even greater market power. It is clear evidence of the complicity of government in the rise of massive corporations.

Ironically, William Shepherd notes that mergers often reduce efficiency: most mergers are actually "empire-building" strategies where a firm's main goal is simply to gain greater control over markets. As telecommunications, petrochemical and financial firms expand their empires, and Table 1 indicates that they are doing that, one might wonder how the individual consumer will fare in these markets. As our choices diminish, do you think we will be provided with better products at lower prices?

Big Firms and Innovation

A common belief about multinational corporations is that they are innovative, constantly designing new and better products for our consumption. Oligopolies are typically depicted in this way because they alone are supposed to have the funds to put into research and development. Others argue that firms in competitive markets will not undertake the cost of innovating because they know that their results will be stolen by competitors. While oligopolies can be sources of innovation, more often they stifle it. Veblen, of course, noted this tendency to stifle innovation in the nineteenth century, and called it a form of "industrial sabotage." Today, corporations manipulate patent and copyright laws to prevent the entry of new competitors, and they repackage items as "new and improved" when the product is essentially the same. Furthermore, instead of inventing new products, corporations often simply buy out path-breaking firms. As Baran and Sweezy observe:

Table 1. **24 Largest U.S. Mergers and Acquisitions, 1998–2000**

Buyer	Seller	Year	Transaction Value (Billions of $)
Pfizer Inc.	Warner-Lambert Co.	1999	116.1
America Online	Time Warner	2000	106.0
Exxon	Mobil	1998	86.5
Travelers Group	Citicorp	1998	72.6
SBC Communications	Ameritech	1998	72.4
AT&T	Tele-Communications	1998	69.9
Vodafone Group PLC	Airtouch Comm.	1999	62.8
NationsBank	BankAmerica	1998	61.6
Bell Atlantic (Verizon)	GTE	1998	60.0
AT&T	MediaOne Group	1999	55.8
British Petroleum	Amoco	1998	55.0
Viacom	CBS	1999	50.2
Deutsche Telekom	VoiceStream Wireless	2000	41.6
Daimler Benz	Chrysler	1998	40.5
JDS Uniphase	SDL Inc.	2000	38.1
Chase Manhattan	J. P. Morgan	2000	36.5
Chevron	Texaco	2000	35.7
Qwest Communications	U.S. West Inc.	1999	34.7
Norwest	Wells Fargo	1998	34.4
Citigroup	Associates First Cap.	2000	30.8
Banc One	First Chicago	1998	29.6
BP Amoco PLC	ARCO	1999	26.6
Monsanto	Pharmacia & Upjohn	1999	25.8
Lucent Technologies	Ascend Comm.	1999	24.1

Source: Du Boff and Herman 2001, 15.

When a new industry or field of operations is being opened up, the big corporation tends to hold back deliberately and to allow individual entrepreneurs or small businesses to do the vital pioneering work. Many fail and drop out of the picture, but those which succeed trace out the most promising lines of development for the future. It is at this stage that the big corporations move to the center of the stage.... The record of the giants is one of moving in, buying out and absorbing smaller creators. (Baran and Sweezy 1966, 49)

Meanwhile, the inventors are only too happy to be cashed out: "Indeed, to be bought out and absorbed is often the ultimate ambition of the small business" (Baran and Sweezy 1966, 74). The Internet boom at the end of the 1990s was the perfect illustration of this, as established firms looking to muscle in on the wave of the future snapped up new startups. In fact, as Shepherd documents, most innovations actually come from individuals or small firms, while corporate research labs account for only about one-third of major innovations. The only reason that we associate big companies with new products is that the big corporations buy up innovations and market them.

Monopoly capital's control of markets and relentless cost cutting can produce an increasing rate of profit – or, to use a term from Baran and Sweezy which we will explain shortly, a growing "surplus." While on the surface, this would seem to be a good thing for firms, Baran and Sweezy argued that it was a source of endemic instability in capitalism.

Rising Surpluses, Crises and Waste

In *Monopoly Capital*, Baran and Sweezy developed the concept of "surplus," which was related to, but not the same as, Marx's idea of surplus value. Baran and Sweezy defined the surplus as the difference between what society produces – its Gross Domestic Product – and the costs of producing it:

$$SURPLUS = GDP - PRODUCTION\ COSTS$$

Let's explore the implications of this formula. First, most costs of production are a reflection of the labor costs incurred – either wages or the cost of building machines and making inputs. Second, the "surplus" is a macroeconomic approximation of Marx's concept of surplus value, the part of the total value of output that does not go to workers but becomes profits or is paid to the government.[35]

Baran and Sweezy argue that in monopoly capital firms work tirelessly to lower production costs. In addition, as they grow, they control larger and larger segments of markets, and they can use this market power to increase prices. With downward pressure on costs and upward pressure on prices, Baran and Sweezy held that *there is an inherent tendency for the surplus to rise.* Hence a key economic issue becomes how the economy is able, or not able, to absorb this growing surplus.

These ideas recall the work of John Maynard Keynes, who discussed the circular flow of income among producers, workers, and consumers. In the Keynesian system, firms take in money and pay most of it out in wages and salaries. They pay some to banks that have loaned them money, some to the government in taxes, and they keep some as profits. When the money goes to workers, they spend most of it on consumer goods, pay some of it in taxes, and save what's left. In Baran and Sweezy's formulation of the surplus, they are looking at this circular flow of income from a slightly different perspective. In the formula above, Baran and Sweezy mean by production costs only those that are truly *necessary,* not all costs of production. As an example, in the auto industry this would include the wages and salaries paid to production workers, and the wages and salaries paid to those at other firms who supplied materials and machines to the autoworkers. If we subtract these *necessary* costs from total output, GDP, we get what's left, and what Baran and Sweezy call the "surplus." With that money, firms pay the owners profits, the banks interest, the government taxes, and they also spend enormous sums on such things as advertising, supervisors whose only job is to help drive down costs, officers of the firm, and so on. Thus, the surplus can be divided as follows:

SURPLUS = PROFITS + INTEREST + TAXES + ADVERTISING+ MANAGEMENT COSTS

Profits and interest payments are usually used to finance investment (I), and taxes are used to finance government spending (G). And Baran and Sweezy see spending on advertising and excess management as waste. So the formula for surplus can also be written as follows:

SURPLUS = I + G + CORPORATE WASTE

We can assume that most of what goes to workers in the form of production costs gets back into the system as consumption spending, but that is not necessarily true in the case of the surplus. Since significant parts of the surplus, particularly that paid to the owners as profits and to the government in taxes, will not automatically get back to the firms in the way of spending, it is a potential source of instability for the entire economy. This is not different, conceptually, from the total "leakages" in the Keynesian system: the surplus leaks out of the circular flow of income, and it must be returned in one form or another. If the entire surplus is not returned, then some income generated from production is not spent, and some goods go unpurchased. The result is stagnation and recession as businesses cut production and lay off workers.[36]

More concretely, why must profits be reinvested? Why wouldn't corporate executives want to hold onto their profits? Fundamentally, firms must use the profits they keep as retained earnings to invest in new capital and grow; otherwise their stock value will fall because they will have a lower rate of return on capital. This means that their stockholders will be displeased, and their competitors will muscle in on their markets. Thus, all profits must find an outlet every year. Or, in other words, the accumulation of capital is an imperative for survival in capitalism: *businesses must grow or die.*

Similarly, profits that firms don't keep, but pay to banks and investors, must also find an outlet. All financial investment firms that earn money one year will want to earn more money next year by buying more stocks, bonds, or other such instruments. Or if the money goes to a bank which pays interest, the bank must find someone to loan that money to at an even higher rate of interest. Banks therefore need good investment opportunities. The imperative for the financial sector to reinvest is clear when one considers that the wealthy save much of their income: most of the surplus they receive from salaries, stocks, and bonds finds its way back into financial markets seeking a high rate of return. Thus, the generation of profits creates additional demands for future profits, the growth of financial speculation generates more speculation, and economic growth creates the demand for more economic growth.

The problem is that *there are only so many good investment opportunities in an economy*. Firms naturally seek out the surest, most profitable investment options and expand into these areas. But if firms run out of good opportunities, the expansion of investment itself becomes a problem. As Baran and Sweezy put it, "Sooner or later, excess capacity grows so large that it discourages further investment" (Baran and Sweezy 1966, 82). When this happens, as we know from Keynes, the dearth of investment and the excess of leakages over injections can cause a downturn. The only way to avoid a recession is to ensure that spending in other sectors goes up.

Are there enough alternative outlets for investment and spending? Baran and Sweezy didn't think so. Once existing investment outlets in an economy have been exhausted, capitalists must find new outlets, such as new techniques of production, new products, and new markets. However, new technology and products will not always be outlets for investment, because giant corporations frequently slow their introduction when it is more profitable to do so. For example, shoes can now be manufactured, and fast food meals cooked and dispensed, entirely by machine. However, corporations still choose to use exploited labor to make these products because it is more profitable to do so. Companies have no incentive to invest in new technology given the current low level of wages.

Similarly, companies are often reluctant to introduce new products into markets that are already profitable. For example, IBM was reluctant to sell networked personal computers as long as its mainframe business was profitable. Microsoft ignored the Internet browser market until Netscape demonstrated the importance of the market for browser software. These examples tend to confirm Baran and Sweezy's conclusion that "new products and new process-es . . . tend to be introduced in a controlled fashion" (Baran and Sweezy 1966, 99). This means that monopoly capitalism is "simultaneously characterized by a rapid rate of technical progress and by the retention in use of a large amount of technologically obsolete equipment" (Baran and Sweezy 1966, 96). This is one example of the irrational nature of the U.S. economic system: corporations are desperately searching for opportunities to invest their profits, and in new technology they have perfect vehicle for profitable investment. But often, com-panies opt instead to hold onto their profits even while there are new techno-logical advances and new products that could be explored.

Similarly, Baran and Sweezy noted that foreign investment cannot be counted on to absorb surplus in the long term (Baran and Sweezy 1966, 106). If foreign investment is profitable, and collectively it is, then it does not solve the surplus absorption problem because even greater profits from previous investments are coming back at the same time that new investments are being made. International flows of money in and out of the U.S. since they wrote their book confirm their argument. The profits from previous investments have been greater than new foreign investments for most years since 1966.

The end of the 1990s boom provided an example of what happens when profitable investment outlets dry up. During the mid-1990s, many firms and individuals invested in Internet startups and telecommunications technolo-gies that were profitable or showed promise. These included startups like Netscape, and wireless telephone technology. By the late 1990s, the "sure things" had been exhausted, yet firms and investors continued to pump money into these sectors. Investors fell over each other to get a piece of com-panies that had never even sold a product, much less made a profit, because they had money to invest and no better place to put it. What was the end result of pumping all this money into the technology sector? In 2000, the sec-tor crashed, slowing the rest of the economy. By 2002, stock prices had fallen to 1997 levels, and dozens of Internet startups and telecommunications com-panies were bankrupt.

Thus, the rising surplus generated by monopoly capitalism must find an outlet, but the investment opportunities are often insufficient. The ongoing problem of insufficient profitable investment outlets for the ever-increasing surplus means that *corporations must find other ways to dispose of the surplus.* One key way to dispose of the surplus is the sales effort: corporations pull out all the stops to sell more products, and simultaneously spend the expanding surplus.

The Sales Effort

Whether or not corporations find outlets for all their profits, the total investment in capital goods, and thus in capacity, constantly expands. Except in cases of deep recession, U.S. firms' overall capacity to produce output has expanded throughout our history. That means that in good times, and even in many bad times, firms continue to add capacity to their production systems. However, a problem looms: as capacity increases, firms must find additional buyers for their products. Consumers buy about two-thirds of all output in U.S. capitalism, and so corporations' survival rests largely on the maintenance and growth of consumer spending.

For the sales effort to work, consumers must have enough income to buy their two-thirds share of the output. But consumers' "purchasing power" is always restricted by the efforts of corporate owners to cut workers' wages and salaries, and get more of the pie for themselves. Most political economists see the current sluggishness of the U.S. economy as a consequence of the redistribution of income since the middle 1990s, when money shifted from most people in the U.S. to those in the top 10%. The bottom 90% of the population spends a greater percentage of its income than the top 10%, so redistributing income from the bottom to the top reduces total consumer spending.

Particularly when workers' budgets are restricted, corporations know that consumers must be persuaded ever more emphatically to buy additional new products. Accordingly, corporations must devote increasing funds to the sales effort. No part of the theory of monopoly capital has proven so absolutely on target than the prediction that this sales effort would be ever more deleterious to society at large.

The sales effort has assumed a huge role in monopoly capitalism to provide outlets for the expanding surplus. Advertising's share of GDP has increased by 86 percent since 1945. In the year 2000, U.S. firms spent well over $200 billion hawking products to consumers here and abroad, filling consumers' attics and basements to capacity.

One result of this explosion in advertising has been a drop in consumers' personal savings. The U.S. savings rate, which since 1940 has averaged 9 percent, reached a post-Depression low of 2.3 percent in 2001. The connection between the sales effort in the U.S. and low savings is direct: as F. M. Scherer documents, in the U.S. the savings rate is lower, and advertising spending as a percentage of GDP is higher, than in *any other industrialized nation* (Scherer 1990).

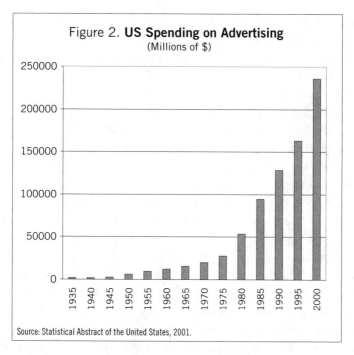

Figure 2. **US Spending on Advertising**
(Millions of $)

Source: Statistical Abstract of the United States, 2001.

As Baran and Sweezy observed, the sales effort has evolved over time. "Price competition," they argued, "has largely receded as a means of attracting the public's custom, and has yielded to new ways of sales promotion: advertising, variation of the products' appearance and packaging, planned obsolescence, model changes, credit schemes, and the like" (Baran and Sweezy 1966, 115). All of us are familiar with the marketing of fraudulent newness for repackaged items, goods that are designed to wear out quickly and need replacing, and ads connecting emotional attachments such as sex, love, family and adventure with products that cannot possibly deliver these things. We are discouraged from buying products for their utility value, from driving cars for their entire useful lives of 10 to 15 years, and from spending our money on things other than the latest consumer goods.

Baran and Sweezy added that the sales effort depends on the manipulative practice of branding. Because consumers know little about most of the products they buy, they are susceptible to labels, trademarks, and brand names which offer a sense of security in the product, whether real or imagined. Baran and Sweezy wrote that studies "show conclusively that individuals are influenced by advertising without being aware of that influence," and that "advertising induces the consumer to pay prices markedly higher than those charged for physically identical products which are not backed by suitable advertising techniques" (Baran and Sweezy 1966, 121). In other words, the sales effort in the 1960s, and more so now, is inherently dishonest and manipulative.

Advertising is an integral part of capitalism: it stimulates aggregate demand by creating new desires, it stimulates production, and it employs non-productive workers in ad agencies and the media. In all these ways, it offsets rising surpluses. Yet while the sales effort props up the system, Baran and Sweezy saw it as "a massive waste of resources, a continual drain on the consumer's income, and a systematic destruction of his freedom of choice between genuine alternatives" (Baran and Sweezy 1966, 122).

As Baran and Sweezy noted after Galbraith, the sales effort is also at war with everything else, which creates a social imbalance. It convinces us to ignore the slums and poverty, crumbling infrastructure and schools, and poisoned air and water. All of our public goods are sacrificed on the altar of products like SUVs—principal culprits in the advance of global warming. Is this truly a rational, optimal outcome that markets are generating— that optimal outcome that mainstream economists extol? Think about your own purchases of consumer goods, and consider some of the following data:

- On average, Americans now spend more than a year of their lives watching commercials.
- By age 20, the typical American will have seen 1 million commercials.
- On average, for every additional hour of television watched in the U.S., consumer spending increases by $200.
- Parents average 6 hours per week shopping, but only 40 minutes per week playing with their children. While some shopping is clearly necessary, shopping for recreation now occupies a more prominent role in families than spending quality time with children.

So, do you think Baran and Sweezy themselves were being rational when in 1966 they characterized the sales effort, and its results, as "wasteful" and "irrational"?

Government Absorption of Surplus

If investment falters and consumers don't buy enough to satisfy corporations, there is still one last great user of the surplus: the government. As monopoly capitalism has evolved, the government sector of every developed country, including the U.S., has expanded, absorbing more and more of the surplus. U.S. government spending as a percentage of GDP increased steadily from 10 percent in 1929 to 32 percent in 1995, before decreasing slightly to about 30 percent of GDP in 2001. Laissez-faire advocates who argue for lower taxes and less government spending miss a fundamental economic fact: if government spending and taxes were reduced, the private sector would have more money to spend, but it would also have more savings. When savings increase, firms must increase investment to prevent a recession. But as we discussed, there are problems with assuming that investment will automatically grow as the economy grows.

Much of the expansion of government spending in the U.S. has been in the area of military spending, which benefits corporations directly through defense contracts. Figure 3 starkly presents the extent to which the U.S. spending on defense exceeds that of other countries.

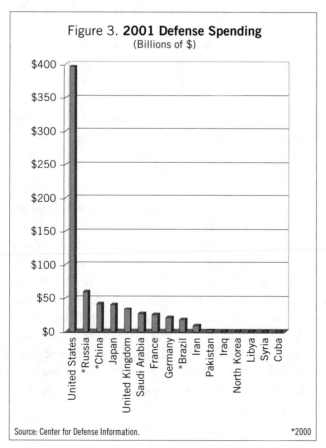

Figure 3. **2001 Defense Spending**
(Billions of $)

Source: Center for Defense Information.   *2000

Even given the events of September 11, 2001 (from which our massive expenditures on defense did not protect us), it is not unreasonable to wonder how much of this spending is truly necessary, and how much is politically demanded by what President Dwight Eisenhower called the "military industrial complex." He was referring to the powerful influence that defense contractors like General Electric, General Motors, and AT&T have on government decisions to buy armaments. For decades, politicians have approved spending on weapons that the military has not asked for and does not want, just to stay in the good graces of defense contractors. For example, according to Senator John McCain, Congress added $7 billion in unrequested spending to the fiscal 2001 Defense Appropriations bill. Thus, some types of government spending, like most of the sales effort, are examples of the "waste" of the surplus. While these funds could refurbish schools—most of which are substandard in urban areas—they are wasted on weapons that even the military does not want.

On top of defense contracts, our government funnels money to corporations in the form of corporate welfare – subsidies and tax breaks amounting to over $150 billion per year. In a recent analysis, Anwar Shaikh and Ahmet Tonak demonstrate that these enormous givebacks to corporations leave very little to fund programs for lower and middle-income people:

> By and large, it is the taxes of the working population that essentially pay for ... state expenditures on health, education, Social Security, unemployment, public assistance, housing, and a host of other social programs. (Shaikh and Tonak 2000, 254)

Though government officials often suggest that poor "welfare queens" are stealing the money of the rich, the truth is that the amount of money transferred from the rich to the poor is negligible, amounting to about one half of one percent of total employee compensation. Baran and Sweezy note that, "[u]ntil the New Deal period of the 1930s, there was not even any pretense that promoting the welfare of the lower classes was a responsibility of government" (Baran and Sweezy 1966, 159). The pretense now exists, but the U.S. is hardly bankrupting itself with its welfare program. In fact, spending on welfare in 2002 was less in real terms than it has been in over two decades. Increasingly, the biggest recipients of welfare spending are corporations, which make sure the government they largely control takes good care of their "needs."

In general, large multinational corporations and their owners support greater military outlays, greater spending on highways, corporate welfare, and other measures that lead to higher profits, but they oppose efforts to increase taxes to meet social needs. Baran and Sweezy argue that these spending priorities are at odds with the goal of creating a just society. They note:

> While massive government spending for education and welfare tends to undermine [the oligarchy's] privileged position, the opposite is true of military spending.... [M]ilitarization fosters all the reactionary and irrational forces in society, and inhibits or kills everything progressive and humane. Blind respect is engendered for authority; attitudes of docility and conformity are taught and enforced; dissent is treated as unpatriotic or even treasonable. (Baran and Sweezy 1966, 209)

Hence, while the government is a key absorber of surplus, the way the U.S. government absorbs surplus is typically most favorable to the giant firms, frequently wasteful, and contradictory to social needs.

We are left with an economy facing regular problems of too much surplus and inadequate levels of consumption and investment—for capitalists, that is, although not for human needs. The sales effort and government spending can absorb some of the surplus, although in the U.S., these are particularly wasteful forms of spending. And even these efforts often fall short. The problem of surplus absorption under monopoly capital is so severe that in the last 150 years, only epoch-making innovations such as the railroads, automobiles, and information technology (computers), along with the sales effort and militarization, have been able to stave off the depressive effects of monopoly capitalism. Even with these innovations, the economy still regularly falls into recessions as demand fails to sustain the system.

Despite all of these problems with monopoly capitalism–the wasteful squandering of the surplus, the control and manipulation of markets at the expense of consumers–the system might still be justifiable if it produced other benefits. In particular, it might be defensible if it created opportunities for creative work that most Marxists see as essential to a decent life. So before we make a final judgment about this economic system we have, we must ask: What is the nature of wage work in the world of monopoly capital?

LABOR AND MONOPOLY CAPITAL

Baran and Sweezy argued that Marx's theory of alienation aptly described workers' experiences in monopoly capitalism. In their book, they wrote:

> Men are ... being specialized and sorted, imprisoned in the narrow cells pre-
> pared for them by the division of labor, their faculties stunted and their minds
> diminished. And a threat to their security and peace of mind which already
> loomed large in Marx's day has grown in direct proportion to the spreading
> incidence and accelerated speed of technological change under monopoly
> capitalism. (Baran and Sweezy 1966, 343)

Baran and Sweezy went on to show in some detail how Marx's arguments about alienation remained applicable to U.S. capitalism. Not long after their book was published, Harry Braverman, one of their associates at Monthly Review Press, wrote *Labor and Monopoly Capital: The Degradation of Work in the Twentieth Century*. In 1996, David Gordon updated the story in another influential book, *Fat and Mean: The Corporate Squeeze of Working Americans and the Myth of Managerial "Downsizing."* We will focus briefly on these two books, which give a good picture of the lot of labor in monopoly capitalism. Many of these writers' conclusions about labor in our times were described with uncanny prescience by Marx in 1844 in his essay on Estranged Labor.

As is typical of capitalism, the problems begin with the accumulation process. The drive to accumulate more capital forces firms to invest in ever more productive techniques. One way to increase productivity and profits is to replace a highly skilled, expensive laborer with a machine operated by an unskilled laborer – a process known as *mechanization* and *deskilling*. When this happens, productivity rises, but workers are often left with mind-numbing jobs and low wages, or no job at all. Another way to increase productivity is by minutely controlling workers' time and motion so that they waste as little time as possible and perform every task in the most efficient manner. This is known simply as "speeding up the process." Again, the result is good for capitalists but bad for workers. Workers lose freedom, and their jobs involve less creativity; and these changes frequently lead to worse mental and physical health, as we explained in the chapter on social class. Braverman documents how this process has unfolded for 250 years, and makes this comment:

> [Deskilling means] the incessant breakdown of labor processes into simplified
> operations taught to workers as tasks. This leads to the conversion of the

greatest possible mass of labor into work of the most elementary form, labor from which all conceptual elements have been removed and along with them most of the skill, knowledge, and understanding of production processes.... [T]he more machinery that has been developed as an aid to labor, the more labor becomes a servant of machinery. (Braverman 1974, 319)

One of the profound ironies of capitalism is that machinery, which is particularly good at performing repetitive tasks, has not replaced monotonous labor. Instead, machines become the regulators of human work, forcing people to work faster and more efficiently at monotonous tasks. As we pointed out earlier, technology now exists that could allow shoes to be made entirely by machine. This would allow workers to do more creative work in design, programming, and overseeing the operations of machinery. Yet most shoes are made by low-wage workers huddling over old machines for long hours every day in unhealthy conditions. The design of production to enhance profit, rather than human creativity, means that most workers are consigned to a work life which denies them the opportunity to use their finest skills.

Braverman spent a good many pages describing mechanization and deskilling in the half century before he wrote his book. His examples included the following:

- Independent, self-supervising clerks and bookkeepers were converted into specialized workers who could not control or do the whole job.
- Skilled office workers, though once fairly independent, eventually became tied to a computer in a cubicle under the direct watch of a manager.
- Secretaries, doing multiple tasks in support of a manager or a few key employees, were replaced by (a) specialized workers in administrative support doing one or two tasks all day long (e.g., typing, copying, mailing, lay out, etc.), or (b) outsourced workers, hired through firms that specialize in generically-structured secretarial tasks. (Notably, outsourced workers often work on a contingent basis, and therefore without any job security.)
- Skilled butchers were replaced by huge, semi-automated meat processing centers.
- Skilled carpenters were largely supplanted by factories that make machine-made components, and reduce the craft to nailing and screwing these parts together.

With the advent of the powerful, small computer, there seems to be no limit to the process of replacing skilled jobs with computer-guided machines and less skilled workers. Unfortunately, as workers have discovered over the last several decades, there is a qualitative difference between a skilled job and less-skilled job involving a computer or machine. A skilled carpentry job involves creativity and craftsmanship, where the worker controls much of the labor process and, because of her skill, is valued by the employer. A worker stapling the same edge of the same type of cabinet using a computer-guided machine has no control over the pace of work, and the work involves no creativity or imagination. And this worker is less likely to be valued and treated well because she can be easily replaced.

In Braverman's view, the drive for greater productivity in monopoly capitalism demands a complete disregard for human beings, the environment, and macroeconomic health. As he put it:

> [T]he increasing productivity of labor is neither sought nor utilized by capitalism from the point of view of the satisfaction of human needs. Rather, powered by the needs of the capital accumulation process, it becomes a frenzied drive which approaches the level of a generalized social insanity. Never is any level of productivity regarded as sufficient. In the automobile industry, a constantly diminishing number of workers produces, decade by decade, a growing number of increasingly degraded products which, as they are placed upon the streets and highways, poison and disrupt the entire social atmosphere – while at the same time the cities where motor vehicles are produced become centers of degraded labor on the one hand and permanent unemployment on the other. It is a measure of the manner in which capitalist standards have diverged from human standards that this situation is seen as representing a high degree of "economic efficiency." (Braverman 1974, 141)

Automobile firms are content to produce unsafe products subject to rollovers and other correctable design flaws. They do so in greater and greater quantities while using less and less labor, usually without considering the human and environmental damage they cause. They apparently give no thought, either, to the fact that as they lay off workers and cut wages, they undermine aggregate demand. Finally, U.S. automobile firms are perfectly comfortable moving operations overseas to take advantage of lower production costs, despite the economic devastation they leave behind. Cities such as Flint and Detroit, which depended on automobile jobs, have been economically destroyed by the flight of auto manufacturers.

The destruction of U.S. auto jobs is part of a century-long decline in manufacturing jobs, as machines have replaced workers. Figure 4 indicates that since 1920 the percentage of workers in manufacturing industries (including mining and construction) has declined substantially, and workers have been forced into the service sector. Because U.S. unions have not traditionally organized the service sector, wages there tend to be lower; thus, wages stagnate as manufacturing jobs are eliminated and laborers are thrust into the service sector. This in turn encourages service-sector employers to use old-fashioned, labor-intensive methods.

The shift to a service economy has helped produce a devastating fall in pay and benefits for U.S. workers. As Figure 5 shows, real wages for non-supervisory workers in the U.S. were lower in 1999 than they were in 1971. And the total compensation of these workers, described Figure 5, has lagged behind that of workers in other developed countries, including our major trading partners, for the past two decades.

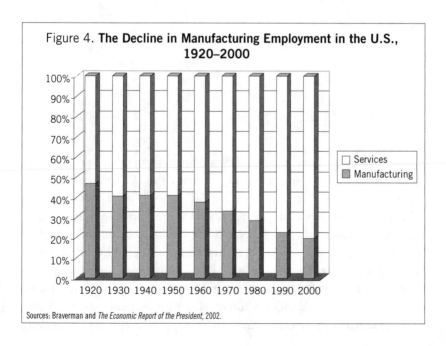

Figure 4. **The Decline in Manufacturing Employment in the U.S., 1920–2000**

Sources: Braverman and *The Economic Report of the President*, 2002.

Figure 5.

Country	Real Compensation Growth per year, 1979–1998
United Kingdom	1.72%
Germany	1.20%
France	1.00%
Italy	0.97%
Japan	0.93%
Canada	0.64%
United States	0.13%

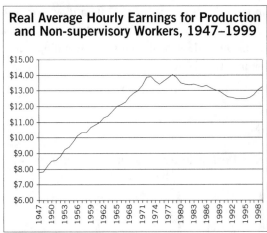

Real Average Hourly Earnings for Production and Non-supervisory Workers, 1947–1999

Source: Economic Policy Institute (www.epinet.org), 2002.

In addition to the relentless downward pressure on wages and the loss of worker control, independence, and creativity, the U.S. labor market has other characteristics that make it bad for workers. In his book *Fat and Mean*, David Gordon demonstrated that U.S. firms are also over-managed and more bureaucratic than firms in other developed countries. According to Gordon, in the early 1970s, U.S. corporations adopted a "stick" strategy to control workers. They broke unions and drove down wages to increase profits. They moved manufacturing operations overseas, outsourced their production to low-cost manufacturers (also often overseas), sped up work, and cut wages in their U.S. operations. In order to keep laborers working hard under these conditions, employers added numerous supervisors to monitor employees. This is, according to Gordon, the "dirty little secret" of the U.S. economy. In 1994, 17.3 million supervisors earned $1.3 trillion in compensation, or 20 percent of national income. How is it possible that we have so many people who boss other people around? As Gordon noted in a 1996 article:

> The basic principle is simple. If a labor-management system relies on hierarchical principles for managing and supervising its front-line employees on the shop and office floors, then it needs more than just the front-line supervisors who directly oversee these workers. Who keeps the supervisors honest? What guarantees that those supervisors won't be in cahoots with their charges? In such a hierarchy, you need supervisors to supervise the supervisors ... and supervisors above them...and managers to watch the higher-level supervisors ... and higher-level managers to watch the lower-level managers. (Gordon 1996b, 27)

Clearly, the only way to keep employees working hard under antagonistic, alienating conditions is to hire an army of supervisors to watch them carefully. Of course, as with so many of these aspects of capitalism, Marx was the first to observe that the factory was more analogous to the military, with several layers of hard-fisted sergeants keeping the troops in line.

Today, U.S. companies have more than three times as many supervisors per production worker as Germany and Japan, and five times as many as Sweden. This difference is explained by the more cooperative model of employment in these countries. Germany, Japan and Sweden employ the "carrot" method to increase productivity: workers are given job security, wage incentives, strong union representation, and a role in making important decisions. Such cooperative environments don't require many bosses because workers are less likely to hate and resent their jobs. Of course, even the "carrot" method of motivating workers is a far cry from the kind of cooperative workplaces that most political economists advocate, where employees would have much more control over all aspects of work. But in the U.S., workers are goaded into working hard via the employment of the "stick": low wages, which might erode productivity, are countered by constant monitoring and the threat of unemployment.

Unfortunately for the U.S., cooperative workplaces tend to be much more productive. As Gordon noted in the same article:

[T]hose economies with more cooperative systems of labor relations also have more rapid productivity growth rates. And with more rapid productivity growth, there is room for financing more productive investments, for affording more rapid wage growth, and for maintaining a competitive edge in the global economy. (Gordon 1996b, 33)

Once again, the U.S. system is efficient at generating profits, but it lags behind other developed countries in terms of other goals, such as productivity and creating a humane workplace.

CONCLUSION

Were Baran and Sweezy reasonable to end their book with a chapter called "The Irrational System" – a sustained, mostly negative critique of U.S. capitalism? Their central claims were as follows:

- The U.S. economy is dominated by huge multinational corporations which do everything in their power to stifle competition;
- Stifling competition involves rigging markets through collusion, mergers, and buying protection from the government;
- The drive to accumulate capital is inherent in the system, as past profits require investment opportunities to generate the highest possible return;
- But the very expansion caused by investment and capital accumulation contains within it the seeds of regular recessions as investment opportunities dry up and aggregate demand proves insufficient;
- The U.S. government willingly participates in the system, shoring up firms with billions of dollars in corporate welfare and defense contracts;
- Multinational corporations are sometimes innovative, but they also stifle innovation when it is more profitable to do so;
- Firms work to expand markets as much as possible, wasting hundreds of billions of dollars annually on dishonest attempts to manipulate consumers;
- U.S. corporations relentlessly lower costs via mechanization and attacks on labor, but the cost savings are not generally passed on to consumers;
- The relentless drive to lower costs results in mechanization, deskilling, alienation, and low wages for U.S. workers, culminating in the employment of the "stick" strategy to coerce alienated workers into working hard.

So, what do you think? Are these arguments believable? And, if they are, do they illuminate an economic system that is fundamentally irrational? It's an interesting question as we leave the 1990s, a decade during which Americans were relentlessly told by the media, the sales effort, and their own government, exactly what the economic mainstream has always maintained: that capitalism, though it has a flaw or two, is the best of all possible systems, a remarkable testament to rational thought and hard work. Maybe so, maybe not.

Perhaps, finally, we should ask another question. Has reading this, and the other chapters, made you wonder if there might be a better way to shape and develop the economy? One that is less unequal – politically and in every other way? One that doesn't systematically destroy its habitat? One that is, well, a bit more *rational* than our own? We know that after reading material in a book like this one, such questions are as inevitable as the loud honk just after the traffic light turns green. That is why we conclude this book with a description of Sweden's modern welfare state – what they call "social democracy." For decades, the Swedes have been constructing a humane, efficient alternative to our kind of cowboy capitalism where the biggest crooks get the biggest paychecks. We will now see what the Swedes have wrought.

Suggestions for Further Reading

Baiman, Ron, Heather Boushey, and Dawn Saunders, editors, *Political Economy and Contemporary Capitalism: Radical Perspectives on Economic Theory and Policy*. Armonk, NY: M. E. Sharpe, 2000.

Baran, Paul and Paul Sweezy, *Monopoly Capital: An Essay on the American Economic and Social Order*. New York: Monthly Review Press, 1966.

Braverman, Harry, *Labor and Monopoly Capital: The Degradation of Work in the Twentieth Century*. New York: Monthly Review Press, 1974.

Gordon, David, *Fat and Mean: The Corporate Squeeze of Working Americans and the Myth of Managerial Downsizing*, New York: Free Press, 1996.

Gordon, David, "Underpaid Workers, Bloated Corporations: Two Pieces in the Puzzle of U.S. Economic Decline," *Dissent*, Vol. 43, Spring 1996, 23-34.

8
The Middle Way: Swedish Social Democracy*

[In Sweden] the state, the consumer, and the producer have intervened to make capitalism "work" in a reasonable way for the greatest good of the whole nation .... That this constitutes a ... middle course seems to me obvious; it is a course between the absolute socialization of Russia [the USSR] and the end development of capitalism in America. In Russia ... the rulers of the state attempted to make all of life conform to an idea, an ideal. In the United States the profit motive was put above every other consideration and it worked to the end of blind self-destruction. (Childs 1936, 143-4)

INTRODUCTION

What Childs describes in the quotation above are two forms of economic extremism. The Soviet Union developed an economic system based on command-style communism, where the state controlled almost all aspects of the economy, while the United States over the course of its history has always had a market system, where capitalists and individuals made most economic decisions. What we will discuss below is an example of what Marquis Childs refers to as the *middle way* between command communism and unregulated capitalism: *social democracy*. Sweden developed an economic system that successfully incorporated many of the ideas of Marx, Keynes, and Veblen into the economy. As a result, we can see in Sweden's system the practical application of many of the ideas of these influential thinkers. The Swedes created a society that demonstrates impressive levels of equality, stability, and productivity.

The Social Democratic Labor Party (Socialdemokratiska Arbetarparti, or SAP) that governed Sweden for most of the twentieth century took its cue from Marx, and actively worked to make Sweden an egalitarian society where

*Our thanks to Ellen Campbell, who helped with the research and writing of this chapter.

there was little poverty and where all persons had the opportunity to build a good life for themselves. The SAP believed that all Swedish citizens should have the right to a decent job, to security in their old-age, to health care, to day care, to a decent standard of living. These rights evolved over the years through the ongoing implementation of innovative policies, which we will show in our brief sketch of Sweden's economic history.

In Sweden's system we also see the application of the ideas of John Maynard Keynes. Sweden was the first industrialized nation to employ Keynesian policies. Moreover, Swedish economists took Keynes' ideas much further than most. During the 1920s, the Swedish government made some small efforts at stabilizing the economy, such as creating low-wage private-sector jobs for the unemployed. But during the Great Depression of the 1930s, under the direction of the "Stockholm school" of economists, the Swedish government began a large-scale implementation of Keynesian stabilization policies.[37] By 1936, the year Keynes' *General Theory* was published, when other developed countries had only begun to consider Keynes' ideas viable, Sweden had already successfully used these stabilization policies to create jobs and raise wages to their pre-Depression level. Beginning in the 1950s, Sweden took even bolder steps, carefully managing the economy so that *even in recessions*, the unemployment rate remained exceptionally low.

Sweden also incorporated the ideas of Thorstein Veblen into its system. Sweden sought to limit the predatory and wasteful aspects of capitalism, such as advertising; and instead emphasized the productive side of the economy. For instance, the media in Sweden is publicly owned and operated, and high-quality programming is aired without commercials. Likewise, companies in Sweden are allowed to keep their profits as long as they are reinvested in productive activities, but wasteful or destructive practices, such as polluting and downsizing, are penalized.

In short, Sweden has a remarkable economic system that is worthy of careful study, as it provides an interesting counterpart both to the command economies of the former Soviet bloc and the unregulated market economies of the United States and Japan. In what follows below, we will outline what it means to have an economic system described as "social democracy." We then take you through a sketch of Sweden's economic history, which describes the evolution of what came to be called the "Swedish model" or the "Middle Way." Finally, we make the argument that Swedish socialism is a humane, productive, and civilized economic system that improves upon many aspects of the U.S. economy. We begin by exploring the curious resistance to forms of socialism seen in America.

WHAT IS A SOCIAL DEMOCRACY?

The terms used to describe the Swedish economic system, as a rule, do not carry positive connotations for Americans. For example, the term "socialism" often draws a suspicious reaction, as does the idea of a "big government" interfering with the "free" market. Consider your own reaction when you see or hear the word "socialism." Does it conjure images of Communist Russia? Anti-Americanism? A vast and inefficient bureaucracy that limits personal freedom and rights?

But what is the *real* meaning of "socialism"? In a 1967 Webster's dictionary, socialism is defined as "any of various economic and political theories advocating collective or governmental ownership and administration of the means of production and distribution of private property." Yet in a 1923 Webster's dictionary, the definition of socialism is "political and economic theory of social reorganization, the essential feature of which is governmental control of economic activities, to the end that competition shall give way to cooperation and that the opportunities of life and the rewards of labor shall be equitably apportioned..." Consider the difference between these two definitions. What happened to the meaning of this word over a period of 44 years? In the early 1900s, the philosophy of socialism was a response to the philosophy of individualism, a *cultural* philosophy and movement that encouraged self-awareness and personal gain (greed). Therefore, this earlier "socialism" was not strictly political, but social, cultural, and essentially philosophical. However, over time its meaning became more and more politically extreme as the opponents of socialism sought to demonize it. As one can see, we have so politicized the term over the years that our more contemporary dictionaries, our supposedly non-biased sources for meaning, have lost sight of its roots and define it only in political terms.

The word "democratic" has also been politicized over the years. In the United States, we promote democracy as government by and for the people. Yet there are other possible applications of democracy. Democracy in the workplace can mean workers having input into how things are produced and how the workplace is run. Democracy in a community can mean people deciding how to allocate health care and jobs. The U.S. focus on *political* democracy, especially electoral activity, over and above other arenas for democratic action, demonstrates the extent to which we narrowly define social philosophies in purely political terms. Similarly, the word "freedom" is heavily politicized in the United States. We are used to referring to "free markets," where the word "free" applies to freedom from a meddling government. But freedom comes in many forms, and historically Sweden's Social Democrats have been more concerned with a broader range of freedoms: freedom from the domination of an employer, from poverty, from the ravages of a recession.

In this essay we will challenge the traditional definitions of "socialism," "democracy" and "freedom" by moving beyond the simplistic, *politicized* uses of these terms. Forget the Republican-Democrat, right-left, conservative-liberal labels we have been trained to apply. Instead, keep in mind the philosophies that originated the meanings of these words. Unlike the caricature of socialism as a massive bureaucracy controlling every aspect of our lives, socialism is an economic system designed to promote cooperation, equality, and a high standard of living, but not necessarily at the expense of individualism. Social Democracy means the freedom for people to control collectively many aspects of their lives, not simply to choose political leaders. As we trace the evolution of the Swedish model below, we will see an example of real, democratic socialism in practice.

THE ORIGINS OF THE SWEDISH "MODEL": 1847-1932

Many books and articles written about Sweden's economic system refer to it as the "Swedish Model." Implied in the word "model" is the idea that this was an experiment, something planned by a centralized group of intellectuals, and then implemented for the world to observe and critique. This was not the case. Sweden's system developed slowly but persistently throughout the twentieth century as a result of many decisions made by many groups striving toward the same goals of equality and quality of life. These groups included the business community, unions, politicians as well as scholars. In other words, the majority of Swedish citizens built this socioeconomic structure democratically over time.

Sweden's democratically created socioeconomic system is also referred to as a "welfare" state. "Welfare" is another term that has been politically demonized. But the fact that Sweden has a welfare state does not mean that its populace doesn't have to work because the government supports it, or that poverty is so pervasive that widespread welfare benefits are required just to keep its citizens in shoes. It means exactly what it says: "welfare" is to "fare well." In other words, the welfare state is designed for the benefit of the whole society.

Historically, Sweden's welfare state evolved from a society that was admirably enlightened long before its Western counterparts, and even before the Social Democrats first came to power in 1920. In 1847 and 1853 Sweden passed "poor relief laws," taking the first step toward implementing its social philosophy of helping those whose impoverished circumstances were beyond their control. In contrast, most of Europe still had debtors' prisons and indentured servitude at this time: people who were too poor to pay their debts were imprisoned, enslaved, or forced into "workhouses" to work for a pittance. As examples, Paris had the Bastille, most of the first colonists in America were indentured servants from Europe, and Australia was a penal colony for Britain's criminals, many of them debtors. Whether it was a mother of three whose husband died, or a worker who was injured and disabled, the cause of indebtedness was irrelevant. The inability to pay one's debts in these countries was treated as a willful, punishable act. But Sweden recognized that poverty was usually neither willful nor deserving of punishment. The Swedes saw poverty as a product of economic factors, and began taking responsibility for helping their people out of poverty.

The Social Democratic Labor Party (SAP) was founded in 1889. Around this time, the philosophy that produced the "poor relief laws" began to mature and expand. Instead of assessing the health of their economic system through stock prices and GDP, the Swedes began to develop a system wherein the health and value of the economy was gauged by the quality of life of its entire population. As early as 1913, Sweden's Liberal Party government (non-socialist), with the support of the populace, began broadening the range of social benefits. It took most other developed countries until the Great Depression of the 1930s to take similar steps.

In contrast, at the turn of the century Mark Twain coined the phrase, the "Gilded Age," to describe the excesses and decadence of wealthy American society. This was when the most powerful people in the American economy, appropriately termed the "robber barons," controlled the direction of our country. It was the economic climax of the Industrial Revolution in the U.S., and the U.S. was an exceedingly wealthy nation—or at least a few people were wealthy. The Gettys, Rockefellers, Vanderbilts, Goulds, et al., held virtual monopolies on our natural resources, banks and railroads, and did business without any significant government intervention. There were few corporate taxes or regulations and no laws to protect labor.

Today we take our labor laws for granted, but we can try to imagine life for the worker who didn't have the protection of the forty-hour work week, or health benefits, or safety in the work environment, or the minimum wage. In the late nineteenth century, workers had few rights in the workplace; those who weren't in unions—the great majority—were completely at the mercy of the employer who understood that the most efficient way to increase profits was to cut the costs of labor, to lengthen the workday, and even to employ children. One out of six American children under the age of 16 worked to support the family, spending twelve-hour days in unventilated, poorly lit mills, operating dangerous machinery without breaks.

This was also a time in American history when the difference in quality of life between those who owned the means of production and those who did not, was strikingly evident. Those who owned property, along with the few who could afford an education, had the means to consume lavishly; the lines of class division were never clearer. But for the poor of the Gilded Age, a lack of income could have devastating consequences. Being poor meant not being able to pay a doctor when sick (there was no medical insurance) or to put food on the table (there were no programs in the United States to keep people from starving).

To view the poles of this class division, begin with Newport, Rhode Island, the lovely ocean resort where the robber barons built their summer homes. Their architectural beauty is breathtaking – imported Italian marble, elaborate frescoes, exotic woods, rare works of art, crystal and gilt. They installed in these palaces every known amenity and luxury, staffed them with dozens of servants, and hosted only the world's most wealthy elite for their soirees. America's laborers, who paid for these displays of decadence with their sweat and sometimes their lives, lived in a very different world. They lived in city slums that a state board of health described as "choked up with garbage, filth and mud." Workers daring to strike against low pay and poor working conditions were sometimes killed, or driven from their homes. In 1886, after sugar laborers went on strike asking for a wage of one dollar a day, thirty were killed and hundreds wounded by local authorities. In the Homestead strike of 1892 at the Carnegie Steel plant, laborers were killed, the state brought in the militia, and the strikers were arrested. Time and again, employers and the government suppressed any efforts by laborers to improve their lot.

The schools, churches and popular literature of the time taught that "to be rich was a sign of superiority, to be poor a sign of personal failure...." This attitude is reflected in the words of James Mellon's father, who declared, after his son paid a substitute only $300 to take his place in the Civil War, that "a man may be a patriot without risking his own life or sacrificing his health. There are plenty of lives less valuable." John Rockefeller, Andrew Carnegie, Philip Armour, and Jay Gould also hired substitute soldiers to go to war for them. These cowardly men were our "industrial giants."

This was laissez-faire capitalism at its *worst*. U.S. governments of this era believed that the economy should be left alone, relying on the arguments of Adam Smith, despite the fact that the economy in the late 1800s little resembled the early industrial economy of Smith's era. Competition was no longer atomistic due to the massive size of corporations, and the "invisible hand" discriminated according to wealth and privilege.

At the same time that the United States became increasingly mired in inequality at every level of society, Sweden took steps toward the development of a more humane, egalitarian system. The Liberal Party government passed the National Pension Act in 1913 to provide security for the aged, more than twenty years before the United States implemented its own social security system. In 1918 a Liberal-SAP coalition government passed a new poor law, turning the responsibility of assisting anyone in need over to local governments, while the central government contributed administrative support. This law was to remain the cornerstone of Sweden's assistance programs for the next 40 years.

By 1918, America had made only a few changes in an effort to dampen the ravages of uncontrolled capitalism, and these small efforts targeted the corporations, not the people. One was corporate taxation, and another was the Sherman Anti-Trust Act, used to inhibit only the worst abuses of the most obvious monopolies. As is typical of the United States, the government did not take actions directly to improve the quality of life for the majority, but acted indirectly, hoping to improve their lot by forcing business to mend its ways. The power and responsibility for the welfare of the worker was still solely in the hands of industry, whose main concern was, of course, profit. In the 1930s, after America's unregulated capitalism burned itself out in the form of the Great Depression, the United States finally implemented some modest social policies. But America spent ten years trying to repair the devastation caused by the Depression, and endured massive suffering in the process. Sweden largely avoided these problems because of its welfare state and Keynesian policies.

THE SAP'S FUNCTIONAL SOCIALISM: 1932-1968

Social and Political Philosophy

The SAP began to influence economic policy immediately after its formation in 1889. At that point, it stated its guiding principles as follows:

1. Legislation to guarantee to every Swedish citizen a simple and decent standard of living...[Social Democrats] hold that it is the duty of society to provide for the needs of the aged, invalids, widows, and those who have lost their income through no fault of their own.
2. Housing and child benefits for needy families so that they should not be forced to lower their standard of living because they have children to raise. [The] idea is to distribute the expense over the entire population as a collective responsibility.
3. Social welfare to be...the inherent right of every citizen irrespective of his financial status.

In order to implement its philosophy, the SAP was forced to compromise with employers and political opponents. Compromise was possible because although the philosophy behind the SAP's ideas was socialist in nature, the SAP was not dogmatic or rigid. The Social Democrats pursued the goal of a better life for all Swedes, and allowed the economy to operate within a capitalist system as long as it could achieve this goal.

The Social Democrats saw the problems associated with free-market as well as with state-controlled systems. From 1920 to 1932, recessions plagued Sweden's free-market economy as a succession of governments, some including the SAP, failed to stabilize the economy adequately. There was also an unequal distribution of income and wealth, and a significant percentage of the population lived in poverty. But the SAP did not adhere to the idea of state-controlled production in response to these problems, fearing the inefficiency that could come from a command-style economy. Instead, once the SAP was firmly entrenched as Sweden's ruling party in 1932, it allowed the capitalist norm of private ownership to continue, intervening in the economy whenever the needs of labor were not met. As in the U.S. capitalist system, there were wealthy entrepreneurs who owned and controlled much of Swedish industry, but the SAP limited their power and influence. The SAP devised taxes on income and profits so that it was profitable for business owners to reinvest in productive activities and to create jobs. Entrepreneurs were allowed to make a fortune in Sweden, but only if they expanded employment, produced socially useful products, and limited the destruction of the environment. Thus the SAP permitted the private sector to pursue profits as long as firms achieved social goals. In some sectors, the SAP organized consumer and producer cooperatives, and in other sectors, such as health care, dental care and child care, the SAP socialized the provision of services, but overall the SAP preserved private ownership.

The Social Democrats established early on that equality and economic growth were not necessarily incompatible. Conservative Swedish economists who followed the ideas of Adam Smith insisted that some measure of inequality was necessary to stimulate growth: if investors, business owners, and the wealthy in general were not allowed to keep what they earned, they would have no incentive to continue investing and growth would stagnate. Thus they argued that measures to improve equality through high taxation of corporations and wealthy individuals would slow growth. Swedish Social Democrats rejected this argument, and demonstrated that public investment, stability, and careful macroeconomic management could stimulate growth, which would ultimately be very profitable for industry and private individuals, providing incentives for continued investment. The Social Democrats prevailed and were able to win over industry leaders to this approach.

By no means did the Social Democrats have free rein when they came into power. The democratic electoral process remained in place, with political parties (socialist and non-socialist) and special interest groups wielding influence and power, keeping partisan measures from dominating the political arena. Powerful interest groups included both labor unions and employers' associations, and all actors within the economic system were included in the decision-making process for negotiating mutually beneficial policy and legislation. The leaders of the SAP could not have achieved their egalitarian goals without the cooperation of employers, and the fact that employers cooperated indicates the benefits all parties realized in a democratic socialist economy. Thus through pragmatism and compromise, the SAP gradually implemented socialist policies and ideals *without* a revolution or large-scale nationalization. It was the first socialist party in the world to do so.

De-Commodification
One of the primary (socialist) goals of the SAP was the de-commodification of the Swedish people. "De-commodification" meant taking people, and what they needed to live decent lives, out of the marketplace as mere commodities to be bought and sold. To Marx, treating people as commodities—buying and

selling labor—is exploitative, because the market value of people is measured simply by how much economic profit (surplus value) they produce. De-commodifying people meant ensuring that all people had decent lives, irrespective of market outcomes.

People need certain basic goods and services in order to live full lives. In the SAP principles mentioned above, for example, child-care is treated as a fundamental need because, as is stated, "[Swedish citizens] should not be forced to lower their standard of living because they have children to raise." In many market systems, families that have children must lower their standard of living because, in paying for the costs associated with caring for and raising children, they have less money to spend on other goods. In the United States, child-care is sold as a commodity only to families that can afford the service. When examined objectively, privatizing childcare is an exploitative practice that impacts the lower wage earners most dramatically.

The same can be said for housing, medical care, dental care, and services for the disabled. In an unregulated market system, these fundamental needs are at the mercy of for-profit industries where the bottom line, and not quality of life, is the only concern, and not everyone can purchase these necessary items. In the United States, those who cannot pay for these basic, life-sustaining services are often forced to go without, and suffer the consequences. But Sweden does not choose to value its people by such standards, and will not deny these necessities to those without money. All Swedish citizens have the *right* to essential goods and services under the Swedish welfare state.

After the Social Democrats were voted into power in 1932, they introduced legislation that began to fulfill the principles of de-commodification embedded in their social philosophy. Augmenting the Pension Act of 1913 and the Poor Law of 1918, the SAP instituted housing subsidies and a national pension scheme in 1935, and in 1938 added socialized dental care. By the 1950s, the SAP had installed a national health plan and laid the foundation for a comprehensive network of de-commodified rights for all Swedish citizens.

To this point, the provisions mentioned are those needed to survive physically. But the SAP wanted to guarantee a full *quality* of life as well. Their two main goals when they came into power were *equalization* and *integration*. Equalization refers to a better distribution of wealth and income, and integration refers not to racial or ethnic issues, but to issues of social class. The primary objective in this realm was full employment. Putting everyone to work would diminish the exploitation of labor, reduce income inequality, and thereby further reduce class divisions. This would also eliminate what Marx referred to as the "reserve army of the unemployed." As we will describe in more detail below, policies designed to achieve full employment were put into action after World War II, policies that went far beyond simple stabilization of the economy and provision of basic services.

Equalization and integration were also accomplished through investment in *human capital*. This was, and is, primarily accomplished through education. Although the primary reforms in the Swedish educational systems took place between the 1950s and 1970s, education had for a long time been considered vital to the well-being of the nation. Schooling is free at all levels in Sweden; as a result, the inequality seen in the U.S., for instance, of personal wealth buying the best education, is non-existent. All citizens are entitled to the best education, regardless of financial status, giving every person a start from a level playing field. Sweden's population is one of the most widely and best educated in the world.

As we can see, the "Swedish model" was not a planned experiment, but in fact an evolutionary process that resulted from a series of actions over long periods of time. And although the pace of structural change picked up in the 1950s, the groundwork had been in place since 1889.

Economic Stabilization and Full Employment

Most countries instituted Keynesian stabilization policies, designed to boost spending and create jobs during recessions, following the advent of the Great Depression. As noted above, Sweden's stabilization efforts preceded the Depression. The national pension system of 1913 and the comprehensive poor law of 1918 both served to boost spending when times were tough, and the Swedes instituted policies to stabilize employment as early as the 1920s. Stabilization policies in the 1930s were even more aggressive and successful. But because capital was privately owned, there was still a natural dependency on industry to stimulate the economy. The state recognized this, and a pattern of compromise between capital, labor, and the government became the method for ensuring stability, equality and growth within a highly regulated, but still capitalist system.

The Swedish government implemented an extensive stabilization policy beginning in the 1930s, spending money counter-cyclically. When an economy enters a recession, tax revenues decrease as businesses downsize and workers lose jobs. In such circumstances, many governments decrease spending to counter the reduction in tax revenues, thereby keeping the budget balanced. But cuts in government spending during a recession put even more people out of work, making the recession even worse. Instead, Sweden *increased* spending in recessions by borrowing money to invest in public works projects, to train workers and to create jobs. This way, the flow of production and income was stabilized, spending didn't decrease dramatically in recessions, industry was encouraged to invest, and the economy was bolstered until industry's investments brought employment back to normal levels.

In addition to using government spending to stave off recessions, the Swedish government instituted a counter-cyclical investment tax credit system called the Investment Reserve in 1938. Firms were allowed to deposit funds with the government which could be invested tax free if invested *in Sweden at specified times*—during a recession. If invested at another time, the firm would have to pay taxes on the funds. Thus the government encouraged the private sector to invest counter-cyclically, stabilizing the economy even further.

In the 1950s, the Rehn-Meidner plan, named after its two economist authors, was implemented to manage the economy more carefully. Included in the plan were two main areas: the solidaristic wage policy, and active labor policies. The primary goal of this plan was to ensure *full employment.*

In the U.S., full employment (or "the natural rate of unemployment") is considered to be an unemployment rate of about 5.5%. Many mainstream economists believe that an unemployment rate of less than 5.5% guarantees inflation. Labor becomes more powerful when unemployment is low because there are fewer workers available to fill jobs, and at the same time firms need labor to increase production because more goods are sold when more people are employed. Workers are able to demand wage increases, thereby driving up costs. In theory, a wage-price spiral would result from dramatically low unemployment: labor's demand for higher wages forces business to raise prices to cover the higher cost of labor; the higher prices of goods force workers to demand even higher wages, and so on. But this theory, that low unemployment always causes inflation, does not necessarily hold true.

With cooperation between unions, employers' associations, and the government, unemployment in Sweden exceeded 3% only *three times* from 1951 to 1991, without causing significant inflation. The agreement was that real wages were increased annually at the rate of one-half percent below the national average rate of labor productivity growth. This meant that if workers increased their productivity by 3%, they would receive a raise of 2.5%, and employers would keep the rest. This formula insured that workers benefited from increases in productivity but also guaranteed that wages did not increase too quickly, thus keeping inflation in check.[38] In other words, wages were voluntarily limited by labor unions so that they wouldn't increase faster than productivity, keeping inflationary pressures down, despite full employment and the accompanying power that a tight labor market gives to unions. As a result, workers did not need to strike to force pay increases, and workers and employers were cooperative rather than antagonistic—both labor and capital had a direct incentive to increase productivity since both groups benefited. Following this pattern of compromise, Sweden had full employment without spiraling inflation for 40 years (1951-1991) and laborers received a substantial share of the benefits from economic growth, equalizing incomes to a significant degree. Sweden's experiences call into question both the theory that equality and growth aren't compatible, as well as the assumption that full employment and low inflation aren't possible. Sweden offers a striking contrast to the U.S. system where productivity increases by laborers often do *not* result in higher wages. From 1973 to 1997, the average productivity of a U.S. worker increased by 34%, but average wages for workers actually *declined* by 14%. U.S. workers actually lost ground when they increased productivity!

Solidaristic Wage Policy

Another key economic policy was Sweden's *solidaristic wage policy*. This meant equal pay for equal work: all workers at all firms doing the same type of work would be paid the wages that workers in the most efficient, internationally competitive firms were paid. Wages were set nationally in a centralized bargaining process that included employers, labor unions, and the government. The equalization of wages reduced competition between workers, creating a more cooperative environment for labor and removing the inequality of less pay for comparable work. An important byproduct of this policy was that women began receiving pay equal to men. All workers then received the same annual wage increases, based on productivity growth. A provision was later added to the solidaristic wage policy to increase the wages of low-wage workers faster than the rest, to make Sweden even more equal.

Another consequence of the solidaristic wage policy was that firms experiencing rapid growth did not have to raise wages faster than other firms did. Typically, firms in growing industries (such as 1990s high-tech firms in the United States) have to pay laborers a premium in order to keep them. But because of the solidarity wage policy in Sweden, the best, most competitive firms did not have to grant additional wage increases when they were doing well, allowing them to make large profits. Meanwhile, firms experiencing hard times were not able to reduce wages. As an example, in a year with 3% average productivity growth, a firm that increased productivity by 10% would only have to raise wages by the national rate of 2.5% (one-half percent below the average rate of productivity growth). A firm with only 1% productivity growth would still have to increase wages at the same rate of 2.5%. The former firm earns excess profits, while the latter firm loses money. Thus the solidaristic wage policy caused expanding industries to do better, and contracting industries to struggle even more. The result was a reallocation of capital to profitable, expanding industries from contracting industries. The systematic elimination of the least efficient, least profitable firms, and the promotion of the most productive firms, was an explicit goal of the SAP – an attempt to encourage the best businesses with the greatest comparative advantage. And it succeeded: from 1950-1970, the golden age of U.S. Keynesian capitalism, Sweden's per capita GDP increased by an average of 4% per year, higher even than the U.S. growth rate of 3.5%. Sweden found that the economy's overall productivity improved as the firms that increased productivity gained excess profits, which were then pumped back into the firm, generating economic growth. The unions, employers associations and government, working to energize the economy, supported this reallocation of capital.

An interesting point here is that declining industries were not "bailed out" by the government, but if they failed, they were reabsorbed by successful industries. This harsh but realistic approach kept the economy growing and competitive. Instead of pouring funds into dying industries, investing resources in growth industries stimulated productivity and improved competitiveness. This is one of the reasons why Sweden's economy performed successfully even with all of the restrictions on corporate behavior imposed by the SAP.

Active Labor Market Policies
Another way of maintaining full employment was via *active labor market policies*. For those who became unemployed, there were generous unemployment benefits with a time limit, training and education with a stipend, and money

for relocation costs if needed. If a worker was still unemployed when the benefits ended, there was employment available in short term public works projects (the Swedish government established itself as the "employer of last resort" for those workers who could not find work after a certain period of time). Unemployed Swedish workers were given money, time, training, and moving assistance to make sure they could find a good job to replace the one they lost. And if they could not find a job, they were put to work in community projects that needed attention.

Active labor market policies, along with stabilization policies, produced full employment without accelerating inflation in Sweden from 1951 to 1991, as noted above. Full employment is beneficial to any economic system: all workers remain productive, the stream of income and spending supports the economy, industry profits and invests, tax revenues support the government, which in turn supports the full employment system, resulting in a self-sustaining economy in which everyone benefits. The cooperation between labor, capital and the government in the institution of the "middle way," and the benefits that each group received as a result of it, helps to explain the widespread support in Sweden for a socialist model of development that is almost inconceivable in the United States. By 1968, Sweden's system was the envy of much of the world. Swedish firms were internationally competitive, Swedish workers were among the best paid in the world, and poverty and homelessness were eliminated. But labor leaders still thought Sweden could be improved.

SWEDEN BECOMES MORE SOCIALIST: THE LABOR OFFENSIVE, 1968-1976

Despite the relative generosity of the Swedish welfare state, labor leaders during this period decided that is was time for Sweden to become even more socialist in nature. They were dismayed at the vast profits being earned by Sweden's huge transnational corporations that in part resulted from the solidarity wage policy that controlled wage increases at the most profitable firms. The SAP believed that the vast wealth being generated for a few individuals was unfair and threatened the integrity of the system. Labor wanted to negotiate a fairer distribution of the excess profits that firms were receiving because of union wage restraint.

Furthermore, labor leaders became increasingly concerned with the boring, stressful jobs, typical in Swedish industries, that Marx would describe as alienating in nature. In keeping with the idea that all Swedes have the right to *meaningful* work, labor leaders began to push for greater labor control over the workplace. A series of strikes and work slowdowns led to concessions from employers and workers did gain more control over the workplace. Factories were redesigned to be more flexible, to increase efficiency, and to give workers more control over the work process. Jobs were rotated so that no one laborer was stuck with a particularly dull task for too long a period; the most repetitive jobs were mechanized and workers were retrained for more highly skilled work. Workers also gained more control over job security and promotion. Thus Swedish workers were able to avoid many of the negative consequences of deskilling that Marx saw as an inevitable part of capitalism.

During this period, the SAP also increased the benefits provided to Swedish citizens. Employees were given the right to take educational leaves to upgrade their skills or change professions, health benefits and industrial safety measures were expanded, and the government instituted new programs to promote gender equality. The SAP also began to move more explicitly towards traditional socialism during this period through the institution of *wage earner funds*: employee investment funds that were to be funded by taxes on corporate profits. The SAP intended the funds to be used to buy up shares of companies, so workers could gradually gain a voice in all business decisions. Once labor leaders became owners, they would sit on corporate boards and directly influence corporate decision making. Laborers could then keep firms from moving overseas, or downsizing workers unnecessarily. The funds would also inject Swedish firms with new capital for investment, and gradually generate a more equitable distribution of ownership and wealth as workers became part owners, and eventually majority owners, in all large Swedish firms. Note that although the principle of worker ownership of the means of production is certainly a Marxist concept, the Swedish vision differed from that of the Soviet Union. The Swedish vision was for workers at each firm to control how it was run. This differs from the Soviet approach in which a centralized government bureaucracy controlled the direction of all firms.

Swedish economist G. Adler-Karlsson eloquently stated the ideals behind the push for wage earner funds:

> Let us look upon our capitalists in the same way as we have looked upon our kings in Scandinavia. A hundred years ago a Scandinavian king carried a lot of power. Fifty years ago he still had considerable power. According to our constitutions the king still has equally as much formal power as a hundred years ago, but today he is in fact powerless. We have done this without dangerous

and disruptive internal fights. Let us in the same manner avoid the even more dangerous contests which are unavoidable if we enter the road of formal socialization. Let us instead strip and divest our present capitalists of one after another of their ownership functions. Let us give them a new dress, but one similar to that of the famous emperor in Hans Christian Andersen's tale. After a few decades they will then remain, perhaps formally as kings but in reality as naked symbols of a passed and inferior development stage. (Adler-Karlsson 1970, 95-6)

Thus the SAP pushed for the gradual transition from highly regulated private ownership to a socialization of the means of production in the hands of the working class—a peaceful transition to socialism. As one can tell from Adler-Karlsson's statement, the SAP believed that socializing the means of production would lead to a superior society. But it was not to be. Wage earner funds were controversial even within the SAP, and they were never fully instituted. Nevertheless, the SAP was able to extend the welfare state during this period, as noted above.

Unfortunately, these demands by labor and concessions by employers came at a time when the world was facing a global recession. The oil crisis of 1973 began a period of world-wide economic instability that would change the economic landscape of many industrialized nations. Sweden in particular suffered, because it was totally dependent on imported oil as its energy source. Inflation reached 10% in 1974, unemployment increased, and capital experienced rapidly rising costs in a highly regulated system that limited the ability of a firm to escape these high costs. This is when profound economic, political and welfare changes began to take place, resulting in what some have termed "the decline of the Swedish model."

CAPITAL'S OFFENSIVE, 1976-1999

The economic difficulties of the early 1970s caused Swedish voters to oust the SAP and elect a center-right government that was more conservative, and more sympathetic to industry. This ushered in an era in which big corporations successfully fought to roll back taxes and the welfare state. The erosion of the Swedish system began when employers abandoned the practice of centralized bargaining with labor that had been in existence since 1938. Instead, they turned to bargaining individually with their labor unions, undermining the solidaristic wage policy that had been a cornerstone of Swedish social democracy. The "divide and conquer" strategy was somewhat successful. With such a vital element of the system disempowered, corporations excluded workers more and more from the decision-making process, and increasingly moved operations overseas.

Along with the center-right government, employers worked to cut taxes and decrease government spending and government control over the economy. For example, the investment tax credit system, which gave businesses incentives to invest during recessions, was abolished. Corporations were now free to invest whenever they wished without tax penalties. But an even more significant change was the deregulation of capital markets in the 1980s, as Swedish firms were allowed to invest abroad instead of just at home, and funds could be moved freely internationally for the first time in many years. The result of the newfound ability of capital to invest wherever it wanted, and tax cuts that increased the amount of money at capital's disposal, was a boom in asset markets. Money flowed rapidly into real estate, art, and other speculative, non-productive assets, resulting in huge price increases for these assets—a speculative boom. Unfortunately, as spending increased but productivity did not, an overheated economy resulted, generating inflation as high as 10.5% in 1990. Gregg Olsen describes the debacle that followed:

> The Swedish credit market . . . was rapidly deregulated throughout the 1980s. By the end of the decade, Sweden's long standing system of controls over foreign investment and exchange and the financial sector were effectively eliminated. Finance houses proliferated during this period, and money flooded into office buildings and real estate, both in Sweden and abroad. However, the speculative boom ended in short order. The Swedish credit system foundered by the end of 1991, forcing the government to divert tax revenues to bail out several of its major banks at a cost of 3% of GDP. The near collapse of the key banks and insurance companies that comprise the financial industry helped to bring the international recession to Sweden. (Olsen 1999, 241ff)

As a result of the collapse of the speculative boom, many assets became worthless, leading to large financial losses for many banks and businesses. Sweden's central bank responded to the overheated economy of the late 1980s with tight money policies, generating huge increases in interest rates to rein in inflation. Real interest rates reached an incredible 14% in 1992, leading to significantly higher unemployment, as consumer spending dropped and business investment collapsed. The combination of high interest rates, the bursting of the speculative bubble of the 1980s, and an international recession all during the same period proved devastating. In 1991, the Swedish economy entered its deepest recession since the Great Depression, with unemployment reaching 8%. The economy has since rebounded, although unemployment remains much higher than it was previously (unemployment was still 8% in 1996, vs. the post-World War II average of 2.4%).

The rise of Sweden's business interests and the subsequent decline of the power of labor unions parallels the experiences of the U.S. as well as other developed nations with the advent of globalization. In essence, globalization erodes the power of labor, because instead of paying organized laborers higher wages at home, businesses will now move to a country where wages are low and where labor unions are suppressed. As a result, we see employers worldwide pursuing a race to the bottom, seeking out the lowest wages and the least organized labor.

The Swedish Welfare State Since 1976

A major goal of the conservatives who ruled Sweden from 1976-1982 and 1991-1994 was to reduce the size of the Swedish welfare state, by reducing taxes and cutting government spending on social programs. They reduced the top tax rate from 85% to 50%, extended sales taxes to make up revenue, and reduced but did not eliminate benefits for parental leave, health and dental care, housing, unemployment, retirement and sick leave. These policy changes helped to produce a doubling of the poverty rate in Sweden from 1978 to 1992, although as we will see below, the Swedish poverty rate nonetheless remains the lowest in the world. Sweden also experienced the inevitable decrease in equality in all areas—the rich grew richer while the poor grew poorer, wage inequality between men and women increased, and opportunities were no longer as equal. The "fare well" state was under attack.

Even more drastic changes in the welfare state were enacted during the 1991-1993 recession. A new center-right government, elected in 1991, instituted corporate welfare programs (subsidies and tax breaks for corporations), and privatized education, child-care, and health care in some cases. Prior to this time, Swedes had widely accepted the idea that benefits should be universal, and not subject to the inequities of the market (i.e., de-commodified), so these changes marked a significant departure in philosophy. Nevertheless, much of the Swedish welfare state remained in place, and the return to power of the SAP in 1994, as voters rejected the conservative government because of its failure to improve Sweden's economic performance, meant a renewed commitment to social democracy. The partial erosion of the welfare state in Sweden led some conservative commentators to talk about the "end of the Swedish model." However, as we will see below, Sweden retains a vast government sector that still safeguards the social and economic rights of its citizens. And overall, Sweden's recent experiences are not unique: the Swedes faced the same hardships that all developed countries faced beginning in the early 1970s.

Sweden's Economic Performance Since 1970

In general, the economic performance of Sweden deteriorated after 1970 due to a number of factors, including globalization, industrial decline, and the aging of the population. With the advent of increased global competition, traditional manufacturing industries that Sweden specialized in, such as cars and household durable goods, faced more competitive markets. Furthermore, Sweden's huge industrial giants were unable to adjust and move out of declining sectors and into rising sectors of the global economy, much as the rust belt industries in the United States had trouble adjusting. Some industries even gave up producing in Sweden and moved operations to less costly locations in the Third World.

Sweden also faces an aging population, which means fewer working people supporting more and more elderly. Gregg Olsen notes that Sweden has the largest proportion of seniors in the world today (Olsen 1999). A natural byproduct of these demographic changes is a less productive economy. The United States will be facing a similar problem in the years ahead as the baby boomers retire in larger and larger numbers.

These forces—global competition in traditional manufacturing, the flight of transnational corporations to the developing world, the aging of the population—have presented problems throughout the developed world. For instance, both Sweden and the United States experienced slower economic growth and a more unequal distribution of income since 1970. Although Sweden faced higher levels of unemployment and stagnation in the 1990s, while the U.S. economy experienced relatively more economic growth, Sweden's average real economic growth rate from 1967-1996 was 2.1%, while the real growth rate in the U.S. was 2.5%.

Conservative commentators argue that the generous benefits of the Swedish welfare state also may have contributed to the difficulties in staying competitive in the global marketplace of today, although the evidence on this issue is mixed. Sweden's welfare state expanded dramatically after World War II, yet as noted above, Sweden's average real economic growth rate from 1950 to 1970 was 4%, one-half percent higher than the U.S. average real rate of growth over the same period. Given this fact, there is clearly no reason to think that the welfare state is inherently inefficient or that it constrains economic growth. In actuality, it was when the welfare state was eroded and markets deregulated that Sweden's economic performance began to decline, a trend we also see in the experiences of the United States.

The problem with the Swedish approach may actually have been that their government was not active enough in guiding industrial development. Unlike the government of Germany that focused government resources on key growth industries such as computers, the Swedish government allowed its industries to determine where to invest their funds. While Sweden's active labor market policies successfully solved their unemployment problem, the lack of an active industrial policy to help Sweden's industries evolve created problems. The efforts the government did make in the last 20 years to prop up declining heavy industries were very costly and did not succeed in making these industries competitive.

The Results of Capital's Offensive

Since capital's offensive began in the 1970s, all Swedish governments have pursued a less regulated form of capitalism. Even when the SAP has been in power recently (the SAP governed from 1982 to 1991 and from 1994 to 1999), it, too, largely pursued a market-based agenda. The pursuit of these policies on the part of all political parties in Sweden is strikingly similar to political developments in England and the United States, where conservative groups pushed the economy in a free-market direction, formerly liberal groups (Democrats in the U.S., the Labor Party in England, the SAP in Sweden) turned to a moderate market-based approach, and organized labor ceased to be as powerful a voice in national politics.

As in the United States, Sweden is now dominated by huge transnational corporations (TNCs). Industrial concentration in Sweden is extremely high (a small number of large firms dominate the economy), in part because of the solidaristic wage policy which made it more profitable for large, efficient, export-oriented companies. As these companies increased in size and power, they pushed for a deregulated market approach to the economy, along with membership in the European Union so that they would have even more mobility and more markets in which to operate. Swedish TNCs now attack any form of government regulation in the popular press, criticizing the "public sector," the "welfare state," and "collectivism," while supporting the market economy, which supposedly generates a "free and good society." Sweden's CEOs now regularly threaten to relocate outside of Sweden unless the government creates a more business-friendly environment for them. And many businesses are carrying out these threats. Despite being profitable, Volvo closed its taxpayer-financed plants that experimented with worker autonomy and a more humane work place, moved some operations overseas, and sold out to Ford.

Meanwhile, as TNCs offer a united front in favor of unregulated markets, Swedish labor unions fight amongst themselves, and the SAP is no longer directly associated with the labor movement. The welfare state is largely intact, shored up by the return of the SAP to power in 1994, but industrial relations between employers and unions have been dramatically altered, and the new government's ability to pursue equality and stability is, in the words of Gregg Olsen (1996, p. 16), "severely circumscribed in a neo-liberal [laissez-faire] environment dominated by TNCs and global financial markets." In order to qualify for the Euro and to appease the huge conglomerates that dominate Sweden, the SAP-led government recently agreed to deeper cuts in the welfare state and new efforts to fight inflation.[39] The cuts in government spending and the high interest rates necessary to fight inflation resulted in chronically high levels of unemployment in the 1990s. But it is important to remember that being unemployed in Sweden does not have the devastating consequences that it can have in the United States, because of the generous welfare system and the potential for retraining for a new job. And Sweden remains committed to equality and to collective decision-making, with the participation of labor, capital and the government. With the SAP continuing to enjoy broad-based support and with labor unions still relatively powerful, the "Swedish model" will be in place for the foreseeable future, albeit in a somewhat less progressive form than its 1970s incarnation.

CONCLUSION: THE CASE FOR SWEDISH SOCIAL DEMOCRACY

Despite the recent erosion in some areas of the welfare state, Swedish social democracy remains intact, and there is no denying the effectiveness of the Swedish model over the last 60 years. The SAP returned to power in 1994, as voters tired of conservative policies that failed to solve Sweden's social and economic problems. Over the last few years, the SAP has resumed its egalitarian approach to running the economy and restored most of the welfare state. Ultimately, Sweden's system for most of this century has been, and still is based on the following general goals and principles:

1. **Economic development and efficiency.** In order to have a prosperous society, the economy must function efficiently, and in a worker-friendly manner. This means cooperative management of the economy to serve the needs of society, but not necessarily government control of the entire economy. Cooperation between labor and capital can increase efficiency and productivity, resulting in fewer strikes, less litigation, more rapid technological change, and innovative forms of work organization.

2. **Economic well-being for all.** The benefits of prosperity should be shared with all citizens. This can only be accomplished with the de-commodification of all basic necessities.

3. **Solidarity.** Individuals are members of a community, not only with rights but with obligations to that community as well. A society based on mutual cooperation is preferable to one based on unmitigated competition.

4. **Universality and equality.** All Swedes rely on the same network of services and participate in deciding how the local government operates these services. This network gives everyone a stake in the system as well as a voice. The provision of a wide range of services is a buffer against the predatory nature of an unregulated market system, while local control over services is a buffer against an overly controlling or inefficient national bureaucracy. This builds both equality and community.

5. **Democracy and cooperation.** Every society needs rules, which should be determined by the people themselves, and not unduly influenced by money. True democracy means that workers should have input into management decisions as well as political decisions, otherwise society degenerates into a barbaric system in which only the wealthiest and most aggressive prosper, and where workers are exploited. Firms influence the direction of the economy, as do labor unions and community groups. These groups must work together and compromise for the economy to work effectively.

6. **Education and access to information.** In order for a democratic society to work, all citizens need to be well-educated and informed. One measure taken by the Swedes is public control of the media in order to insure an unbiased flow of information. Swedish radio and television are run by the Swedish Broadcasting Corporation and contain no commercials. Programming emphasizes education and information in addition to entertainment.

7. **Pragmatism.** The SAP is remarkably free of dogmatism, and has shown itself to be quite flexible. The goal is to establish a society that benefits all people, and if this can be achieved without worker control of the means of production then the SAP accepts that. On the other hand, the SAP refuses to accept the social costs associated with unregulated capitalism.

In Sweden, social democracy resulted in an economy that is remarkably prosperous, and one that has the least poverty, the most equitable income distribution, and the highest levels of spending on health and education in the developed world.

Further, Sweden has succeeded in Keynesian stabilization policy and the pursuit of full employment far better than any other developed country. From 1950 to 1991, a period of 42 years, Sweden's unemployment rate only exceeded 3% a total of three times, whereas U.S. unemployment exceeded that level 38 times. Sweden's average rate of unemployment, even including the deep recession of 1991-1993, is amazingly low when compared with other European and developed (OECD) countries, as Table 1 indicates.

Table 1. **Average Unemployment Rates for Sweden, the U.S. and Other Developed Countries, 1960–1994**

Country or Group of Countries	Average Rate of Unemployment
Sweden	**2.4%**
All OECD countries	5.2%
15 European Union Members	5.6%
United States	**6.0%**
Canada	7.3%

Source: Olsen 1999.

Sweden was able to maintain full employment because of the following factors: 1) wage restraint on the part of labor, as part of the nationwide collective bargaining agreement; 2) an unemployment benefit system with a fixed duration of benefits, a wide range of labor-market programs to promote the acquisition of skills, and strict work requirements; 3) an active labor-market policy in which the government created jobs through public works and employment subsidies, provided training, assisted people in finding jobs and moved them to areas where there were jobs (there is a nationwide labor-market exchange which matches job seekers with jobs).

Sweden demonstrated conclusively that there is no reason for a country to live with a high "natural" rate of unemployment in order to have price stability. As Swedish economist Rudolf Meidner stated, "There is no such thing as a natural rate of unemployment. The level of employment and unemployment is significantly influenced by what the government does. It is a result of economic policies. . . . Price stability and full employment are not incompatible goals" (Quoted in Silverman 1998, 86). Sweden's inflation rate averaged 6.4% from 1961-1996, 33% higher than the U.S. average inflation rate of 4.8% over the same period, but the average unemployment rate in the United States was *150%* higher than Sweden's unemployment rate.

Despite the existence of extensive benefits for those who do not work, Sweden has the highest labor participation rate in the world. Whereas mainstream economists predict that generous welfare benefits provide a disincentive to work, the Swedish experience demonstrates that people *want* to be productive (recall Veblen's idea of the instinct of workmanship), and that if work is not drudgery people will work willingly and enthusiastically.

Sweden's experiences with economic growth are similar to those of the United States, with relatively high rates of growth for much of the 1870-1970 period, and slower growth since 1970. The build-up of the welfare state in Sweden was quite compatible with economic growth. The benefits of social peace and stability along with public investment in infrastructure and human capital more than offset the high taxes and the restraints on businesses. The cooperative nature of economic decision-making, with businesses, labor unions, and the government all participating, insured that economic growth could occur in a socially responsible context.

Meanwhile, Sweden also succeeded in creating one of the most peaceful, crime-free, egalitarian societies in the world. It de-commodified many aspects of the market system, thereby insuring that all citizens have the right to a good education, housing, health care, and a job. As Table 2 indicates, the rights of a Swedish citizen are much more extensive than the rights of an American citizen. If you came from an average family, which society do you think would be most pleasant place to live in?

Because of its extensive system of benefits and rights, proportionally Sweden has the largest government sector in the world. The Swedes believe this to be necessary to control aspects of life that should not be left to the market. As Figure 1 indicates, Sweden and the other social democracies of Europe

Table 2. **Rights of a Swedish Citizen vs. Rights of a U.S. Citizen**

	Sweden	U.S.
Parental Leave	All parents have the right to stay home and care for an infant for up to one full year per child at 90% of normal salary. All parents also receive a child allowance to cover the costs of raising children.	All parents have the right to six weeks of unpaid leave to care for a newborn child. Some parents receive monetary assistance for a limited period of time if they are very poor.
Vacations	All workers get at least five weeks of paid vacation per year plus extensive sick leave benefits.	U.S. workers *may* get at least two weeks of unpaid vacation per year *if* they are permanent employees; there are no mandatory vacations for temporary employees, and no one is guaranteed sick leave.
Health Care	All citizens receive high-quality health and dental care, with modest co-payments up to a maximum yearly payment. Care is generally so good that even the wealthy use public health care.	Medicare and Medicaid provide health insurance to the elderly and very poor. Many workers receive health insurance through their employer, but over 43 million Americans, including 10.7 million children and many of the working poor, have no health insurance.
Education	Free education is provided for all citizens at all levels, including college, vocational and adult education (for those people who want to explore new careers). Adult students receive time off from work and a stipend. The quality of education is so universally high, that even the children of the Swedish King attend public schools.	Free primary and secondary education is available to all citizens, with the quality varying widely depending on where one lives. People living in poorer school districts generally receive inferior educations. Limited funding is available for college students, but college is often beyond the reach of the poor and the lower middle class. What funding is available is usually in the form of loans, creating long-term debt for most.
Job Training	Free training is provided to all citizens who desire it. Those undergoing training receive a stipend from the government.	Some training programs exist, but they are limited in nature, and usually only to the poor. Trainees do not usually receive a stipend.
Employment	The Swedish government believes that every citizen has the right to meaningful work. Unemployed persons receive unemployment benefits, retraining, or a job in a public works project.	*Some* of the unemployed receive up to 6 months of unemployment benefits and job search assistance. After six months, benefits are cut off.
Social Security	All Swedish citizens receive a pension from the state, which pays people at least 75% of what they earned when they were working, or a guaranteed minimum amount if they did not work.	Most U.S. citizens receive social security benefits, but often the payments are not enough to live on.
Housing	If Swedish citizens cannot afford a house, they receive a housing subsidy. Sweden does not have a problem with homelessness due to the success of their housing and anti-poverty programs, and they have no slums.	Some U.S. citizens receive housing subsidies or a spot in public housing. But many citizens do not qualify for these benefits, and the U.S. has a significant number of homeless people. Every major U.S. city has slums.

have the largest proportional governments, while the United States, United Kingdom and Japan have among the smallest governments. This is a clear indication of the economic philosophies of the different countries. Sweden, Denmark, France and the Netherlands, to name a few, believe that all citizens have the right to a decent standard of living and real opportunities. They use government programs to insure that all citizens have these rights. The U.S., the U.K. and Japan do have substantial governments, but these countries leave much more up to the market than does Sweden.

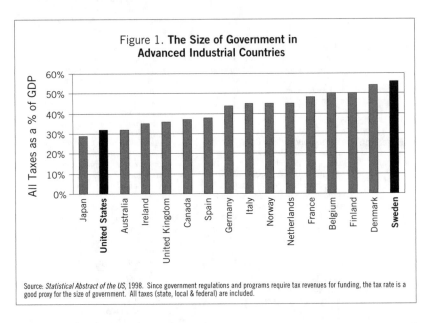

Figure 1. **The Size of Government in Advanced Industrial Countries**

Source: *Statistical Abstract of the US*, 1998. Since government regulations and programs require tax revenues for funding, the tax rate is a good proxy for the size of government. All taxes (state, local & federal) are included.

As Figure 2 shows, through extensive spending on education and social programs, Sweden has virtually eliminated poverty. Sweden's large government is accompanied by the lowest poverty rate in the world, a byproduct of its highly regulated economy and generous allocation of rights. Meanwhile, the U.S. has one of the smallest governments in the world, but also the highest poverty rate of all developed countries. Many, if not most, poor people in the U.S. are not able to lift themselves out of poverty through their own efforts, and often they are characterized as lazy or incompetent by those who are more privileged. The reality is that most poor people want to work, but do not have the necessary resources (education, a car, work clothes, child care, or opportunities) available to them that would allow them to find self-sustaining employment. Together, Figures 1 and 2 conclusively demonstrate that a country *can* eliminate poverty if it is willing to spend the money, but without such intervention, many people will remain poor.

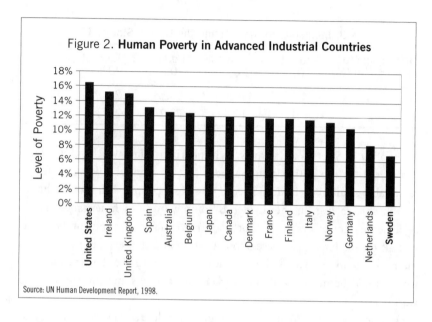

Figure 2. **Human Poverty in Advanced Industrial Countries**

Source: UN Human Development Report, 1998.

In addition to eliminating more poverty than any other country, Sweden has one of the most egalitarian societies in terms of income distribution. Its highly progressive tax and transfer system insures that those who have the most contribute the most, and those who have the least are guaranteed a decent income. Table 3 shows how much more equal Sweden is than the U.S. as a result of its different tax and transfer system. The bottom 80% of the population does much better in Sweden than in the United States. Sweden's highly progressive tax system contains within it a value judgment about different kinds of consumption based on the ideas of Thorstein Veblen. It is assumed that the consumption of basic necessities by all people is more important than the consumption of additional conspicuous luxury goods by the wealthy. In contrast, most U.S. politicians argue that the wealthy have the right to spend all their money as they see fit. Many conservative politicians in the U.S. even want to create a flat tax, where the rich and the poor would pay the same marginal tax rate. In the United States, with the central position given to individual choice in consumption decisions, there is no stigma attached to a rich person spending $1 million for a yacht, but politicians who propose that society has a responsibility to spend an equivalent amount on health insurance for

250 uninsured children are criticized for advocating big government. Swedes find this U.S. method of allocating resources immoral and barbaric.

Table 3. **Inequality in Sweden and the United States, 1989**

GDP going to each group (%)	Poorest 20%	2nd Poorest 20%	Middle 20%	2nd Richest 20%	Richest 20%
U.S.	4.6	10.6	16.5	23.7	44.6
Sweden	8.1	12.1	16.7	25.3	37.8

Explicit in Sweden's extremely high inheritance tax, which helps reduce incomes at the top, is the egalitarian idea that everyone should start life at a reasonably similar level. Most Swedes agree that people with money should not be able to live on the dividends coming from an inheritance simply because their ancestors made a fortune. True equality of opportunity means that all people have equal access to education and that even the children of the rich should have work. Furthermore, in order to avoid alienation, that work should be meaningful and workers must have some control over the workplace.

In another nod to Veblen, Sweden dramatically restricts advertising and instead channels funds into productive areas such as research and development. As noted above, the Swedish Broadcasting Corporation runs television and radio and airs all programming commercial-free. Newspapers receive state subsidies so they are not entirely dependent on ads. Again, Swedes make a value judgment about economic activity: advertising is wasteful and commercial impulses distort the content of television and newspapers. While the U.S. media resists "restrictions" on programming, most Swedes believe the commercial nature of the media in the United States is much more restrictive, and not in society's best interests. Can we really depend on the huge corporations that own the media to present a balanced version of the news? If so, then why haven't we all heard more about the success of Sweden's economic system?

It is often said that the United States is the land of opportunity, yet most working people do not have an equal opportunity to succeed because they lack access to equal education and training. In Sweden, *all* citizens have access to a high quality education. The United States is spoken of as the land of the free because we have few government regulations over the marketplace. This gives us the freedom to succeed and to keep most of the money we make. We also have the freedom to work wherever we want—but often for next to nothing! This is, of course, a freedom much admired by some Swedes: the corporate bosses.

Swedish economists also question whether the United States is truly prosperous in any meaningful sense. Despite rapid GDP growth during the 1990s relative to the rest of the world, should the U.S. be boasting about a level of prosperity that is benefiting only a small percentage of the population and that was built on the low wages of workers with declining, or no benefits? Shouldn't U.S. citizens be concerned that despite this supposed prosperity, millions of people in the United States are condemned to poverty, including many children, and over a million poor people are in prison? The debtors' prisons of the 1800s are reviled in history books, but is imprisoning poor, desperate people who resort to crime really so different? Is the purpose of an economy to generate billions for Bill Gates or to generate the greatest standard of living for all that belong to that society? In all of these ways and more, the social democracy of Sweden serves most people better than the (largely) unregulated capitalism of the United States.

Thus the experiences of Sweden demonstrate the possibility of a "Middle Way" between unregulated capitalism and command communism: social democracy. Sweden may not be a paradise on Earth. Sweden has problems just like all other countries. People there complain about their high taxes and their sometimes inefficient government. But building on the ideas of Marx, Keynes and Veblen, Sweden proved that a country can maintain full employment, be efficient and productive, and give every citizen the right to decent levels of food, clothing, health care, to a job, and to some control over their lives. Ultimately, each country must decide what things to leave up to the market and what things should be determined by the collective decisions of all citizens. In the United States, most things are allocated based on how much money a person has, which gives unprecedented levels of freedom and choice to the very wealthy, but leaves much of the population without the basic necessities of life. Perhaps the United States is the land of the free—if you're rich. But for everyone else, social democracy seems to provide more freedom and better opportunities.

Works Cited

Adams, Walter, and James Brock, eds. 1995. *The Structure of American Industry*. New York: Prentice-Hall, Inc.

Adams, Walter, and Hans Mueller. 1986. The Steel Industry. *The Structure of American Industry*. Edited by Walter Adams and James Brock. New York: MacMillan Publishing Co.

Adler-Karlsson, Gunnar. 1970. *Reclaiming the Canadian Economy: A Swedish Approach Through Functional Socialism*. Toronto: Anansi.

Amott, Teresa. 1996. Class. *A Dictionary of Cultural and Critical Theory*. Edited by Michael Payne, et al. Lewisburg, Penn.: Bucknell University Press.

Amsden, Alice H. 2002. Gilded Age II, review of Kevin Phillips, *Wealth and Democracy*, New York: Broadway, 2002. *The Nation*, September 2.

Andrews, Edmund. 2001. Bush Angers Europe by Eroding Pact on Warming. *New York Times*, April 1.

Baran, Paul, and Paul Sweezy. 1966. *Monopoly Capital: An Essay on the American Economic and Social Order*. New York: Monthly Review.

Bartlett, Donald, and James Steele. 1994. *America: Who Really Pays the Taxes?* New York: Simon and Schuster.

Benjamin, Lois, ed. 1997. *Black Women in the Academy*. Gainesville: University of Florida Press.

Bourdieu, Pierre. 1984. *Distinction: A Social Critique of the Judgment of Taste*. Cambridge, Mass.: Harvard University Press.

Bowden, Elbert, and Judith Bowden. 1995. *Economics: The Science of Common Sense*. 8th Edition. Cincinnati: Southwestern Publishing Company.

Braverman, Harry. 1974. *Labor and Monopoly Capital: The Degradation of Work in the Twentieth Century*. New York: Monthly Review.

Brown, Paul. 1998. Greenhouse Effect Worse than Feared. *Manchester Guardian Weekly*, November 9.

Burros, Marian. 1999. High Pesticide Levels Seen in U.S. Food. *New York Times*, February 19.

Canterbury, E. Ray. 1995. *The Literate Economist*. New York: Harper Collins College Publishers.

Cassidy, John. 1996. The Decline of Economics. *The New Yorker*, December.

———. 1998a. Rich Man, Richer Man. *The New Yorker*, May 11.

———. 1998b. The New World Disorder. *The New Yorker*, October 22.

———. 1999. No Satisfaction. *The New Yorker*, January 25.

Chandler, Alfred D., Jr. 1977. *Visible Hand*. Cambridge, Mass.: The Belknap Press of Harvard University Press.

Chernow, Ron. 1999. *Titan*. New York: Random House.

Childs, Marquis. 1936. *The Middle Way*. New Haven: Yale University Press.

Coleman, Richard, and Lee Rainwater. 1978. *Social Standing in the United States*. New York: Basic Books.

Collander, David, and Alfred W. Coates, eds. 1998. *The Spread of Economic Ideas*. New York: Cambridge University Press.

Cushman, John H. 1997. U.S. Reshaping Cancer Strategy as Incidence in Children Rises. *New York Times*, September 29.

Dahrendorf, Ralf. 1979. *Life Chances*. Chicago: University of Chicago Press.

Dews, C. L. B., and Carolyn Law. 1995. *This Fine Place So Far From Home: Voices of Academics from the Working Class*. Philadelphia: Temple University Press.

Dillard, Dudley. 1967. *The Economic Development of the North Atlantic Community*. Englewood Cliffs: Prentice-Hall.

Domhoff, G. William. 2002. *Who Rules America?* 4th Edition. New York: McGraw-Hill.

Dorfman, Joseph. 1961. *Thorstein Veblen and His America*. New York: August M. Kelly.

———. 1973. *Essays, Reviews, and Reports*. New York: August M. Kelly.

Du Boff, Richard, and Edward Herman. 2001. Mergers, Concentration, and the Erosion of Democracy. *Monthly Review*, May.

Engels, Frederick. 1975. *Socialism: Utopian and Scientific*. Peking: Foreign Language Press.

Frank, Robert H. 1999. *Luxury Fever*. New York: Free Press.

Friedman, Milton. 1963. *Capitalism and Freedom*. Chicago: University of Chicago Press.

Fussell, Paul. 1983. *Class*. New York: Ballantine.

Galbraith, John Kenneth. 1958. *The Affluent Society*. Boston: Houghton-Mifflin.

——. 1967. *The New Industrial State*. Boston: Houghton-Mifflin.

——. 1972. Introduction to *The Theory of the Leisure Class* by Thorstein Veblen. Boston: Houghton-Mifflin.

——. 1977. *The Age of Uncertainty*. Boston: Houghton-Mifflin.

——. 1982. *The Anatomy of Power*. Boston: Houghton-Mifflin.

——. 1987. *Economics in Perspective: A Critical Analysis*. Boston: Houghton-Mifflin.

——. 1998. *The Affluent Society*. Boston: Houghton-Mifflin.

Gallup Organization, Inc. 1999. *Giving and Volunteering in the United States*. Washington, D.C.: Gallup Organization.

Gerth, H. H., and C. Wright Mills, eds. 1946. *From Max Weber: Essays in Sociology*. New York: Oxford University Press.

Gilbert, Dennis. 1998. *The American Class Structure in An Age of Growing Inequality*. 5th Edition. Belmont, Calif.: Wadsworth.

Goode, Erica. 1999. For Good Health, It Helps to be Rich and Important. *New York Times*, June 1.

Gordon, David. 1996a. *Fat and Mean: The Corporate Squeeze of Working Americans and the Myth of Managerial Downsizing*. New York: Free Press.

——. 1996b. Underpaid Workers, Bloated Corporations: Two Pieces in the Puzzle of U.S. Economic Decline. *Dissent*, Vol. 43, Spring 1996.

Grimes, Michael D., and Joan M. Morris. 1997. *Caught in the Middle::*

Contradictions in the Lives of Sociologists from Working-Class Backgrounds. Westport, Conn.: Praeger.

Hamilton, David. 1991. *Evolutionary Economics.* New Brunswick, New Jersey: Transaction.

Heilbroner, Robert. 1999. *The Worldly Philosophers.* New York: Touchstone Books.

Henwood, Doug. 1997. *Wall Street.* New York: Verso.

Herbert, Bob. 1997. Bad Air Day. *New York Times*, February 10.

Hollingshead, August, and Fredrick Redlich. 1957. *Social Class and Mental Illness: A Community Study.* New York: Wiley.

Holt, Douglas. 1999. Does Cultural Capital Structure American Consumption? *Journal of Consumer Research*, June.

Kadi, Joanna. 1996. *Thinking Class: Sketches from a Cultural Worker.* Boston: South End Press.

Karasek, Robert and Tores Theorell. 1990. *Healthy Work: Stress, Productivity, and the Reconstruction of Working Life.* New York: Basic Books.

Keynes, John Maynard. 1933. *Essays in Biography.* New York: Harcourt-Brace.

——. 1936. *General Theory of Employment, Interest, and Money.* New York: Harcourt, Brace, and World.

——. 1963. *Essays in Biography.* New York: W. W. Norton and Co.

Kong, Delores. 1999. Jobs Don't Kill People, But Stress in the Workplace Can. *Boston Globe*, August 30.

Korten, David. 1996. *When Corporations Rule the World.* West Hartford, Conn.: Kumerian Press.

Lerner, Max, ed. 1976. *Portable Veblen.* New York: Penguin Books.

Leonhart, David, and Kathleen Kerwin. 1997. Hey Kid, Buy This! *Business Week*, June 30.

Marx, Karl. 1967. *Capital.* Vol. 1. New York: International Publishers.

——. 1981. *Capital.* Vol. 2. New York: Vintage.

Marx, Karl, and Frederick Engels. 1978. *The Marx-Engels Reader.* Edited by Robert Tucker. New York: Princeton University Press.

——. 1998. *The Communist Manifesto*. New York: Verso.

Mayer, Caroline E. 2000. It's Becoming a Mad Ad World. *Manchester Guardian Weekly*, June 1-7.

Miller, Roger Leroy. 1997. *Economics Today: The Micro View*. New York: McGraw-Hill.

Mills, C. Wright. 1962. *The Marxists*. New York: Dell.

Mirowski, John, and Catherine Ross. 1989. *Social Causes of Psychological Distress*. New York: deGruyter.

Myrdal, Gunnar. 1965. *The Political Element in the Development of Economic Theory*. Cambridge, Mass.: Harvard University Press.

Navarro, Vincente. 1991. Class and Race: Life and Death Situations. *Monthly Review*, September.

Olsen, Gregg. 1999. Half Empty or Half Full? *Canadian Review of Sociology and Anthropology*, May.

Polanyi, Karl. 1944. *The Great Transformation*. New York: Farrar and Rinehart.

Porter, Glenn. 1973. *The Rise of Big Business*. Arlington Heights, Illinois: Harlan Davidson, Inc.

Rachel's Environmental and Health Weekly. Edited by Peter Montague. Annapolis, Maryland: Environmental Research Foundation.

Ratner, Sidney, James Soltow, and Richard Sylla. 1993. *The Evolution of the American Economy*. New York: MacMillan Publishing Co.

Reich, Robert. 1999. Galbraith in the New Gilded Age. *Between Friends: Perspectives on John Kenneth Galbraith*. Edited by Helen Sasson. Boston: Houghton-Mifflin.

Riddell, Tom, Jean Shackelford, and Steve Stamos. 1998. *Economics: A Tool for Critically Understanding Society*. 5th Edition. Boston: Addison-Wesley.

Rohlf, William. 1999. *Economic Reasoning*. 4th Edition. Reading, Mass.: Addison-Wesley.

Routh, Guy. 1977. *The Origin of Economic Ideas*. New York: Vintage Books.

——. 1986. *Unemployment: Economic Perspectives*. London: MacMillan.

Ryan, Jake, and Charles Sackrey. 1984. *Strangers in Paradise: Academics from the Working Class*. Boston: South End Press.

———. 1996. *Strangers in Paradise: Academics from the Working Class*. Rev. ed. New York: University Press of America.

Samuelson, Paul. 1964. *Economics: An Introductory Analysis*. 6th Edition. New York: McGraw-Hill.

Scherer, F. M. 1990. *Industrial Market Structure and Economic Performance*. Boston: Houghton-Mifflin.

Schor, Juliet. 1999. *The Overspent American*. New York: Basic Books.

Schumpeter, Joseph. 1954. *History of Economic Analysis*. New York: Oxford University Press.

Shaikh, Anwar, and Ahmet Tonak. 2000. The Rise and Fall of the U.S. Welfare State. *Political Economy and Contemporary Capitalism*. Edited by Ron Baiman, Heather Boushey, and Dawn Saunders. New York: M. E. Sharpe.

Shepherd, William. 1997. *The Economics of Industrial Organization*. Upper Saddle River, New Jersey: Prentice-Hall.

Silverman, Bertram. 1998. The Rise and Fall of the Swedish Model. *Challenge*, Vol. 41, No.1.

Stanfield, James Ron. 1996. *John Kenneth Galbraith*. New York: St. Martin's Press.

Stiglitz, Joseph. 2002. The Roaring Nineties. *Atlantic Monthly*, October.

Stockman, Alan. 1999. *Introduction to Economics*. 2nd Edition. Chicago: Dryden Press.

Tilman, Rick. 1993. *Veblen Treasury*. Armonk, New York: M. E. Sharpe.

Tokarczyk, Michelle, and Elizabeth Fay, eds. 1993. *Working Class Women in the Academy*. Amherst: University of Massachusetts Press.

Uchitelle, Louis. 1999. Reviving the Economics of Fear: In Bad Times, Consumers Might Simply Refuse to Spend. *New York Times*, June 2.

Vanneman, Reeve, and Lynn Weber Cannon. 1983. *The American Perception of Class*. Philadelphia: Temple University Press.

Veblen, Thorstein. 1919. *The Place of Science in Modern Civilization*. New York: B. W. Huebsch.

———. 1973. *The Theory of the Leisure Class*. Boston: Houghton-Mifflin.

———. 1978. *The Theory of Business Enterprise.* New Brunswick, New Jersey: Transaction.

———. 1990. *Engineers and the Price System.* New Brunswick, New Jersey: Transaction.

———. 1997. *Absentee Ownership.* New Brunswick, New Jersey: Transaction.

———. 1998. *The Nature of the Peace.* New Brunswick, New Jersey: Transaction.

Weinstein, Michael. 1999. Students Seek Reality Amid the Math of Economics. *New York Times.* September 18.

Winter, Greg. 2001. Contaminated Food Makes Millions Ill Despite Advances. *New York Times,* March 18.

Wolff, Richard, and Stephen Resnick. 1987. *Economics: Marxian vs. Neoclassical.* Baltimore: Johns Hopkins University Press.

ENDNOTES

1. On this matter of what to call the various schools of economics that we have discussed above, there are several possibilities. John Kenneth Galbraith has called the dominating school of economics, from Adam Smith until our own time, the "central tradition." We will use that term on occasion. Typically, we will draw from a fusion of terms used by Marx, Keynes, and Samuelson, as follows: we will refer to the central tradition in economics from Adam Smith until Keynes' *General Theory*, in 1936, as "classical" economics. For economists in the central tradition after 1936, we will continue to use the term "mainstream" or "neoclassical."

2. In talking about modes of production, Marxists use a few terms that one should know. The *forces of production* include all things needed to produce output: machinery, tools, natural resources, and human effort and human capital (skills and knowledge). By themselves, the machinery, tools, and resources are the *means of production*. Those who own them are the *bourgeoisie*, or *capitalists*. Those who don't own such capital goods, who must live by wage labor, are *proletarians*. The *social relations of production* in capitalism are the ongoing interactions between capitalists and laborers in the workplace, in particular the conditions by which workers will produce enough output to guarantee a profit to capitalists.

3. Adam Smith had also noticed the negative effects of the division of labor on workers. In *Capital*, Marx quotes from Smith's *The Wealth of Nations* (1776) that divided labor can "make the worker as stupid and as ignorant as it is possible for a human creature to become." To appreciate the argument that both make, one only has to imagine performing the same mind-numbing task hundreds, or thousands, of times per day for decades.

4. As our consulting example shows, in terms of the extraction of surplus value in a particular firm, it makes no difference whether the output is an intangible service or a can of beans. However, in considering how

surplus value flows through the economy, Marx did distinguish between services which are "necessary" costs of production and those that aren't. A consultant, Marx might have noted, does not produce any value at all but simply allows her employer to obtain surplus value produced elsewhere. This matter goes beyond the level of our introduction, but for those interested, it is discussed clearly in Wolff and Resnick 1987.

5. This "enclosure movement" in England meant that land in villages traditionally set aside in "commons"—groups of plots farmed by individual families—were by Parliamentary acts taken over by large landowners or by the British Crown. In eliminating the commons, these enclosures made it impossible for most rural families to sustain themselves on the land. This was, of course, the first step in the process by which rural families found themselves headed to cities and into the factories of the emerging class of capitalist owners.

6. Smith devoted considerable effort in *The Wealth of Nations* to a critique of monopolies, so much so that many interpreters of the book see it as a polemical attack on the existing government policies as well as an exposition of classical economic theory. Smith believed that the great joint stock companies such as the British East India Company were products of the mercantilist policies that had granted these companies monopolies over the trade between England and certain parts of the world. See Canterbery 1995, 49, as well as the *The Wealth of Nations* itself.

7. Cumulative causation is contrasted to simple cause and effect, where action a results in reaction b, end of story. Cumulative causation suggests that reaction b may become a cause of reaction c, and in turn reaction c may be a cause of reaction d, and on and on ad infinitum.

8. In an example of his irony Veblen notes that "it may even be that the men's work contributes as much to the food supply and the other necessary consumption of the group" (Veblen 1973, 23).

9. Ron Chernow discusses this in depth in his biography of Rockefeller. The opportunity for railroads to get large and steady shipments of oil lowered their own costs, so the rebates were a way of sharing those benefits with the shippers; as Rockefeller himself said, "It was a large, regular volume of business such as had not hitherto been given to the roads in question" (Chernow 1999, 113). Rockefeller was further aided by the fact that railroads like the Erie and the New York Central were very interested in promoting Cleveland as an oil-refining center, in order to boost the shipments through their own railway networks.

10. Rockefeller also used less brutal tactics to compete. He was the first oil refiner to build his own pipelines for shipping oil, to set up his own marketing operations, and to reduce his costs further and further. At the same time, by owning his own pipelines and setting up marketing operations, he closed off the distribution markets from the wholesalers and railroads in favor of his own divisions, thus centralizing even more power over the national oil refining market in the hands of the Standard Oil Trust (Chandler 1977, Ch. 10).

11. He is often accused of moving into an activist stance with his book *Engineers and the Price System*. In this book, he advocated for engineers and others of an industrial state of mind to take over the nation's industrial apparatus and reorganize it to provision the entire economy.

12. There are many ways to classify the different schools of economics, and we will use the following one: the "classical school" refers to the mainstream of economics from Adam Smith to John Maynard Keynes; the "neoclassical school" refers to the mainstream of economics since the 1930s, with its two broad branches of microeconomics and macroeconomics. The "central tradition" refers to both the classical and neoclassical schools, thus the mainstream from the time of Adam Smith to our time. "Political economy" refers to schools of thought outside the mainstream, particularly those that emerged in the thinking of Karl Marx and Thorstein Veblen, and in the works of critics such as Keynes who worked inside the mainstream school but were highly critical of it.

13. In our brief discussion of Say's Law we must leave out two important additions by later economists that made the macroeconomics of the classical more sophisticated than his simple law. These additions are an explanation of how interest rates equilibrate the market for loans, and a theory of the role of money in capitalist societies. Omitting these two, we are thus presenting an oversimplified version of classical macroeconomic theory, yet the parts that we are discussing – Say's Law and its theory of unemployment – were its central tenants and can reasonably be discussed on their own.

14. These savings come from two sources: *retained earnings*, which is the part of total profits the capitalists keep for the firm rather than paying them as dividends to the stockholders; and *depreciation allowances*, funds they also retain out of sales revenue that are used for replacing used-up capital goods and for buying new capital goods.

15. All economic majors must pay their dues in part by taking a course in intermediate macroeconomics. In such a course, if it is a thorough one,

the principal critics of Keynes, as well as the post-Keynesians, will be given the necessary coverage.

16. The practices of the IMF, World Bank, and the WTO, have in recent years been given wide coverage in academic and popular presses, in other media, and from all points of view. Thus, one can easily add the details and perspectives we are necessarily ignoring here. For a sustained, readable, and highly critical analysis of the practices of the IMF and the World Bank (and of many other aspects of international capitalism), one should see: Korten 1996. Korten is an ex-professor at Harvard's Business School, was an official with a U.S. international development agency, and his book has gotten wide attention.

17. Dennis Gilbert, whose work we will report on below, reports that studies on children's attitudes about social class show that 3rd graders have begun to recognize different social classes, that 70% of 6th graders see about the same class alignments as their parents, and that most 12th graders will see such alignments the same as do their parents (Gilbert 1998, 116-7).

18. One reviewer of this essay, John Boylan, wrote us these wise words of warning about the narrow focus we were taking. "While economics and class structure play a significant role in the creation of culture, they must be factored in with a whole pattern of other elements... Individuals also develop their individual personalities from countless influences, forces, and circumstances, including, of course, class background, many of which they are only dimly aware... [We] live in [and are shaped by] a culture that is a tremendous ever-shifting web of words, images, rules, lies, taboos, prejudices, fears, hopes, and dreams. It pervades laws, norms, rules both stated and unspoken...[Once] you start examining it, it shifts, changes, camouflages itself, and envelopes the observer. I think of it is as a huge tinker toy in which the pieces are constantly being reassembled...We tend to understand it the same way that the blind men know the elephant by describing only the part of the animal that each is actually touching."

19. In addition to Vincente Navarro, mentioned in the text, two other scholars have been making these arguments for a long time. One, Leonard Sagan, covered much the same territory as Navarro in *The Health of Nations* (1987), particularly in Chapter 8 on "Mortality Gradients Among Social Classes." Another, Harvey Brenner, has for twenty years produced a long series of books and articles about the relationship between socioeconomic variables and health, with a particular focus on unemployment.

20. The following is an example of "controlling statistically" for these kinds of characteristics. Assume we were to select randomly two groups, one from poor families and one from rich families, and all members of both groups had similar diets and exercise habits, smoked about the same number of cigarettes, drank similar amounts of alcohol, and all were in reasonably happy marriages. Even though these were all the same, we would expect statistically to find the rich people living longer than the poor ones on average. That would then lead us to look for other variables to explain this difference in longevity between the two groups, such as the nature of their work, where they lived, and a host of other things.

21. Since 1990, structural changes in the U.S. economy, such as more and more people being shoved into low-paying service jobs and – related to it – increasing income inequality in the U.S., have almost certainly increased the rigidity of class barriers. Thus, given these changes, our argument about the difficulty of upward mobility may actually be *understated*.

22. In this research we based our conclusion on the most influential study of the time: Coleman and Rainwater 1978.

23. A good discussion of the theoretical complexities of looking at social mobility data is presented in Grimes and Morris 1997.

24. In our analysis we have dropped the last category of farm workers because they represent less than 3% of all workers, and because they are such a mix—ranging from migrant workers to more highly paid workers in corporate farms—that their *average* circumstances do not give us useful information.

25. Concerning this 60%, how do these people arrange to stay in the social classes of their privileged parents? We have used the idea of "cultural capital" to provide an abstract, structural answer to the question. For much greater detail on this intriguing question, but one too is too broad to take up here in an adequate fashion, we think the best book is Domhoff 2002. Since 1967, when he wrote the first edition, Domhoff has studied the upper classes in the U.S., who they are, how they behave, and how they got there. We very highly recommend his work.

26. We should emphasize a point we mentioned briefly before, that all these barriers to upward mobility are greater for most women than for men with similar circumstances and in particular if they have children along the way. Tokarczyk and Fay 1993, a book we mentioned above, has a number of essays making this point, particularly the one by Donna Langston. Another book that focuses on the relatively greater barriers to upward mobility for black women, is Benjamin 1997.

27. We have focused in this chapter on Galbraith's theory of social balance rather than on a larger slice of his work because we believe it is his most important contribution to modern social analysis. Also, his books are readily accessible to any adult reader, and there are numerous readable overviews of Galbraith's writing, such as Stanfield 1996.

28. This estimate was given by Sut Jhally, who narrates a documentary film, "Advertising and the End of the World," by the Media Education Foundation. This film provides compelling evidence that Galbraith's 1958 theory of social balance was genuinely prophetic.

29. Some of Galbraith's critics have argued that he overestimated the power of the technostructure to direct the operations of the giant firms and that globalization has shifted some of its power to high-profile CEOs and, especially, investment banking firms. While no doubt there is merit to these criticisms, they are actually not particularly relevant to the theory of social balance. Suffice it say that the world economy is under the sway of giant firms, getting more giant-like as we write, thoroughly committed to maximizing profits, and their effects on social balance are the same whether they are themselves dominated by owners, the technostructure, financial interests, or all three.

30. Each September, *Advertising Age* publishes a list of the 200 largest advertisers in the U.S.

31. *The Anatomy of Power*, like so many of Galbraith's works, is highly recommended for those who seek to understand our economic order. We can only mention its argument in passing because to give it the credit its many insights merit we would need to go considerably beyond the limits of a short chapter. The bright side of this situation is that *The Anatomy of Power* is another of Galbraith's most clearly written books.

32. A further complication for producers in this regard is that if the average consumer decides to save more income this year than last year, some companies will lose customers no matter the intensity of their advertising efforts. This is the familiar "underconsumption" problem in capitalism that our readers will take up in the chapter on J.M. Keynes, or in any discussion of macroeconomics.

33. The world press, to which this report was promulgated in 1992, virtually ignored it. The report was reprinted in the newsletter cited. This newsletter is an exceptionally valuable resource for research on environmental pollution, one written for the general public. Each issue lists ample source material for those interested in more information on a subject The newsletter is typically referred to as *Rachel's*, and there is more information about it at the end of this essay.

34. For the evidence, ranging from a recent EPA "reassessment" of the effects of dioxin, to an enormous array of other sources, see *Rachel's* #640, March 4, 1999. For virtually unlimited information, search under "dioxin" on the Web. In short, human exposure to dioxin has been shown to be related to cancer; chloracne, a skin disease that can cause acne-like sores all over the body, sometimes lasting for years; decreased testosterone in blood of dioxin-exposed males; a variety of disorders in the development of human reproductive organs; and diabetes. Rats exposed to dioxin had decreased sperm production (and during the last 50 years, sperm production of men through the industrialized world has dropped 50%).

35. Baran and Sweezy's idea of surplus derives from Marx's idea of surplus value, but it is not the same. For example, Marx's measure of surplus value would not have included all taxes, but taxes are a key component of Baran and Sweezy's definition of surplus. Baran and Sweezy's development of the idea of surplus was the first of many efforts by contemporary Marxists to refine the concept of surplus value.

36. For a more detailed explanation of this idea of the surplus as it relates to the aggregate economy, the best source is Wolff and Resnick 1987.

37. Although Swedish economists were writing about and implementing stabilization policies at the same time Keynes was advocating them, these ideas came to be known as "Keynesian" policies because of the widespread influence of Keynes' masterwork, *The General Theory*.

38. The key point here is that if workers increase their productivity by 3%, this lowers firms' costs by 3%, since the same work force is now producing 3% more than before. Because firms' costs have decreased by 3%, firms can increase wages by as much as 3% without having to increase prices at all. Ultimately, wage increases only cause inflation if wages increase *faster* than productivity increases.

39. Sweden signed the Maastricht treaty to link their currency with other European currencies, with the ultimate goal being the establishment of one currency in Europe — the Euro. Hence, the Euro is the currency that all European countries that sign the Maastricht treaty will use in the future. But in order to qualify for the EURO, Sweden must obey the following strict macroeconomic rules: 1) budget deficits cannot exceed 3% of GDP; 2) the national debt cannot be greater than 60% of GDP; 3) inflation cannot be more than 1.5% above the average of the inflation rates of the three EU members with the lowest level of inflation; 4) long-term interest rates cannot be more than 2% higher than that achieved by the three nations with the lowest inflation rates; and 5) exchange rates must fall within the Exchange Rate Mechanism.